böhlau

Legal Area Studies

Edited by
Martin Löhnig and Anna Moszyńska

Volume 7

Argita Malltezi / Armela Kromiçi

History of Law in Albania

Bibliography of Legal Research

BÖHLAU

Bibliographic information published by the Deutsche Nationalbibliothek:
The Deutsche Nationalbibliothek lists this publication in the Deutsche Nationalbibliografie; detailed bibliographic data available online: https://dnb.de.

Cover design: Michael Haderer, Vienna
Proofreading: Elizabeth Phelps, Tirana
Typesetting: le-tex publishing services, Leipzig

Printed and bound: Hubert & Co. BuchPartner, Göttingen
Printed in the EU

Vandenhoeck & Ruprecht Verlage | www.vandenhoeck-ruprecht-verlage.com
ISBN 978-3-205-22008-4

Foreword

Albania, as immediately becomes clear when reading general accounts of the history of south-east Europe, must be a country full of legal history. And yet we in Germany (and the names of many other countries could also be mentioned here) know next to nothing about Albania's legal history and the academic work that has been done on it. This is of course due to the fact that Albania was isolated for decades. But this ignorance has not changed to this day, even though Albania is now part of a network of international relations and will soon be a member of the European Union.

The work of Argita Malltezi and Armela Kromiçi fundamentally changes the situation. The "History of Law in Albania. Bibliography of Legal Research" is a pioneering work that makes all Albanian legal history research accessible and documents its findings. In addition, the work, modestly titled "Bibliography", offers original descriptions in its extensive commentaries on the individual publications, which make central areas of Albanian legal history accessible to the reader. As a standard academic work, this "Bibliography" is therefore the basis for all further legal-historical research on Albania and as such is of inestimable value.

Prof. Dr. Martin Löhnig

Table of Contents

History of Law in Albania. Bibliography of Legal Research

The course of the evolution of law, beginning with its sources and tracing its development through time, not only highlights the peculiar features of a nation's legal order, but also reveals its fundamental ligature with the essence of the nation's conscience. The collection of titles that we had the opportunity to review during the preparation of this book unfolds the extraordinary journey of Albanian legal thought and legal systems, which developed their own particular features, despite the fact that during long periods of history the Albanian territories have been under the rule of the greatest empires of the times and their legal regimes. The Albanian legal regimes borrowed from the regimes of these empires, or the neighbouring countries, but preserved and consolidated their own unique identifying features.

The effort to document the history of legal research in Albania first began with the modest aim of reflecting the research published in recent years. From the onset we noticed that, whilst several general or thematic bibliographies had been previously published, none of them focused on the history of law. We therefore decided to expand the scope of our work and attempt the recollection of all publications on the history of the legal research in Albania that we could find.

The bibliography of the research on the history of law aims to provide Albanian and foreign researchers with a chronological picture of the works that have explored the history and evolution of law in the Albanian territories. The research studies listed in this bibliography discuss topics pertaining to the applicable legal regimes, spanning from Illyrian times until the present day. This book is the result of extended research conducted at the National Library of Albania, the Library of the Academy of Sciences, the Library of the Parliament of Albania, libraries of the Faculty of Law and the Faculty of History of Tirana University, School of Magistrates, University Libraries of Shkodra, Durrës and Korça, the Central State Archive, the Library and the Archive of the Institute of History.

The titles listed in this study include books, articles and other scientific works of scholars, which highlight key moments in the evolution of law, or its branches, in the Albanian territories. The publication is organized in four chapters. Within each, the titles are listed chronologically by year of publication and are accompanied by an explanatory paragraph. The first chapter contains works that explore the history of law from a legal point of view. Their authors are lawyers, whose research focuses on matters pertaining to the history or evolution of law. In addition to publications by legal scholars, the research in this domain has also attracted the attention of historians, whose significant contribution to the fond of such studies is evident. The books included in the second chapter are publications of a philosophical, historical, and diplomatic nature, as well as studies on Albanology, which have dedicated a part of their research to aspects of the history of the Albanian law and state. The third chapter lists doctoral theses and various scientific articles in this domain. The fourth chapter is dedicated to sources from the library and the archival fond of the Institute of History and the Central State Archive. The appendix lists compendium editions of legal acts adopted in different time periods, and a compendium of High Court and Constitutional Court jurisprudence, which in our opinion will be useful references for legal scholars, practicing lawyers and magistrates.

The titles listed in this bibliography demonstrate that the main focal areas for these bodies of literature include the study of the legal regime in Illyria, the role of liturgic and chronographic codices, the statutory law of medieval Albanian cities, the customary law of the *kanuns* (canons) of different areas, the law under the Albanian principates, the legal regimes of the Albanian *pashaliks*, the law of the ruling empires in the Albanian territories, as well as the positive law of the Albanian state as of its declaration of independence.

Studies on the state and the legal regime of Illyria and of the later Byzantine period are rather few, published mainly between 1960–1990 with some major reprints and new contributions after this year. They are important stepping stones in the research on this period, which still remains relatively unexplored.

Codices, canons, statutes, as well as the law of the Albanian *pashaliks* of Shkodra and Ioannina, testify to the creation of Albanian legal regimes which were developed and applied independently of the positive law of the ruling empires in the Albanian territories in the same period. They also bear evidence of the evolution of the national consciousness among Albanians.

The recently published codexes and ensuing studies on them affirm their impact on the creation of the secular legal regimes amongst the Albanian population. The path from the early codices to the codex of Korça and Selasfori, the codex of Fier, and other similar codices illustrates how the codices exceeded their initial liturgical object and included in the range of their recordings mandatory rules for the lay community, statutes and decisions of community guilds or different contracts of the inhabitants of their parish.[1] This dynamic influenced the development of the legal language and the secular legal regimes. The statutes of the chapters of the Cathedral of Drishti sanctioned in their rules that the ancient customs of the elders ought to be considered as a legal source,[2] which shows not only common ancestral sources of this regime with the customary law, but also the persistent validation of the customary law principles by the positive law of the period. The codices have been

1 Drejtoria e Përgjithshme e Arkivave. Kodikët e Shqipërisë. Tiranë, 2003.

2 Ahmeti, Musa. Lala, Etleva. Statutet dhe Urdhëresat e Kapitullit të Kishës Katedrale të Drishtit. Statuta Et Ordinationes Capituli Ecclesiae Cathedralis Drivastiensis. 'Ombra GVG'. Tiranë, 2009, Chapter 23, p. 161.

researched and interpreted in a number of publications, but this bibliography has listed only those works which analyse the influence of the codices on the evolution of law in Albania. We remain hopeful that the still unexplored fund of the Albanian chronographic codices will further attract the interest of legal researchers.

A plethora of Albanian and foreign authors have written about the Albanian customary law, considering it to be a continuation of Illyrian and Roman law. Despite the many different powers that have invaded and ruled Albania over the centuries, this corpus of laws has withstood the test of time, preserving its originality while also being enriched by legal developments of different epochs. Contributors in this field have written extensively about the different Albanian *kanuns* that operated in various areas of Albanian territories and have drawn comparative analyses between them, as well as between the *kanuns* and the positive law applicable in the same area, during a given period of time. Many highlight the fact that, during the Ottoman rule, the High Gate recognized certain autonomy of the areas governed by the Kanun of Lek Dukagjini, and several other *kanuns* in the north and the south, acknowledging the *kanun* as the law of these areas and its bodies as the governing bodies of their respective community.

The studies on the role of the *kanun* in the development of the law cited in this book offer not only a legal analysis of its norms, but also of its impact on Albanian legal thought and on the profile of the legislation adopted after the declaration of Albania's independence. The regime of the Albanian *kanuns*, as a unique and the most long-lasting legal regime, has played a significant role in catalysing national consciousness among Albanians. The national conscience, which pushes the coordinated action of the subjects of a territory for the cause of the nation's survival, despite religious and regional differences, is impressively demonstrated in the case of the fights of the northern Albanian tribes against the decisions of the Congress of Berlin, which severed Albanian territories in favour of the neighbouring countries. The *kanun's* instrument of *besa* united the Albanian tribes in this common cause. *Besa* and other instruments of the *kanun* helped the tribes put aside blood feuds, overcome religious differences and property conflicts, and behave as one nation. Their epic fight to protect Plava, Gucia, Hoti and Gruda, revealed the common national consciousness as they pledged to fight for the Albanian lands regardless of their differences. The Catholics of Hoti and Gruda fought against the Christian Montenegrins. The Muslims of Plava and Gucia fought against the Turkish Empire—all together for the lands of their common nation. Although arguably not the first, these fights were amongst the most important manifestations of the reawakening of the Albanian national consciousness after the centuries long Ottoman occupation.

The statutes of Albanian cities have been a constant topic of interest to historians and legal scholars, who have published well-known research in the field of the history of law. These publications were revived after the discovery of the Shkodra

Statutes by Lucia Nadin in 1997, as well as the translation of the complete edition of the Statutes of Drishti Cathedral by Musa Ahmeti and Etleva Lala in 2009, following earlier efforts by the prominent Croatian Albanologist Milan Sufflay at the beginning of the 20th century. Many authors have studied these statutes as evidence of a developed and diverse regime of positive law in Albanian cities during the Middle Ages. These authors have also noted that the statutes of the Albanian cities were formed as independent legal regimes. Despite the influence of Italian law schools, the Albanian statutes developed inherent characteristics which distinguished them from the statutes of the other Adriatic coastline cities. Interestingly, whilst coastal cities like Shkodra were governed by these statutes, the adjacent highlands were governed by the Kanun of Lek Dukagjini. Despite the different sources and paths of formation, the two regimes shared common core principles which are unmistakably identified with features of the Albanian people. For instance, the Statute of Shkodra distinctively based some judicial procedural aspects on *besa (bessare)*, a core principle, minutely regulated in the Kanun of Lek Dukagjini.[3]

The impact of the Ottoman Empire's legal regime in the Albanian territories is another extensively explored topic of the history of law. Authors have researched its influence on the Albanian customary law (*kanun*), the legal regime of the Albanian feudal *pashaliks* and the evolution of their positive law, as well as the publications of different public registers in various areas, which attest to the administrative organization of Albanian territories, the economic life, traditions and structure of its communities. Many of the works listed in the bibliography discuss the Albanian resistance against the Ottoman Empire and its various reforms, as well as the Albanian struggle for autonomy and independence. On the latter, regarding the historical events until the 19th century, particular attention has been paid to the League of Prizren and its legal framework.

Authors who have studied the *pashalik* of Ioannina, of Ali Pasha Tepelena and the *pashalik* of Shkodra of the Bushatli dynasty, have come to the common conclusion that they developed their own legal regimes, different from that of the Ottoman Empire, as part of their efforts to break away from the High Gate. In this context, little has been written about the law of other *pashaliks*, as for instance the *pashalik* of Berat.

The declaration of independence and the creation of the new Albanian state in 1912 paved the way for the structuring of a new and modern legal system, which became the subject of many studies, especially after the 1990s. In a short period of time, the historical course of events, intertwined with the adoption of a

---

3 Sinani, Shaban. Kodikët Kronografikë të Shqipërisë – Shkrime dhe Dorëshkrime prej Rilindjes Europiane deri në Rilindjen Kombëtare. 'Naimi'. Tiranë, 2014, p. 272.

pyramid of legal acts and by-laws, resulted in radical changes of the legal regime in Albania. Many publications offer insights into the Law of the Jury *(Kanoni i Zhurisë)*, manifestly influenced by the customary law; the Interim Law of the Civil Administration *(Kanuni i Përtashëm i Administratës Civile)*; the Organic Statute of Albania under the reign of Prince Wied; the Statute of Lushnja; the Fundamental Statute of the Republic of Albania of 1925 and later, that of the Kingdom of Albania of 1928, and other important legal acts. Noticeable are the works of Albanian jurists who contributed during the reign of King Zog to the drafting of a number of codes, according to the best Western European models of the time, and the publication of important legal works. Some of these jurists, whose works are cited in this bibliography, were later persecuted by the communist regime installed in 1945 and, as a result, their works were banned from references and circulation. After the 1990s, many of these works were re-published in several editions.

This bibliography includes publications from the period of the communist regime (1945–1990), marked by the terminology and ideological tones of the mandatory propaganda of the time. Whilst many of its standard phrases echo the abhorrence of the struggle of classes, the proletarian dictatorship and the lip service that the propaganda provided to the genocidal campaigns of the communist regime, we have chosen to include the publications of this period in this bibliography for several reasons. First, despite the obligatory propaganda tones and restrictive censorship, some of the titles are valuable works, without which we would know much less of our legal history and its evolution, for better or for worse. Secondly, publications which cite the legal acts that served as the basis for the change of regime and the establishment of the new economic model after the Second World War, are helpful in the study of history of law of this period. Thirdly, these works will help legal scholars, especially young scholars, to understand the restriction of basic human rights under the communist regime and its ideology. In our belief, it is only by facing the events of our history directly and analysing them scientifically, without bias or hiding the truth, that we will be able to avert repetitions of the same mistakes over the course of the history.

The fall of the Iron Curtain and the restoration of pluralism in the country in 1990 brought a new era in the development of the state and law, as well as thorough reforms in the pyramid of legal acts. There are many publications dedicated to these transformations in the economic, political, legal and justice system. This period also includes numerous works which, free from censorship, have retaken on aspects of the Albanian customary law, the state and legal regime during the reign of King Zog, as well as that of the period of the communist dictatorship.

In order to follow a unified standard for the selection of titles listed in this bibliography, we have included herein only works that are part of the fonds of the main libraries in Albania, mentioned above. This effectively constitutes a selection criterion and the reason for which some published titles do not feature.

Some works on the history of law, despite market availability, are not found in the fonds of libraries. Another reason for which there may be works that have not been listed in this publication is the lack of a unique standard in the key terms upon which the cataloguing of titles in the National Library or other libraries is based. Erroneous classification keywords may make it impossible to find titles digitally. In order to lessen the impact of these deficiencies, the book has relied on the fond of several libraries. Each title is accompanied with its coordinates in one or more libraries, the corresponding code (if any), or the library file. In cases where a publication is available in several libraries, we have prioritized the libraries where access of the text is easier.

The generous support of many academic and library professionals, to whom the authors are immensely grateful, has been crucial to the conception and advancement of this work. We are especially thankful to Prof. Dr. Martin Löhnig for suggesting we undertake this project and for his continuous support throughout this journey, to Prof. Dr. Nada Dollani and Prof. Assoc. Dr. Eneida Sema for their helpful comments, Prof. Dr. Luan Malltezi, for his constant support and suggestions regarding the sources of this work, Prof. Dr. Valentina Duka, Prof. Dr. Arenca Troshani, Prof. Dr. Ledina Alolli, Prof. Assoc. Dr. Andon Kume, Dr. Ardit Bido, Prof. Dr. Afrim Krasniqi, Prof. Dr. Aurela Anastasi, Dr. Etleva Pepo, Dr. Alketa Bekteshi for the help in carrying out the research in the archives and libraries of their institutions. The dedicated library employees Mirela Mihali, Eva Sefa, Ylkena Këllezi, Teuta Sula, Elektra Haxhia, and Dasara Malltezi who assisted in the identification and collection of materials for revising the early drafts of the English edition.

We hope that this monograph will assist Albanian and foreign legal scholars in their further research. The works contained herein reflect also the challenges of the times during which their authors lived; the shocks from the collapse of systems and the rise of new systems; world wars and challenging historical choices; extreme governmental censorship and individual self-censorship; the transition to pluralism and freedom of expression, accompanied with scientific freedom, which in balance has an essential need for guidance in those domains and projects that are important for the Albanian nation. The scientific works published in different periods depict the journey of Albanian legal thought across different stages in history, the evolution of the distinctive features of the Albanian legal regimes, forged in times of war and freedom, oppression and the rise against it, through examples of virtue and steadfastness or contrasting mistakes. They are the map of a time-tested path, which jurists, historians, legislators and judges must keep in mind when designing the journey of the Albanian legislation on the path towards the future.

Prof. Dr. Argita Malltezi — Dr. Armela Kromiçi

Abbreviations

In order to find each book referenced in the bibliography, its records with abbreviations are provided. The books that are located at the National Library and the Central State Archives are accompanied with the specific code. Regarding the books located in other libraries, the author's name or its title is sufficient.

AQSH	Arkivi Qendror i Shtetit
BK	Biblioteka Kombëtare
BFDUT	Biblioteka e Fakultetit të Drejtësisë, Universiteti i Tiranës
BFHFUT	Biblioteka e Fakultetit të Historisë dhe i Filologjisë, Universiteti i Tiranës
BKSH	Biblioteka e Kuvendit të Shqipërisë
BIHGJL	Biblioteka Shkencore, Akademia e Studimeve Albanologjike
BUSH	Biblioteka e Universitetit të Shkodrës
BUD	Biblioteka e Universitetit të Durrësit
BSHM	Biblioteka e Shkollës së Magjistraturës

Part 1:
Books on the History of Developments of a Legal Regime, or Its Branches

This first part of the bibliography is devoted to publications whose main focus is on the exploration and interpretation of historical development of the Albanian law and institutions, and on the regulatory frameworks of specific legal regimes and their historical development.

1. **Gjeçovi, K. Shtjefën.** Kanuni i Lekë Dukagjinit. Posthumous Work. Summary and Codified by Gjeçovi, K. Shtjefën. Preface by Fishta, Gjergj. The Author's Biography by Bardhi, Pashk. Shtypshkronja 'Françeskane'. Shkodër, 1933. BK: S 59 A 27
2. **Gjeçovi, K. Shtjefën.** Kanuni i Lekë Dukagjinit. Posthumous Work. Summary and Codified by Gjeçovi, K. Shtjefën. Preface Fishta, Gjergj. The Author's Biography by Bardhi, Pashk. Third Edition, Anastatic. 'Botimet Françeskane'. Shkodër, 2010. BK: S 332 A 9.
3. **Gjeçovi, K. Shtjefën.** Kanuni i Lekë Dukagjinit. Posthumous Work. Summary and Codified by Gjeçovi, K. Shtjefën. Preface Fishta, Gjergj. The Author's Biography by Bardhi, Pashk. Fourth Edition, Anastatic. 'Botimet Françeskane'. Shkodër, 2013. BK: S 429 A 48

The Kanun of Lek Dukagjin (KLD) is the most emblematic code of Albanian customary law. It was the absolute legal regime of the areas in the north of Albania, including the highlands of Kosova, regardless of religion. Some of the areas that followed the KLD regime were isolated terrains, where the tribes' unceasing armed efforts in the pursuit of freedom made access of foreign invaders difficult, if not impossible. These areas continued to be governed by the KLD for centuries, despite the various invaders that ruled the country. The High Gate recognized factual autonomy of the northern tribes, as well as that of other areas in the south, and allowed them to be governed by their *kanuns*. This autonomy enabled these regions to apply, transmit and develop the KLD, to preserve their characteristics of organization in the social and public domain, and to resolve matters of criminal and civil law in accordance with their millennia old customary law. It is for these reasons that the KLD has always attracted the attention of researchers, becoming the subject of numerous publications.

Other mountainous or plains rural areas followed other *kanuns*—the publications of which are cited further in this book. However, the provisions of the KLD were collected and published during the time when this set of norms was still being applied with absolute rigor, in every aspect of social and private life, in the respective territories. For this reason the KLD is considered to be the most authentic reflection of Albanian customary law as compared to other *kanuns*.[1] Despite various debates, including the etymology of the word *kanun*, or its eponym after the 15th century prince Lek Dukagjini, the academic consensus is that the *kanun* is the customary law of the Albanian territories; it is believed to have its genesis in pre-state pagan societies, and has been enriched over centuries with further norms that suited the stages of development of social relations and historical conditions.[2]

The provisions of the KLD were verbally transmitted from generation to generation as unwritten customary law until the end of the 19th century, although several attempts of codification of the KLD are reported in the titles quoted in this bibliography.[3] Franciscan priest Father Shtjefën Gjeçovi (1874–1929) was the first to publish his collection of the norms of the famous *kanun*. Gjeçovi spent most of the active years of his life as a parish priest in the Northern Mountains of Albania, where he systematically collected data on the ethnology, folklore, and in particular the customary norms of KLD. He began publishing the collection of KLD norms in parts between the years 1897–1899, in the periodical journal *Albania*, which was published in Brussels by Faik Konica. Later, from 1913 until 1924, the partial publications of KLD continued in Shkodra at the periodical *Hylli i Dritës*.[4]

---

1 Elezi, Ismet. E Drejta Zakonore e Labërisë në Planin Krahasues. 'Libri Universitar'. Tiranë, 1994, p. 22.

2 Studime Historike. Vol. 9, Tiranë. Akademia e Shkencave, Instituti i Historisë. 1972, p. 107–110. Yamamoto, Kazuhiko. The Ethical Structure of Homeric Society. Collegium Antropologicum. Qendra 'Drejtësi dhe Paqe'. Shkodër, 2001, 164 f.; Gjeçovi, K. Shtjefën. Kanuni i Lekë Dukagjinit. Codified by Gjeçovi, K. Shtjefën. Annotated by Pupovci, Syrja. Enti i Teksteve dhe i Mjeteve Mësimore. Prishtinë, 1972, p. 18; Gjeçovi, K. Shtjefën. Kanuni i Lekë Dukagjinit. Edited and Annotated by Nova, Koço. Akademia e Shkencave. Tiranë, 1989, p. 14; Valentini, Giuseppe. Studime dhe Tekste juridike I. (Seria Valentini). 'Plejad'. Tiranë, 2009, p. 29.

3 There are references on the tentative of the administration of the Ottoman Empire to codify the Albanian customary law, as a way of putting them under control, but these attempts were futile. Gjeçovi, Kanuni, Annotated by Fishta, p. 21; Gjeçovi, Kanuni, Annotated by Nova, p. 40.

Another Catholic priest, father Nikollë Ashta, author of several works on the KLD, collected and edited a compilation of KLD rules which he began publishing in 1897, in the Albanian journal published in Brussels by Faik Bey Konica. See Elsie, Robert. Der Kanun. Das Albanisce Gewohnheitsrecht nach dam Sogenannten Kanun des Lekë Dukagjini Kodifiziert von Shtjefën Gjeçovi ins Deutche Űbersetzt von Marie Amelie Freiin von Godin Einfuhrung von Michael Schimdt-Neke. Osteuropa Zentrum. Berlin, 2014, p. 6.

4 Elsie, Robert. Der Kanun. Das Albanisce Gewohnheitsrecht nach dem Sogenannten Kanun des Lekë Dukagjini Kodifiziert von Shtjefën Gjeçovi ins Deutcheubersetzt von Marie Amelie Freiin von Godin Einfuhrung von Michael Schimdt-Neke, Dukagjini. Pejë, 2001, p. 6; See also Gjeçovi, Kanuni, Annotated by Fishta, p. 23; Elezi, Ismet. Kanuni i Labërisë. 'Toena'. Tiranë, 2006, p. 21.

The integral text of KLD was published for the first time in Shkodër, by *Botimet Françeskane* in 1933.

The Kanun of Lek Dukagjin has, since then, been widely reprinted in Albanian and in other languages, with prefaces and interpretations by various authors. These reprints and translations can be found in the National Library of Albania as well as the other libraries mentioned in this publication.

Gjeçovi's KLD publication of 1933 is organized in 12 books, which codify legal provisions that regulate life within the community, norms pertaining to the sphere of criminal, public and private law. The provisions span the relationship with the church, family relations, civil law relations, sanctioning of the criminal offenses, the social organization and order of the community, the role of elders and tribal leaders who held public functions, rights and obligations of the individual, as well as the public bodies organized in accordance with the *kanun*. The first book deals with the role and status of the Catholic Church, the parish priest, church wageworkers and staff, the church's properties and related guarantees. The second and third books are dedicated to the family, the role of each of its members, and a detailed regulation of the institution of marriage, arranged marriages, engagements, and inheritance. The fourth book focuses on relations of a civil legal nature and regulates the regime of movable and immovable property, the methods for determining property boundaries. The fifth book regulates trade conduct, types of employment and the rights arising from such relationships. The sixth book encompasses the regime of loans, pawns, the promise to perform an obligation and the relinquishment of claims. The seventh book establishes rules on verbal communication and the consequence of speech, the manner of taking an oath, and its importance and types: such as the oath upon the cross, the oath upon the house *(be për derë)*, or the oath for not knowing (*be me sedije)*. The eighth book is dedicated to a fundamental institute of Albanian customary law: *honor* and the different regimes that provide for its protection. Part of the regime of this chapter is the protection of the guest, which is considered essential for the honor of the host house. The institutions of mediation, bail, fraternity, and the institute of godfather—equally applicable to Christian and Muslim areas according to customary law procedure—are also addressed here. The ninth book establishes the legal regime for damages. The tenth book regulates criminal offenses, including theft, robbery, and murder. The eleventh book, which deals with aspects of public law, is centered on the role of the eldership (*pleqësia*), the different assemblies of the elders (based on the village, the brotherhoods and the flag (*bayrak*), the manner of summoning the eldership, the right of participation in its meetings, the eldership competences and decisions, as well as the implementation of these decisions by the bailiff (*gjobtarët*). The rules of the last book regulate the rites in case of death and the honoring of the deceased. The famous

Albanian customary law institute of *besa*[5] is regulated in different parts of the KLD. For instance, the eighth book regulates the protection of the guest and establishes the most severe regime for guaranteeing his safety.[6] Although this part does not specifically mention the word *besa*, the implication is evident as it refers to the breach of it (*t premt'*). The tenth book defines the *besa* given to the killer and his family for a limited number of days before beginning the period of revenge. At the end of the work there is an analytical-alphabetical index and a glossary of terms and phrases. Despite some terms, borrowed from foreign legal regimes, the code has always preserved its uniqueness and distinctiveness as an Albanian legal regime. This aspect is emphasized in most of the books listed in this publication.

The publication of Gjeçovi's compilation is the starting point of any subsequent study or translation of KLD. It offers biographical notes on Father Gjeçovi, prepared by Father Pashk Bardhi, as well as a preface by Father Gjergj Fishta. The preface underlines the importance of the national folklore and of the collection of customary laws, as well as the legal significance of the Kanun of Lek Dukagjin. The reprints have faithfully preserved the organization of the norms according to the original edition.

4. **Gjeçovi, K. Shtjefën.** Kanuni i Lekë Dukagjinit. Collected and Codified by Gjeçovi, K. Shtjefën. Preface by Pupovci, Syrja. Enti i Teksteve dhe i Mjeteve Mësimore. Prishtinë, 1972. BK: S 90 A 49. BFDUT

This edition of the Kanun of Lek Dukagjin is accompanied by legal interpretation by Syrja Pupovci. The author elaborates on the origin and evolution of Albanian customary law as a legal framework brought about by the daily life of people, rather than being imposed by various governing authorities.

He points out that KLD has two versions. One is the version followed by the tribes of Northern Albania, whilst another variation is widespread in the villages of the Dukagjin plain, among Albanians living in Kosova. The author notes that from a legal point of view, Albanian customary law distinguished class elements, and that the KLD was developed in a tribal patriarchal societal order, which recognized and accepted the personal initiative of the tribe leaders, or elders, who were distinguished for the weight of their personality and the respect they enjoyed amongst

5 *Besa* is a promise or allegiance. The *Albanian Encyclopedic Dictionary* explains *besa* as an institute of the customary law, that consist in keeping up a promise, the word of honor, and honoring at all costs the undertaken obligation. *Besa* has been widely relied on in alleviating consequences of blood vendetta; Fjalori Enciklopedik, Akademia e Shkencave të Shqipërisë, Tiranë, 2008, p. 220.

6 See §640 et seq. To be noted that §649, for instance, stipulates that in case of murder of the closest family, the claim for revenge could be relinquished, whereas in cases of murdering of a guest, the host could not give up his obligation to revenge the guest's death.

other elders. He highlights the collegial powers of the assemblies (*kuvendit*) to issue or change provisions of the *kanun*. The author considers the KLD as evidence of the development and interweaving of different legal systems, with old institutions that are no longer enforced in other European countries. He locates the origin of the KLD in the application of customary law in a slave-owning society and analyzes the different doctrinal positions on the origin of KLD, as well as the consequences of the Islamization of Albanians after the Ottoman occupation. He notes that the unwritten norms of the KLD have coexisted with the various legal systems that have ruled in the Balkans. The text surveys other *kanuns* that operated in the north and south of Albania, and presents a broader comparative analysis between the KLD and the Kanun of Skanderbeg. The author interprets selected norms from different legal spheres of the kanun, including blood feuds, legal actions, private property, institutions of family law and customary procedural norms of criminal and civil law as an overview of the kanun's legal regime. This preface, which can be considered as the first part of the publication, is followed by the complete text of the Kanun of Lek Dukagjini.

5. **Gjeçovi, K. Shtjefën.** Kanuni i Lekë Dukagjinit. Edited and Annotated by Nova, Koço. Akademia e Shkencave e RPSSH. Tiranë, 1989. BK: S 181 F 63

In 1989, the Albanian Academy of Sciences published the Kanun of Lek Dukagjin, collected and codified by Shtjefën K. Gjeçovi, with annotations by Koço Nova. This official edition of the Academy of Sciences, on the brink of changes in the governing system in Albania, indicated a change in the official position of the Albanian government towards the Catholic clergy's contribution in the collection and preservation of the customary law. The publication analyzes the importance of the norms of the Kanun of Lek Dukagjin (KLD) from a legal standpoint. The editor acknowledges the contribution of Albanian and foreign authors in researching and preserving the Albanian customary law: from chroniclers and travelers of the Middle Ages—where he notes Andronicus III of Byzantium, who differentiates between the Albanian customs of punishment by death (*dënim me vrasje*) from the provisions of the nomocanon of Byzantium—to authors in the Middle Ages, who have written about the social structure of the Albanian mountains, regulated according to inherited *kanuns* and without any intervention from Ottoman laws or judges. He also notes the work of foreign Albanologists of the 19th century and their precious contribution to the study of Albanian customary law. The editor highlights that despite bearing the name of Lek Dukagjin, the medieval prince of an Albanian northen tribe, the origin of this customary law is much more ancient. He notes the importance of the local *kanun* acts, which starting from the second half of the 19th century influenced the enrichment of special institutes of Albanian customary law. Among these local kanuns, the author mentiones (i) the Kanun of Kastrati (1891 and

1892), (ii) *Kanun of Usulli*, which is a decision of 1892 of Vukli village, that aimed at limiting the scope of blood vendetta, (iii) the Kanun of Kashnjeti (1904), which again aimed at limiting murders between tribes, (iv) the Kanun of Kurbin, which forbade carrying out blood vendetta arbitrarily, without first consulting the elders, while also prohibiting the residents of Kurbin from consulting Turkish authorities on these matters, as well as other local *kanuns*. Nova's publication of the Kanun of Lek Dukagjini is structured in two parts, further divided into chapters and sub-sections. In the first part, at the forefront of the first chapter, titled "Social order", it regulates the family relations, the institution of marriage, family ties and the basic principles of the KLD. The chapter continues with the main bodies and institutions of the KLD: vengeance, mediation and reconciliation; as well as the role of the Church and religious service. The second chapter, entitled "Economic order", reflects the customary norms dedicated to private and common property, the modalities for determining borders, the farming and agricultural organization of the society. A focal topic of this part is the regime on inheritance and obligations, which are further subdivided into general obligations and obligations arising from damages. The third chapter, known as the "Punishment part", regulates types of punishments, the modality of their enforcement and the punitive liability. The fourth chapter, titled the "Special part", focuses on offenses (*mbrapshtinat*) against the social order, church, life, health, wealth, and the norms that regulate exemptions. The second part of the publication, titled *"Appendices" (Shtojcat)*, includes information on the Kanun of Lek Dukagjin, the district of Dukagjin and notes on the life of Gjeçovi. The second chapter also offers decisions of assemblies regarding the application of the KLD, as well as special *kanun* acts of a local character. Further on, the work contains documents that depict the role of the church and of the Turkish authorities, including the law of *jibal*[7] and other customs implemented in the Northern areas of Albania. An English translation of the introduction is provided at the end of the publication.

6. **Gjeçovi, K. Shtjefën**. Kanuni i Lek Dukagjinit. Preface by Fishta, Gjergj. 'Albiform'. Tiranë, 1993. BK: S 97 G 60. BFHFUT

7 *Jibal Kanun* was the Ottoman term for the law (the kanun) of the mountains and in this context referred to the Kanun of Lek Dukagjini. In the second half of the 19th century, within the framework of the centralizing reforms of the Tanzimat, the Turkish government created a commission called the "Highland Commission". Also known as the Jibal Commission, it was placed under the supervision of the Vali of Shkodra and aimed to bring the areas governed by customary law under the control of the Ottoman administration. Its members, representatives of 26 *bayraqs* of Shkodra Vilayet as well as 26 Bolukbashis, were paid appointees. The President of Jibali was appointed by the Governor (Vali) of Shkodra. The commission and the executive role of the *bylykbashes* sought to replace the authority of the canonical institutions. For further, see Gjeçovi, Kanuni, Annotated by Nova, p. 40; Gjeçovi, Kanuni, Preface by Pupovci, p. 68.

7. **Gjeçovi, K. Shtjefën.** Kanuni i Lekë Dukagjinit. Preface by Fishta, Gjergj. Kuvendi i Shqipërisë. Lezhë, 1998. BK: S 193D 42
8. **Gjeçovi, K. Shtjefën.** Kanuni i Lekë Dukagjinit. Preface by Fishta, Gjergj. Second Edition. Kuvendi i Shqipërisë. Lezhë, 2001. BKSH; BK: AL 30 B13

The 1933 edition of KLD from the publishing house *Botimet Françeskane*, is reprinted in full, together with the preface by Father Gjergj Fishta. These reprints highlight the role of the KLD in the preservation of national identity in the areas of governance, noting that during the Ottoman occupation the High Gate (Porta e Lartë) allowed the provinces historically governed by the KLD to maintain this regime instead following Ottoman law, effectively granting autonomy to the mountainous areas of Albania.

A dictionary of rare words and expressions is included at the end of the text; these are instrumental in understanding the content of the provisions of the KLD.

9. **Gjeçovi, K. Shtjefën.** Codice di Lek Dukagjini ossia Diritto Consuetudinario delle Montagne d'Albania. Tradotto dal Albanese in Italiano dal Dodaj, P. Pal. A Cura di Fishta, Gjergj. e Skiroi, Zef. (Schirò, Giuseppe). Con Introduzione di Patteta, Federico. Reale Accademia d'Italia. Roma, 1941. Italian Edition. BK: Al 25 C 23

Paolo Dodaj completed the first translation of KLD, into Italian. Father Gjergj Fishta and Zef Skiroi supervised the translation a few years after its first publication in Albanian.[8] The initial publication emphasizes the importance of the KLD and Albanian customary law in the preservation of national identity and notes that, although unwritten, the *kanun* was valued as imperative, with the same authority as if the norms were codified in writing. For this reason, it is considered a customary code. The Italian edition has preserved the structure of Shtjefën Gjeçov's *kanun* divided into twelve books, each accompanied by explanatory notes. The translation was first published in Rome in 1941 and has been reprinted in Italian in 1996 and in 2009, with the following coordinates:

10. **Dodaj, Paolo.** Il Kanun di Lek Dukagjini. Le Basi Morali e Giuridiche della Societá Albanese. Con Introduzione di Resta, Patrizia. 'Besa Editrice'. Lecce, 1996. Italian Edition. BK: AL 20 E 91

8 Gjeçovi, K. Shtjefën. Codice di Lek Dukagjini ossia Diritto Consuetudinario delle Montagne d'Albania. Traduzione dal Albanese in Italiano Dodaj, Pal. A cura di Fishta, Gjergj e Skiroi, Zef (Schirò, Giuseppe). Con Introduzione di Patteta, Federico. Reale Accademia d'Italia. Roma, 1941, p. 8.

11. **Dodaj, Paolo.** Il Kanun di Lek Dukagjini. Le Basi Morali e Giuridiche della Societá Albanese. Con Introduzione di Martucci, Donato. 'Besa Editrice'. Nardo, 2009. Italian Edition. BK: pp. 3(496.5). Ka

12. **Gjeçovi K., Shtjefën.** The Code of Lekë Dukagjini. Kanuni i Lekë Dukagjinit. Edited by Fox, Leonard. 'Gjonlekaj'. New York. 1989. Albanian and English Edition. BK: Ar 61A 30; PP.3/Gjeç.

This edition of the Kanun of Lek Dukagjin, as collected by Shtjefën Gjeçovi, was translated by Leonard Fox. The bilingual edition, in English and Albanian, is presented with a foreword by Martin Camaj. The edition has retained the original structure of the division into twelve books.

13. **Gjeçovi, K. Shtjefën.** Kanonot na Lek Dukagjini: (Posthumno Delo)/Sobral i Kodificiral. Prevel od Albanski Jazik Mehmeti, Kim. Urednik Gafur Abdiu. Fi & Ga. Tetovë, 1994. Macedonian Edition. BK: P 524C 21

The translation of the KLD into the Macedonian language by the writer and publicist Kim Mehmeti retains the original structure of the KLD, divided into twelve books. Besides an introduction from the editor, the publication also provides a summary of cases arising from the practical application of the kanun.

14. **Elsie, Robert.** Der Kanun. Das Albanisce Gewohnheitsrecht nach dem Sogenannten Kanun des Lekë Dukagjini Kodifiziert von Shtjefën Gjeçovi ins Deutcheubersetzt von Marie Amelie Freiin von Godin Einfuhrung von Michael Schimdt-Neke. 'Dukagjini'. Pejë. 2001. German Edition. BK: Al 30 C 17
15. **Elsie, Robert.** Der Kanun. Das Albanisce Gewohnheitsrecht nach dem Sogenannten Kanun des Lekë Dukagjini Kodifiziert von Shtjefën Gjeçovi ins Deutche Űbersetzt von Marie Amelie Freiin von Godin Einfuhrung von Michael Schimdt-Neke. Osteuropa Zentrum. Berlin, 2014. German Edition. BK: PP 3 (496.5) El

Renowned Albanologist and publicist Robert Elsie prepared and annotated this publication of the KLD. Elsie highlights the importance of the collection of the *kanun* by Shtjefën Gjeçovi and the history of the publication of the KLD in several foreign languages, as well as the work of various authors, Albanian and foreign, who have published studies about the KLD. He notes the Kanun of Labëria, the Kanun of Papa Zhuli and other *kanuns* that applied in other areas of Albania. He highlights the German translation of the KLD by the Bavarian Baroness Marie Amelie von Godin (1882–1956), who collaborated closely with Ekrem bej Vlora (1885–1964) beginning in the 1930s, with the aim of publishing a translation based on an earlier Albanian edition of the *kanun* collected by Shtjefën Gjeçov, rather than the version published in 1933. This translation was published in the 'Stuttgart Periodik Zeitschrift für Vergleichende Rechtswissenschaft' between 1953 and 1956. Elsie's publication is based on this version, which retains the structure in 12 books.

16. **Gjeçovi, Shtjefën.** Kanuni i Lekë Dukagjinit. El Kanun de Lekë Dukagjini. Traducción Española por Ajazi, Erida. Edición de Texto por Maria Moreno Molina. 'EDFA'. Tiranë, 2016. Spanish Edition. BK: S 492 A 34[9]

The Spanish translation of the Kanun of Lek Dukagjini preserves the original structure of the publication in 12 books.

17. **Gjeçovi, Shtjefën.** Kanuni i Lekë Dukagjinit. Preface, Additions and Appendix by Dema, Benedikt. O.F.M. Codified by Tedeschini, Emid. Second Edition. 'Botimet Françeskane'. Shkodër, 2018. BK: S 540 A 13
18. **Gjeçovi, Shtjefën.** Kanuni i Lekë Dukagjinit. Preface, Additions and Appendix by Dema, Benedikt. O.F.M. Codified by Tedeschini, Emid. Third Edition. 'Botimet Françeskane'. Shkodër, 2022. n.c.

The publication reflects the joint effort of father Benedikt Dema (1904–1971) and the well-known lawyer and author Emid Tedeschini (1909–1989), in which the norms of the kanun of Lek Dukagjin, collected by father Gjeçovi, are re-organized into chapters, according to their affiliation in private and public law. Despite the early attempt to publish this codification in 1944, the complete text was published only in 2018.[10] This version of the KLD is divided into two parts. The first part entitled "Private (law) Kanuns" is organized in 184 articles and structured in sub-titles. The first subtitle regulates personal relations, which include family law institutions, extended family and tribe relations, guardianship and the guest. The second title is dedicated to the regime on inheritance. The third title deals with goods and posessions, whilst the fourth title regulates obligations. The second part entitled "Public Laws" codifies 182 articles, structured in four sub-titles: (i) the first title is dedicated to governance; (ii) the second title regulates crimes; (iii) the third title provides the rules on trials, and (iv) the fourth title deals with the organization and rights of the (Catholic) Church. The publication contains ample bibliographic references, an analytical-alphabetical index, appendices and a glossary of rare terms and phrases.

---

9 The book cannot be withdrawn from the library archives.

10 Gjecovi, Shtjefën. Kanuni i Lek Dukagjinit. Third Edition. With the Introduction and Additions by Dema, Benedict. O.F.M. Codified by Tedeschini, Emid. 'Botimet Françeskane'. Shkodër, 2022, p. 6.

19. **Benussi, Baltazar.** Komentari i Kodit Civil. Sendet, Zotënimi dhe Modifikimet e Tija. Libri i Tretë i Kodit Civil. Ministria e Drejtësisë. Shtypshkronja 'Mbrothësija' Kristo Luarasi. Tiranë, 1931. BK: S 84 A 20
20. **Benussi, Baltazar.** Komentari i Kodit Civil. Sendet, Zotënimi dhe Modifikimet e Tija. Libri i Tretë i Kodit Civil. Ministria e Drejtësisë. Second Edition. Tiranë, 1997. BK: S 205 A 26

The Commentary of the third book of the Civil Code of 1929 is authored by one of the main contributors to the Albanian Civil Code of 1929. The code was drafted according to the best contemporary practices of European countries, breaking away from the Ottoman legislation that was implemented until that time in Albania.

21. **Benussi, Baltasar.** Komentari i Kodit Civil. Obligimet dhe Kontratat Përgjithësisht. Titulli i II i Librit të IV të Kodit Civil. Second Edition. Tiranë, 2012. n.c.

The second edition is the publication of the original version published by the Ministry of Justice in 1932.

22. **Tsitsos, Niko Ev.** Parime të Përgjithshme të së Drejtës Civile. Shtypshkronja 'Dhori Koti'. Korçë, 1931. AQSh: vendi: J.s 4

"General principles of the civil law" systematically interprets the general principles of the civil law of the time. The work is organized in five parts. In the first part, the author deals with the definition of positive law, morality, sources of civil law, the constitutional control of laws, the collection of evidence and its types, abrogation of laws, interpretation and criticism of laws, doctrine and jurisprudence. The second part analyzes the scope of application of the law, land boundaries, inheritances, donations and contracts, as well as other civil law institutions. In the third part, the author dwells on the classification of rights, focusing on real rights, personal rights, intellectual property rights, transferable and non-transferable rights, subjects of law, and categories of objects. Further, the work analyzes the concept of wealth, coins and currencies. The fourth part deals with the elements and the validity of legal acts, their legal regime and prescription. In the fifth and final part, the author reflects on aspects of the judicial protection of rights. This publication, despite not being a book on the historical developments of the law, it is included in this bibliography because it reflects a period of major legal transformation in Albania, which the author aimed to elucidate by interpreting the newly implemented regime and by drawing a comparison with the European jurisprudential traditions and legal developments of the time.

23. **Shkoza, Haxhi.** Financat e Shqipnis (1839–1934). Shtypshkronja 'Nikaj'. Tiranë, 1935. BK: S 88 B 75

"The finances of Albania" is one of the key sources on the history of financial law in Albania, for the centenary period of 1839–1934. It lists the categories of public revenue in Albania during this time span; their legal regime under the rule of the Ottoman Empire, which partially remained in force even after Albania's independence in 1912; and the legal reforms undertaken by the Albanian governments during the republican and the monarchic form of the regime. It includes sources of public revenues, such as taxes; duties; revenues from public services; monopolies; income generated from sales or rents of public real estate; fishing and hunting permits; revenues from forests, mining, concessions, customs, courts and public services. A special section is dedicated to the constitutional provisions and the main financial laws that applied during the period covered by the study. This section includes: (a) the applicable tax regime before the Tanzimat reform of 1839; (b) taxation under a unified legal system on 1839 (19 Zil-Kade 1255) and its exemption cases; (c) the regulation of the Ministry of Finance on the legal representative and lawyers (*hakuk mushaviri*) of 1886 (27.9.1302); (d) the law of the tithes (*ligjin e të dhjetave*) of 1905 (9.VI.1321), which remained in force during the monarchy of Ahmet Zog; (e) the Founding Statute of the Monarchy of 1928; (f) the law On The Establishment Of Chambers Of Commerce, dated 14.3.1929 and its appendix dated 9.9.1929; and (g) the Law on the State Accounting (1928). The book also notes the framework of commercial agreements between the Ottoman Empire and third countries and the applicability of this regime in Albania, as well as agreements between the Albanian independent state and other countries. The author analyzes the establishment of popular banks in 1890, approved by the law dated 19 *Zil-hixhe* 1305, which later became the Agricultural Bank, its reformation on 1930, and the adoption of the Commercial Code of 1932. In addition to this book, which can be found in the National Library, the fond of Haxhi Shkoza can be accessed at the Central Archive and provides a number of important documents of the time.

24. **Toçi, Terenc.** Tri Mbrojtje Ndëshkimore. Për Lirin e Shtypit, për Vrasjen e nji Mësuesi, për Nderin e Familjes Shqiptare. Shtypshkronja 'Tirana'. Tiranë, 1940. BK: 88 F 162; S 11 D 172

The author presents his legal viewpoints on three cases in which he acted in the capacity of the defense attorney, and which had sparked considerable debate in the doctrine and public opinion of the time. The book, despite its limited focus on the material law of a particular matter, is useful in understanding the interweaving of elements from the newly emerging Albanian state law with elements that were historically regulated by customary law, such as matters of honor and family law.

25. **Giannini, Amedeo.** L'Albania D'Indipendenza all'Unione con L'Italia (1913–1939). Instituto per gli Studi di Politica Internazionale. Fourth Edition. Varese, 1940. Italian Edition. BK: Al 40 33 G

The Italian edition titled "Albania from independence to its union with Italy" addresses important issues of the history of the Albanian state, bringing the full text of a series of documents and legal acts, including in particular: (i) the status of Albania according to the decision of July 29, 1913 of the Conference of Ambassadors in London (in French); (ii) The Statute of Albania drawn up by the International Control Commission; (iii) the decision of the Durrës Assembly of December 15, 1918 (in French); the Agreement of July 29, 1919 signed by Tittolini-Venizelos (in French); (iv) the founding statute of the Republic of Albania dated March 7, 1925; (v) the treaty on the alliance between Italy and Albania on defense matters, dated November 22, 1927; (vi) the statute of the Kingdom of Albania dated December 1, 1928; (vii) the founding statute of the Kingdom of Albania, issued by the decision of the Constitutional Assembly, convened in Tirana on April 12, 1939, which determined the legal union of Albania with Italy as a constitutional monarchy; (viii) the economic-customs and currency agreement between the Kingdom of Italy and the Kingdom of Albania dated April 20, 1939.

26. **Ricca, Alfonso.** Legislacione Faschista e dell'Lavoro in Albania. Con Commento, Note e Riferimenti alla Legislacione Italiana e dell'Impero. Arti Grafiche 'Italia Imperiale'. Napoli. 1942. Italian Edition. BK: 82 B 34

Divided into three parts, this publication contains several legal acts approved after the Italian occupation of Albania, such as (a) the statute of the Albanian Kingdom after its union with Italy, (b) the statute of the Albanian Fascist Party, law no. 6 July 1939-XVII, n. 1066 which made enforceable the agreement signed between Albania and Italy on the rights of the citizens of the respective countries, (c) law no. July 13, 1939-XVII, n. 1115 for the union of the Albanian and Italian armed forces, (d) the regulation dated April 18, 1940-XVIII on the creation of the Fascist Corporate Superior Council. The second part reflects the legal agreements between Albania and Italy, pertaining to customs, currency and the economy. The third part is dedicated to the provisions of labor law and its respective by-laws.

27. **Studime e Tekste Juridike.** Studime e Tekste, Nr. 1, Instituti i Studimeve Shqiptare. 'Vallechi'. Romë, 1943. BK: In the File Cabinet under "Studime Filologjike. Italian and Albanian Edition." BK: Arp 13 A 20

This bilingual edition, in Italian and Albanian, titled "Studies and legal texts" includes works from different Albanian authors on the Albanian customary law and legal tradition. It begins with the open lecture entitled "Albanian Kanun Law and the Roman Law" held by Ernest Koliqi at the Royal Institute of Roman Studies in Rome, dated March 27, 1942, in which the author analyzes the close relationship between the norms of *kanun* and the Illyrian-Roman influence, and the preservation of these elements during the Turkish occupation. The author analyses several institutions of the *kanun* of the Mountains and compares them with similar regimes of the Roman law. Giuseppe Valentini's article "Preliminary and general thoughts on the Kanun named after Lek Dukagjini" analyzes the etymology of the word *kanun*, the reasons why it bears the name of Lek Dukagjini, as well as the content of the *kanun* regimes with regard to private and public law. Valentini reflects on the changes that the *kanun* has incurred throughout history, as well as the the criminal provisions of the *kanun* that bear unique characteristics as compared to the customary law of other countries in the Balkan region. The work of Father Bernardin Palaj, "On the *kanun* of the mountains" and its application in the Northern regions of Albania analyzes several important institutes of the *kanun*, such as the *bayrak* and the commoners, or youth of the tribe *(Djelmia e Fisit)*. Giuseppe Valentini's "Albanian Corporations" delves into the topic of Albanian guilds, their origin and role in Albania. He argues that the institution of corporations was borrowed from Roman law. This institution flourished with the revitalization of Albanian medieval cities, where the corporations of various professions, the guilds, undertook the regulatory framework for the exercise of the pertinent professions, as well as the procedural rules of dispute resolution between its members. Under Ottoman rule, these guilds were known as *esnaf*. The paper discusses some of these Albanian corporate bodies and their impact on the development of civic life, offering examples of their by-laws.

These articles have been republished in 2009, with the following coordinates:

28. **Valentini, Giuseppe.** Studime dhe Tekste Juridike I. (Seria Valentini). 'Plejad'. Tiranë, 2009. BK: S 327 D 4

In addition to the articles of the aforementioned title, the 2009 publication known as the *Corpus* includes several documents collected by Valentini in various Albanian and foreign archives and published here for the first time. Valentini interprets norms of the customary law based on legal documents from antiquity, the Middle Ages and the modern times to elucidate the Albanian legal tradition consolidated over the centuries, and reflected in the Albanian *kanuns*. The author explores the origin of the Albanian legal mentality to the legal tradition of Justinian and notes that the Albanian customary law has adapted to historical changes and has interacted with other legal cultures of the time. He argues that the *kanun* of the Albanian mountains provides a foundation of principles and social morality that characterizes constitutional law and that is common to all tribal *kanuns*. The work is structured in two parts, with the first part consisting of three books. The first book focuses on the

Albanian tribes of the North and the civil law applied in these. The second book is dedicated to criminal law, while the third considers the political organization of the tribe and its governing bodies. Articles from other authors[11] are also presented in full. The second part includes various legal writings by Albanian authors, alongside materials extracted from the archives of the Spanish embassy near the Holy See and the Archives of Vatican.

29. **Dindi, Mark P.** Gjëmëtime Juridike. Shënime nga Jurisprudenca Shqiptare Dega Penale 1929–1942. Tiranë, 1943. BK: S10 E 4;

The summary of the Albanian High Court decisions on criminal matters during the period 1929–1942 aimed to provide legal professionals with the correct interpretation of the provisions of the Albanian Penal Code and the Albanian jurisprudential standing of the time. This document can serve legal researchers in understanding the evolution of the legislation in the mentioned time span.

30. **Dindi, Mark P.** Çelës i Kodit Penal. 'Luarasi'. Tirana, 1943. BK: Ar 57 G 25; S 9 E 57
31. **Dindi, Mark P.** Gjëmëtime Civile-Proceduriale nga Jurisprudenca Shqiptare dhe e Huaj. Tiranë, 1944. BK: Ar 57 G 26

In a similar fashion to the previous texts, the author examines several important institutes of the Albanian criminal code and trends in Albanian jurisprudence on civil procedure matters. Discussion on the latter includes prescription, deed-acknowledgment, the role of the lawyer, litigation, promise of sale, divorce, expropriation, and damage. Although the focus is not on the history of the development of law, the paper is of interest to researchers of history of law, because it touches on issues of co-existence with, and the influence of the Ottoman legal regime on, the newly approved Albanian criminal and civil law legislation, inspired by West European developments. We also note another publication from the same author, a manual of the civil procedure, which clarifies the legal terminology applied in the provisions of Albanian Civil Procedure Code.[12]

32. **Saatçiu, Andrea.** Historia e Përgjithshme e të Drejtës në Shqipëri prej Fillimit të Mesjetës gjer në Pavarësinë e Shqipërisë. Tiranë, n.d. BFDUT.

---

11 See Studime e Tekste Juridike (Legal Studies and Text).

12 Dindi, Mark P. Çels' i Procedurës Civile Shtojcavet dhe gjithë Modifikimeve të saj. 'Gutenberg'. Tirana, 1943. BK: S 12 105 D.

The book, titled "The general history of law in Albania from the beginning of middle ages until the independence", explores the evolution of Albanian law in the mentioned period, highlighting the important foreign legal systems that have influenced this development in different eras; such as Roman law, the old statutes of Venice, or the codes of the Napoleonic period. The author also delves into the development of Albanian customary law and the development of its various branches. Of interest is his analysis on the penetration and implementation of Ottoman and Sharia law into Albanian law, where special attention is paid to the Timar system in Albanian lands. The work also touches on issues of the development of Albanian ecclesiastical law and the coexistence of three religious faiths.

33. **Xhai, Vasil. Çevi, Kristo.** Regjimi Juridik i Tokës në Shqipëri. Ministria e Bujqësisë. Stabilimenti "Mihal Duri". Tiranë, 1956. BK: S 82 E 76

"The legal regime on the land in Albania" offers an overview of the historical developments and all the important reforms undertaken in Albania with respect to the land property regime. It extends from the regime in force before and during the Ottoman reform of Tanzimat, initiated by Sultan Abdulmejid I in 1839, until the implementation of the agricultural reform of the communist regime in post-war Albania, introduced by law no. 108, of August 29, 1945. The expose offers a detailed description of the land ownership categories according to the reform of Tanzimat,[13] its abrogation by the Fundamental Statute of 1925, as amended in 1928,[14] and the agrarian reform of 1945. The latter receives emphasized attention, together with the ensuing reforms which created cooperatives and nationalized land. Despite the propagandistic tones, the text is of interest to researchers as it provides in chronological order all the agrarian reforms implemented in Albania up to the moment of its publication. It also constitutes a good source for the study of the process of violent nationalization of private property and the collectivization of Albanian agriculture.

34. **Taushani, Riza. Nova, Koço.** Ligjshmëria Socialiste dhe Roli i Organeve të Drejtësisë në Ruajtjen dhe Forcimin e saj. Ministria e Drejtësisë. Stabilimenti 'Mihal Duri'. Tiranë, 1958. BK: S 35 D26

---

13 The author also explains that by means of the Land Law (*Erazi Kanuni*) the land was divided into five categories: (a) simple ownership lands (*Erazi Mamluk* or *mulq*); (b) public or state lands (*erazi mirie*); (c) *waqf* lands (*erazi mefkufe*), (d) lands left for collective use (*erazi metruqe*) and (e) abandoned or deserted lands (*erazi mevat*).

14 The statute proclaimed that all lands within the territory of the Albanian State were simple properties (*mylq*), owned by the state, legal entities and natural persons.

Titled "The socialist legitimacy and the role of the judiciary organs in its strengthening", the text aimed at highlighting the advantages of the monist system and the control of the executive power over the judiciary. The propaganda tones aside, the book provides a window for understanding the historical developments of the laws of this domain and the sub-ordination of the Albanian justice system to the party ideology during the communist regime and the creation of special courts, which were established *ad hoc* for specific cases.

35. **Nathanaili, Andrea. Papuli, Nonda.** Disa Çështje mbi Pronësinë dhe Trashëgiminë. Ministria e Drejtësisë. Stabilimenti 'Mihal Duri'. Tiranë, 1961. BK: S 28 8 U

The work, which focuses on the regime of ownership and inheritance, is helpful in understanding the legal changes that led to the progressive restrictions of property rights during communism. Amongst other issues, the authors analyze the legal changes brought about by decree no. 1892, dated 07.05.1954 and other subsequent acts, that limited testators in passing on to heirs only property which served to meet personal needs.

36. **Kotini, Dhimitër. Struga, Xhavit. Veizi, Fane. Kleanthi Dedi, Mediha.** Qeveria e Përkohëshme e Vlorës dhe Veprimtaria e saj: Nëntor 1912 – Janar 1914. Drejtoria e Përgjithshme e Arkivave Shtetërore të RPSH. Tiranë, 1963. AQSH: A/1 s 9; BFHFUT

The book "The interim government of Vlora and its activity: November 1912 – January 1914" is an archeo-graphic elaboration of the acts of the first Albanian government after its Independence in November 1912 until January 1914. It documents official communications of the government and its members, and various decisions of the government on matters of criminal, administrative and the economic law. To illustrate, we note the Circular for the organization of the judicial administration in all the provinces, issued by the chief judge of the Provisional Government; the act of concession for the creation of the Albanian National Bank, which was not finalized; the standard contract for admission to the gendarmerie corps; as well as acts regarding relations between Albania and the Great Powers. A portion of the acts are translations into Albanian from official communications with international actors. Other documents are communications between different state bodies such as prefectures, mayors, decisions of the representatives of the highlands, or communications between ministers. Given the time of publication, the book reflects shades of the regime's communist ideology, however it provides accurate archival references for the documents it compiles.

37. **Taushani, Riza. Papuli, Nonda. Nova, Koço.** (Prepared). Komentar i Kodit Penal të Republikës Popullore të Shqipërisë. Pjesë e Posaçme. Ministria e Drejtësisë. Vol. I. Tiranë, 1964. BK: S 47 A 52

The Special Part of the Commentary of the Criminal Code reflects the changes that were made to the Albanian Criminal Code of 1952 with Decree no. 2477, dated 3.VI.1957, and law no. 2804 dated 04.12.1958. It also sheds light into the jurisprudence, mainly of the High Court, pertaining to the implementation of the criminal code of 1952. The most important changes are reflected in the first two chapters, dedicated to crimes against the state and against the socialist economy, as interpreted by the jurisprudence of the time. The third chapter deals with the new criminal offenses against trade, finance, and the exercise of a prohibited profession. The fourth chapter analyzes crimes against life, health, freedom and dignity. The last two chapters are dedicated respectively to crimes against marriage and family and crimes against citizens' property. In the context of the history of law, the text provides insight to the pace and typology of changes of the criminal laws in Albania, whilst the socialist system was developing peculiar features, more restrictive than in other countries of the socialist block.

38. **Pulaha, Selami.** Lufta Shqiptaro–Turke në Shekullin XV. Burime Osmane. Universiteti Shtetëror i Tiranës. Instituti i Historisë dhe i Gjuhësisë. Tiranë, 1968. BK: S 36 65 A

"The Albanian Turkish war during the 15th century" relies on documents extracted from the archives of the Turkish Prime Ministry, the High Gate Museum (*Muzeu i Portës së Lartë*) and other data from Ottoman historiographical sources, which pertain to Albania of the 15th to 17th centuries. Among the documents presented, an important part consists of the Registry (*defteri*) of the Sanjak of Dibra, from the year 1467, which provides information on the *timar* system in the lands of the Vilayet of Mati, Uraka, Benda and the lands of Dhimitër Jonima, during Sultan Mehmet II's campaign in 1466. Additionally, the appendix contains a document which the author suggests was written between 1438–1443, where Skanderbeg requests the High Gate to grant him possession of the *ziamet* of Mysje (which is situated between Kruja and Mat River).[15]

15 Pulaha, Selami. Lufta Shqiptaro–Turke në Shekullin XV. Burime Osmane. Universiteti Shtetëror i Tiranës. Instituti i Historisë dhe i Gjuhësisë. Tiranë, 1968, p. 10.

39. **Valentini, Josephi.**[16] Acta Albaniae Iuridica. Tomos I. Ed. Rudolf Trofenik. München, 1968. BK: Al 8 28 B

The compendium is a reprint of Valentini's work of 1944,[17] on the *corpus* of Albanian customary law. It also includes other previously unpublished documents, issued by the State Archives in Venice, Vatican Apostolic Archive and other important archives, which include reports and summaries dedicated to Albanian customary law and its characteristics. The documents, mainly written in Latin and Italian, were compiled in chronological order and published by Dr. Rudolf Trofenik. All acts and contents provide information on the date, place, author, origin of the act, whether or not it is bibliographic, and the pertinent references to the chapters of Albanian customary law. The introduction, written in Latin and Italian, clarifies that the Greek, Slavic and Albanian texts are included in the original language, and translated into Latin and Italian, while the Italian and French texts are provided without translation. The documents in English and German have been translated into Italian.

40. **Valentini, Josephi.** Acta Albaniae Iuridica. Tomus II. Ed. Rudolf Trofenik. München, 1973. BK: AL 10 30 B

The documents of the second volume in this two-volume work were extracted from the State Archives in Venice, and the bibliographic references are the same as *'Acta Albaniae Veneta'*, by the same author.[18] This volume presents materials and documents dating up to 1423. A glossary of terms and their translation from Albanian to Italian can be found at the end of the text.

The work, in Albanian and Ottoman Turkish, contains a series of important acts arranged in chronological order, dating as far back as 1384. These reveal the relations between the Republic of Venice and Albania until the mid-fifteenth century. The

16 The National Library's online catalog on the works of the Italian authors and researchers provides detailed information on the contents of this two-volume publication and the documents it contains. See Sharrexhi, Afërdita. Basha, Nermin. Vepra të Autorëve dhe Studiuesve Italianë për Shqipërinë dhe Shqiptarët (Shek. XV–XX). Katalog. Opere di Autori e Studiosi Italiani sull'Albania e gli Albanesi (Sec. XV–XX). National Library. 221 f. and 228 f. in https://bksh.al/uploads/_/originals/61b90437-9ca9-4ef1-aad1-14699f112f19.pdf [last access16.10.2023].

At the National Library there are also several other articles by the same author, dedicated to Albanian customary law. For instance, Lo Satuto Personale in Albania all'Epoca di Scanderbeg (Appunti dagli Archivi della Repubblica Veneta). Shejzat. Roma, 1967, p. 118. BK: A 15 10 C; Il Concetto della Giustizia Specialmente nel "Kanun" Albanese. in rev.: 'Criminalia', 1942, an. VI. fasc. 2–3, Aprile – Settembre, p. 79–92. BK: 81 C 2.

17 Testi, in 'Studi e Testi'. Instituto di Studi Albanesi. Serie I, Giuridica, n. 1. Tirana/Firenze, 1944.

18 Valentini, Josephi. Acta Albaniae Iuridica. Tomus II. Ed. Rudolf Trofenik. München, 1973, p. 6.

text contains an index of acts. The series was translated and published in Albanian in 2010, with the following coordinates:

41. **Valentini, Giuseppe.** Akte Shqiptaro–Juridike I. (Seria Valentini). Shtëpia Botuese '55'. Tiranë, 2010. BK: S 358 E 9

This publication contains a translation of the study of Giuseppe Valentini on the Albanian customary law and the diversity of Arbëresh law. It also includes an analysis of the Illyrian and Thracian-Illyrian legal concepts, from the author's Italian language manuscript entitled "Notes on the Albanian cultural history and on the role of the church in the Illyrian period" (*Appunti di storia culturale albanese e sul ruolo della chiesa nel periodo ilirico*). Additionally, the book contains Valentini's works on "Acta Albaniae Iuridica" and "Acta Albaniae Veneta Saeculorum", also known as "Corpus I" and "Corpus II", mentioned above, which were published in 1968 and 1973 in Munich.

42. **Valentini, Giuseppe.** La Legge delle Montagne Albanesi, nelle Relazioni della Missione Volante 1880–1932. Ed. da Leo S. Olschki. Firence, 1969. Italian Edition. BIHGJL; BK: Mfa 517C; Microfilmed

This edition contains the notes of Jesuit missionaries who lived in the northern parts of Albania and recorded the manner in which the *kanun* provisions were applied. The detailed recollection of customs is also important from a legal perspective, as they constitute accurate evidence of the daily application of Albanian customary law. The edition was translated and published in Albanian in 2007 and can be found through the following coordinates:

43. **Valentini, Giuseppe.** Ligji i Maleve Shqiptare. Nga Relacionet e Misionit Shëtitës Jezuit në Shqipëri 1880–1932. 'Plejad'. Tiranë, 2007. BK: S 275 E 4; BIHGJL; BKSH

"The Law of the Albanian Mountains. Reports publication" refers to the various reports of the Jesuit clergy, preserved in the Collection of Annual Volumes '*Ad usum manoscripti*' entitled "Official Letters of the Province of Venice from the Campaign of Christ", as well as to several extracts from the "Official Letters. Corpus III" of the same author.[19] The systematic reading of these acts provides evidence of the ancient legal tradition of the Albanians and the principles on which the unwritten

19 Valentini, Giuseppe. Ligji i Maleve Shqiptare. Nga Relacionet e Misionit Shëtitës Jezuit në Shqipëri 1880–1932. 'Plejad'. Tiranë, 2007, p. 18.

norms have been implemented and passed down through generations. According to the author, the fundamental principle on which the *kanun's* foundations are laid is the principle of "protection of honor".[20] This principle, together with the principle of "essential equality" between individuals and "freedom of action", constitute the pillars on which the entire system of legal norms of Albanian customary law is built.[21] Among other related topics, the author dwells on the origin of the name of the *kanun* and on the various functions of the decision-making institutions it regulates.

44. **Fishta, Iljaz.** Sistemi Monetar dhe i Kreditit në Shqipëri (1925–1944). Shtypshkronja 'Mihal Duri'. Tiranë, 1971. BK: S 86 A 30

"The monetary and credit system in Albania (1925–1944)" analyzes issues pertaining to the creation of banks, the monetary and credit systems, during the period of King Zog's reign until the end of the Second World War. The paper is structured in two parts. In the first part, the author focuses on the efforts to create the Albanian monetary and credit systems, from the proclamation of independence in November 1912 until 1925. The analysis sheds light on foreign investments, with evidence of the priority granted to investments of Italian and Austrian capital. Within this first part, the author also explores the main joint stock companies established during this period in Albania, as well as the agreement for the creation of the central bank and the agreement on the SVEA loan (*Società per lo Sviluppo Economico dell'Albania – Association for the Economic Development of Albania*) between the Albanian government and the Italian financial group[22] which provided the capital for the creation of the National Bank of Albania. This part of the book also analyzes other economic agreements entered between Albania and Italy until the official occupation of Albania by Italy in 7 April 1939. The second part discusses the reforms relating to the monetary and credit systems during the years of the Italian and German occupation and the problem of the inflation during this period. Although influenced by ideological tones of the time of publication, the publication is a source of information for scholars focusing on the history of commercial and banking laws and provides archival references.

45. **Pulaha, Selami.** Defteri i Regjistrimit të Sanxhakut të Shkodrës i Vitit 1485. Akademia e Shkencave e RPSH. Instituti i Historisë. Shtypshkronja 'Mihal Duri'. Tiranë, 1974. BK: S 119 B 20

---

20 Valentini, Ligji i Maleve, p. 11.

21 Ibid.

22 The work provides references fo the agreement, which was signed on March 15, 1925, and published on the Official Journal no. 40, dated July 31, 1925.

The Official Registry (*defter*) of the Sanjak of Shkodra of 1485 is considered as one of the most important documents of the Middle Ages, due to the detailed nature of the records regarding ownership registration and feudal relations after the Ottoman occupation.[23] This document, along with the Venetian Cadastre of Shkodra and the Register of Concessions, drawn up for the same purpose (cited below in this bibliography), provide insights into key aspects of the development of the feudal system in Albanian regions over the mentioned period of time. They also allow for comparisons between the regimes after the changes brought about by the Ottoman occupation and the reform of *timar*. In addition to the Registry, this edition also includes an appendix with the registration of the areas (*nahije*) of Piper and Kelmendi, drafted in 1497.[24] As the author notes, in 1485, the *Sanjak* of Shkodra was divided into four administrative subdivisions (*kaza)*: the *kaza* of Shkodra, Podgorica, Peja and Bihor. The *kazas* themselves were further divided into smaller administrative units (*nahije*) for which the Registry (*defter*) provides extensive information. This data also refers to several villages that were part of the *sanjaks* of Vučiterni and Prizren. The Registry was drawn up following the model of detailed ledgers (*mufassal*), which were based on the size of the fiefs and their type, rather than on the division of the administrative units within the *sanjak*.[25] The author draws attention to the systematic approach of the registry, which reflects (a) *hasset*—the land owned by the empire, with an annual tax revenue of over 100,000 *akçe*, (b) the *ziamet* lands, i. e., properties of the feudal aristocracy created upon state-owned lands, that were given by the Sultan as a reward mainly to military leaders and had an annual tax revenue between 20,000 to 99,999 *akçe*, (c) *timars*—lands given by the Sultan as a reward, mainly to the *Sipahis (Timarli Sipahi)*, with an annual tax revenue value of no more than 20,000 *akçe*.[26] Feudal rent is also noted in the Registry, where a clear distinction is made between areas which were settled under the *timar* system and rural areas of the North of Albania that continued to pay rent without being subject to the common fiscal (*raja*) obligations. It record also shows that the *timar* system did not fully penetrate the northern areas of Albania. The Registry (*defter)*, in the Ottoman language, preserved in the Turkish Archives, is a valuable resource for scholars of medieval law history. The French translation of this publication can be found with the following coordinates:

---

23 Pulaha, Selami. Defteri i Regjistrimit të Sanxhakut të Shkodrës i Vitit 1485. Akademia e Shkencave e RPSH. Instituti i Historisë. Shtypshkronja 'Mihal Duri'. Tiranë, 1974, p. 4.

24 The data on these areas did not feature on the first publication of the summary (icmal) registry of the area of Kuç and Hoti, prepared by B. Djurdejev. Pulaha, Defteri, p. 4.

25 Pulaha, Defteri, p. 6.

26 Pulaha, Defteri, p. 9.

46. **Pulaha, Selami.** Le Cadastre de l'An 1485 du Sandjak de Shkoder. Academie des Sciences de l'Albanie. Shkodër, 1974. French Edition. BK: S 118 B 18

The Albanian edition has been republished in 2018 by the Academy of Albanological Studies, Institute of History in Tirana, and can be found with the following coordinates:

47. **Caka, Eduart.** (Sci. Ed.) Defteri i Regjistrimit të Sanxhakut të Shkodrës i vitit 1485. Akademia e Studimeve Albanologjike. Instituti i Historisë. Tiranë, 2018. BK: S 540 C 7; BIHGJL; AQSH: A/1.s1

The reprint has preserved the original work and is accompanied by a short biography of Selami Pulaha. The annotations of the reprint provide an overview of the historical context of the drafting of this registry and the approach that was adopted for the registration of the *timars*.

48. **Omari, Luan.** Revolucioni Popullor në Shqipëri dhe Çështja e Pushtetit. Universiteti i Tiranës. Tiranë, 1977. BFHF

Focusing on the invasion of Albania and the first years after the Second World War, in "The popular revolution in Albania and the issue of power" the author first analyses the creation and development of the national-liberation councils, and then the establishment of the Albanian state according to the communist ideology after the war. The text bears the tone of glorification of the communist party, in accordance with the propaganda of the time of publication, but provides references to the legal acts that served as grounds for institutional building of the new regime.

49. **Zamputi, Injac.** Regjistri i Kadastrës dhe i Koncesioneve për Rrethin e Shkodrës 1416–1417. Akademia e Shkencave e RPSSH. Instituti i Historisë. Tiranë, 1977. BFHF

The Register of Cadaster and Concessions for the region of Shkodra and its surroundings (1416–1417) was drafted during the time of Venetian rule, based on a special ordinance of Venice. It dates from August 1416 and reflects the conditions until the first months of 1417. The author notes that the register of cadaster and that of concessions, although divided into two parts, is a unitary act of a special nature due to the purpose it pursued, which distinguishes it from the many other acts of ordinary administrative character adopted at that time. He explains that the register aimed at recording the properties and the part of the feudal rent that was paid to Venice, otherwise called "the land master", or *signoria*. This included tithes on production and income from land that was administered directly from Venice, such as customs, concessionary fees and other contracts.[27] The cadastral records for the area of Shkodra include all its villages, the names of the inhabitants, the rights and obligations of each one, as well as the lands and vineyards of the Venetian municipality—a state fund that also included confiscations. The author notes that the second part, which is a register of concessions, was intended to record transactions made on lands, such as the leasing of land, vineyards, or other properties owned by Venice, where as a general rule, the rights and obligations of the parties were determined in a separate bilateral agreement. The register mentions typical acts of feudal law such as the institution of *pronia*,[28] but the author explains that their mention is not systematic, as it was not part of the object of the register.

50. **Bozhori, Koço.** Dokumente të Periudhës Bizantine për Historinë e Shqipërisë (Shek. VII–XV). Akademia e Shkencave e RPSSH. Tiranë, 1978. BK: S 148 26 B

"Documents of the Byzantine period on Albanian history (7th–15th century)" presents in chronological order data on the legal status of the land property in Albania during the Byzantine rule, and highlights the predominance of the individual property of free peasants. The documents and the legal acts summarized in the book have been issued by various foreign administrations that ruled in Albanian lands. They include acts of public administration of the Byzantine Empire, the administration of the Despotate of Epirus, acts of the Serbian Kingdom, then of the Ottoman Empire, as well as documents of ecclesiastical nature. The author argues that the economic differentiation between different classes of the population began around the 8th century in the Albanian territories, which in turn influenced the formation of feudal property and relations. The work discusses the evolution of contracts of sale and purchase of property, its limitations by means of pre-emptive rights in the 5th–8th centuries, and later, the elimination of these restrictions by the 10th century. Consideration is also given to inheritance rights, legal and testamentary, pursuant to the Basilica legislation of 887–892, which continued to apply in the Albanian territories until the 13th century. Of interest is also the regime of privileges granted to religious institutions, such as exemption from taxes, and

---

27 Zamputi, Injac. Regjistri i Kadastrës dhe i Koncesioneve për Rrethin e Shkodrës 1416–1417. Botim i Akademisë së Shkencave të Republikës Popullore Socialiste të Shqipërisë. Instituti i Historisë. Tiranë, 1977, p. 5.

28 The institute of *pronia* refers to the taxes that the different feudal lords levied on the peasantry. The *pronia* included rent for the main lord (heads)—the emperor or the king—which was determined by fixed annual sums for each farm house; as well as the rent for the other feudal lords (*proniar*), based on the system of tithes, payable in industry, cash or in-kind contributions. This regime was abolished after the Venetian occupation of Shkodra. Zamputi, Regjistri, 5 f.

the property of *parik*.[29] The publication highlights the trade fairs of this period and the income they generated. It also includes the Agrarian law of the 7th–8th century, and the agreement of October 1324 between the Byzantine Empire and the Republic of Venice, which allowed the latter to trade in all the provinces of the empire, including the Albanian lands. The documents presented in this book are translated into Albanian. The work is of great interest to researchers of the history of law and public governance, as well as researchers of private law branches.

51. **Banja, Hasan.** Prona Socialiste në R.P.S të Shqipërisë. '8 Nëntori.' Tiranë, 1979. BK: S 149 P 48

This work, despite its propagandistic tones that glorify the proletarian revolution and the confiscation and nationalization of private assets, may serve as a source of information to understand the types of properties that were regulated by the Albanian socialist legal order. The author delves extensively into the regime of state socialist property (*prona socialiste shtetërore*), cooperative socialist property, and the regime of their administration.

52. **Pepo, Petraq.** Materiale Dokumentare për Shqipërinë Juglindore të Shekullit XVIII – Fillimi i Shekullit XX. Kodiku i Korçës dhe i Selaforit. Pjesa e I. Akademia e Shkencave të RPS të Shqipërisë. Instituti i Historisë. Tiranë, 1981. Maket. BIHGJL
53. **Pepo, Petraq.** Materiale Dokumentare për Shqipërinë Juglindore të Shekullit XVIII – Fillimi i Shekullit XX. Kodiku i Korçës dhe i Selaforit. Pjesa e II. Akademia e Shkencave të RPS të Shqipërisë. Instituti i Historisë. Tiranë, 1981. Maket. BIHGJL

The two-volume publication was republished in a single volume in 2018.

54. **Pepo, Petraq.** Kodiku i Korçës dhe i Selasforit. Materiale Dokumentare për Shqipërinë Juglindore. Akademia e Studimeve Albanalogjike. Qendra e Botimeve Enciklopedike. Tiranë, 2018. BK: Ar 201 A 9; BIHGJL

Originally published in 1981, "The Codex of Korça and Selafor" is an important source of information for the researchers of legal history, because it accurately reflects part of the legal regime, traditions and social customs for the period between

29 The term *parik* refers to destitute farmers, who were obliged to live and work on the land of the feudal lords. The latter, including the church, were referred to as *dinat*. See Bozhori, Koço. Dokumente të Periudhës Bizantine për Historinë e Shqipërisë (Shek. VII–XV). Akademia e Shkencave e RPSSH. Tiranë, 1978, p. 5.

18th–20th century in Korça, Devoll, Voskopoja, Vithkuq, Opar, Përmet, and other areas of this region. The Codex includes chronicles, letters, wills and various legal acts that reflect the life of the city. It also contains a long report on the territory of Korça dated in 1879. The original, written in Greek, is kept at the Albanian State Archive. The author highlights that following the Ottoman occupation, the Empire organized the conquered Albanian territories in a separate *sanjak* in 1431, called the Sanjak of Albania, while the surrounding areas of Korça, Kolonja and Përmet continued to remain as separate administrative feudal units until 1457. He notes that during the first century of Turkish rule the area of Korça was included in the *timar* system, and from the end of the 15th century a part of its lands turned into properties (*mylq*) of Mirahor Iljaz Bej. The latter, by means of a *waqfia* (*vakëf-name)*[30] drawn up in 1505, converted a number of properties from his personal estate into *waqfs.*[31] The purpose of *waqfia* was to promote the development of various trades and professions such as masonry, bakery, cooking, tinsmithery, and apprenticeships, through the establishment of charities founded by Iljaz Bej. The annotated documentary materials of the Codex of Korça and Selafor reveal Korça as an important center for crafts and commerce in the region. The cultural and economic strengthening of the city influenced in turning the *kaza* of Korça into a prefecture (*mytesarif*) in 1865. The notes of the codex indicate the presence of guild organizations of various trades, which had buildings designated for their gatherings; a role in the regulation of their pertinent market and profession; trade organizations in the old bazaar of Korça; and types of coins that circulated. The Codex contains notes on Korça's commercial relations with Voskopoja, other Albanian cities, and foreign cities in Italy, Austria, and Hungary. An interesting part of the Codex are the notes dedicated to the Orthodox community of Korça, its rights during the Ottoman occupation, rules for its representation with third parties, its internal organization and mode of operation. The second volume of the 1981 edition provides a series of documents that deal extensively with the status of the Orthodox Church, its relations with the Ottoman administrative apparatus, its properties, the use of income, internal governance and other aspects of its operations. The 2018 edition comprise both volumes of the 1981 edition in one. The publication contains a glossary of terms.

55. **Nova, Koço.** Zhvillimi i Organizimit Gjyqësor në Shqipëri. Universiteti i Tiranës. Tiranë, 1982. BK: S 163 F 5

30 The deed of charity donation under the Islamic law.

31 A charity donation in kind, money or real estate, under the Islamic law, given for the purpose of supporting a religious institution, of vulnerable groups, or for improving the community living standart.

The book, structured in two parts, provides an analytic overview of the development of judiciary in Albania. The first part discusses the main features of the judicial process under the Albanian customary law; the role of the representative bodies of the society according to this law; the eldership, the assembly, and the types of decisions they rendered. The discussion expands to the organization and activity of the courts under the Ottoman occupation, the organization and functioning of judicial power pursuant to the acts of the League of Prizren, the judicial system after the independence, and amendments after the Congress of Lushnja and during the government of King Zog. The second part deals with the structure and judicial activity of partisan courts and the legal grounds for their functioning.[32] The author offers an analysis of the post-World War II law, no. 275, dated 13.08.1946, "On the judicial organization" and its amendments made by law no. 1284 dated 09.06.1951 "On the judicial organization", which provided the principles of the organization and operation of the judiciary according to the Marxist model, and the control of the party and executive power over the judiciary. Despite of the propaganda tones dictated by the censure of the time of publication, the work offers an opportunity to understand the Albanian model of the Marxist state and the role of the justice component within it.

56. **Elezi, Ismet.** E Drejta Zakonore Penale e Shqiptarëve dhe Lufta për Zhdukjen e Mbeturinave të saj në Shqipëri. '8 Nëntori'. Tiranë, 1983. BFDUT

The publication was republished in 2003 with the following coordinates:

57. **Elezi, Ismet.** Njohuri për të Drejtën Zakonore Mbarëshqiptare. Prishtinë, 2003. BFHFUT; BFDUT.

The book focuses on the historical and social conditions that led to the formation of the customary law and the different *kanuns* that emerged in the Albanian territory. It analyzes the Kanun of Lek Dukagjin, the Kanun of Arbëria, the Kanun of Labëria and other special *kanuns* that have applied for centuries among Albanians. In the 1983 edition, the author analyzes the construction of criminal norms in Albanian customary law, the elements of the criminal offense, as well as some institutes of the general part of criminal law that were also regulated by the customary law. Further, it focuses on the meaning and content of the special part of the customary criminal

32 Circular no. 2 dated 24.12.1944 of the Chairmanship of the Anti-fascist National-Liberation Council (*Kryesisë së Këshillit Antifashist Nacional-Çlirimtar)* "On the Interim Organization of the Judiciary" (*Mbi Organizimin e Përkohshëm të Gjyqësorit*).

law, where it discusses murder, blood vendetta, criminal offenses in family and marital relations, and criminal offenses against private property.

The 2003 reprint expands on the study of the Albanian customary law applicable in Kosova, and highlights its role in the survival of national identity. The author examines the sources of the main *kanuns* of the customary law, highlighting the original elements of the institutes these regulated, such as *besa*, honor, hospitality and manliness (*burrëria*). The comparative analysis more fully develops interpretation of specific institutes of family law regulated in the *kanun*, such as engagement, marriage, inheritance and its types, and property relations. The role and competences of the elders (*pleqtë*), the assemblies (*kuvendet*) and military organization, as part of the public law institutes regulated in the *kanun*, are also discussed. Special attention is devoted to the institutes of customary criminal law and its special part in addressing offenses against persons, against family relations, against the normal functioning of self-governing bodies and the delivery of justice, false oath *(beja e rreme)* and the main procedural aspects provided for in the Albanian customary law. The work contains a glossary of terms of the Albanian customary law.

58. **Omari, Luan. Luarasi, Aleks.** (Sci. Ed.). Historia e Shtetit dhe e së Drejtës në Shqipëri. Part I, Dispensa 1. Universiteti i Tiranës, Fakulteti i Shkencave Politike e Juridike. Maket. Tiranë, 1982. BK: S 6 D 59
59. **Omari, Luan. Luarasi, Aleks.** (Sci. Ed.). Historia e Shtetit dhe e së Drejtës në Shqipëri. Part I, Dispensa 2. Universiteti i Tiranës, Fakulteti i Shkencave Politike e Juridike. Maket. Tiranë, 1982. BK: S 6 D 61
60. **Omari, Luan. Luarasi, Aleks.** (Sci. Ed.). Historia e Shtetit dhe e së Drejtës në Shqipëri. Part II. Universiteti i Tiranës, Fakulteti Shkencave Politike e Juridike. Maket. Tiranë, 1984. S 47 25 A
61. **Omari, Luan. Luarasi, Aleks.** (Sci. Ed.). Historia e Shtetit dhe e së Drejtës në Shqipëri. Part III. Universiteti i Tiranës, Fakulteti Shkencave Politike e Juridike. Maket. Tiranë, 1987. BK: S 128 A 35

"The History of state and the law in Albania" is considered a cornerstone legal study in this domain. It was initially published in three volumes, from 1982 until 1987, and has been republished later in different formats.

62. **Omari, Luan. Luarasi, Aleks.** (Sci. Ed.). Historia e Shtetit dhe e së Drejtës në Shqipëri. Part I. 'Luarasi'. Tiranë, 1997. BK: S 191 68 F; BFDUT

The first volume of "The History of state and the law in Albania" is divided into five chapters. The first chapter, authored by **Krisafi, Ksenofon** focuses on the state and law in Illyria (*Shteti dhe e drejta në Iliri*). The author analyzes the development of the state and law in Illyria and the different researchers' viewpoints on the matter.

He notes that the Illyrian state was organized as a slave-owning monarchy, with the power concentrated in the hands of the king, who was assisted in the exercise of his functions by the "friends of the king"—either people close to him or representatives of the slave-owning aristocracy. The main sources of law were both the customary law and the legal acts issued by state bodies. The chapter provides insight into the institution of different branches of law that were regulated in this era, the subjects of law (noting that the subject of law in Illyria were only free natural persons who enjoyed legal capacity), and different types of punishments for criminal offenses. The author further analyzes the state and the legal regime implemented in Epirus, the role of the king, the *prostati* and the council.

The second chapter, titled "Political and legal institutions in Albanian lands during the centuries V–XII" (*Institucionet politike dhe juridike në tokat shqiptare gjatë shekujve V–XII*), is authored by **Ballanca, Zejnulla.** This text analyzes the economic and social organization of the free communities that appeared during the 7th–8th centuries, as well as the features of the ensuing Albanian feudalism, which did not emerge from the slave-owning society, but rather as a result of the disintegration of the free peasant communities. He notes that the legal regime operating in the Albanian lands between the 9th–12th centuries included the coexistence of three legal systems: (i) the Byzantine law system; (ii) the ecclesiastical law, which included the laws of the Catholic and the Orthodox churches; and (iii) the domestic customary law. According to the author, until the 8th century, Justinian's Code was the main source of law in the territories ruled by the Byzantine Empire. The evolution of the Byzantine feudal law extended its influence in the Albanian territories, a process which the author illustrates with the adoption of the law Ecloga (y.726)—the agrarian law that was promulgated during the second half of this century—as well as other acts. He highlights several major legal instruments that influenced the formation of positive law in Albanian territories: (i) Nomocanons, a mixture of imperial norms and church rules; (ii) the Law of Photius of the year 883; (iii) Prochiron of the year 879,[33] which completely revised the Code of Justinian and brought a new regime of civil, criminal and ecclesiastical feudal norms; (iv) Espanogoga of 884–886, which revised previously adopted legal principles; (v) the Basilica approved in the years 888–889, which repelled the regulation of the Ecloga and aimed at destroying the free peasant communities and subjugating them to the emerging feudal order; (vi) the *Chrysobullos logos,* or imperial bulls, that gained importance in the 10th century as legal means for recognizing financial and administrative privileges; and (vii) the Book of the Eparch from the beginning of the 10th century, containing feudal legal norms for the organization, operation and

33 Omari, Luan. Luarasi, Aleks. (Sci. Ed.). Historia e Shtetit dhe e së Drejtës në Shqipëri. Part I. 'Luarasi'. Tiranë, 1997, p. 74.

supervision of corporations of merchants and craftsmen. The chapter also explores the administrative reforms undertaken by the Byzantine emperors, and the tax system that imposed collective liability to community members and contributed to the destruction of rural communities.

The third and fourth chapters, written by **Luarasi, Aleks** are dedicated respectively to the Albanian feudal principates of the 12th–15th century (*Principatat feudale shqiptare të shekullit të 12të–15të*), and to the independent Albanian state led by Skanderbeg (*Shteti i Pavarur Shqiptar i Udhëhequr nga Skënderbeu*). The author highlights the creation of Albanian feudal principates, their applicable law, the social and administrative structure, and the legal status of peasants in their different categories. The third chapter also elaborates on the organization of Albanian medieval towns, their class division and the applicable law. The fourth chapter focuses on the characteristics of state and the law under the leadership of Skanderbeg. It notes that the state of Skanderbeg applied the feudal law, widely based on decrees, but that elements of the Byzantine law remained applicable. The author delves into the legal nature of the Assembly of Lezha (*Kuvendi i Lezhës*), which convened on 2 March 1444, emphasizing its features similar to a constitutional body.

The fifth chapter, by **Gjika, Grigor** titled "Ottoman institutions and albanian feudal pashaliks" (*Institucionet osmane dhe pashallëqet feudale shqiptare*), analyzes the public administration during the rule of the Ottoman Empire, the ruling feudal classes, and the regime of *timar*. He notes the sources of the Ottoman Empire legal regime: the Sharia – the sacred law that applied to the Muslim population, the *kanun-name*, also known as the state law, the *capitulations*, which were concessionary agreements by which the Ottoman Empire favored citizens of European states by giving them special privileges and rights, and other legal acts, such as *berats* and *fermans*. The chapter also provides an overview of the categories of land property under the Ottoman rule. The author notes that the law of the Albanian feudal pashaliks emerged alongside this law, developing distinctive features illustrated in depth by the features of state organization and the applicable law of the *pashalik* of Shkodra and the *pashalik* of Ioannina. Another aspect the author addresses is the autonomy of the highland provinces. Resisting the *Tanzimat reforms* and the Ottoman law, the autonomous provinces of the highlands continued to apply their customary law and organized their community life in accordance with this. Besides the northern areas of Albania, where the precedence of the *kanun* was absolute, the author analyzes the organization of autonomous villages in Southern Albania, where the Turks failed to fully extend the *timar* system. The case of Himara, where the High Gate recognized special privileges (*venome*) in 1492, is upheld as an example. The chapter also provides a description of the Albanian guilds, closed commercial and artisan legal entities, which aimed to regulate the activities of its member producers, craftsmen, or traders and their protection from competition, similar to corporations or brotherhoods developed in the 13th century, before the Ottoman conquest. Similar to the functioning of these organizations in other European countries, the decree of Sultan Mustafa III (1773), recognized the Albanian guilds as possessing some quasi-judicial functions for the resolution of civil disputes arising between guild members.

63. **Omari, Luan. Luarasi, Aleks.** (Sci. Ed.). Historia e Shtetit dhe e së Drejtës në Shqipëri. Part II. 'Luarasi'. Tiranë, 1997. BK: S 191 72 F; BFDUT

The second volume's first chapter, entitled "The Albanian customary law" contains works from different legal scholars. "The Meaning of Albanian Customary Law. Its Main Sources and Principles" (*Kuptimi i së drejtës zakonore shqiptare. Burimet dhe parimet e saj kryesore*), authored by **Luarasi, Aleks** analyzes the origin of the term *kanun* from the Greek-Byzantine term *nomokanon* and reviews the uninterrupted application of customary law in Albanian territories from antiquity until the mid-20th century. Among the main sources of the Albanian customary law he includes the *Kanun of Lek Dukagjin, the Kanun of Scanderbeg*, and the respective *Kanuns of Puka, Luma, and Labëria*, from which he draws the common basic principles of the customary law.

In his work *"The patriarchal family and its role in tribal societies" (Familja patriarkale dhe roli i saj në shoqërinë fisnore)*, **Zaganjori, Xhezair** delves into the regime of arranged marriage and engagement, as well as the types of marriages provided for in the Albanian customary law. The analyses sheds light on ownership relations and obligations under customary law, on family relations and its well-known institutions, such as brotherhood, godparents, adoption, and legal and testamentary inheritance. Attention is given also to some types of specific contracts and liabilities regulated by Albanian customary law.

Under the title "Criminal customary law" *(E drejta zakonore penale)*, **Elezi, Ismet** deals with the criminal offense and its constituent elements, accomplices and their responsibility, as well as the different types of punishments. This text interprets well-known institutes, such as *besa*, brotherhood, blood feud, the norms for preliminary investigation and the burden of proof, the role of *kapucari,*[34] and *porota.*[35] A more in-depth analysis is dedicated to the norms of customary criminal law of the Kanun of Lek Dukagjin.

Nova, Koço, on his presentation "*Procesi Gjyqësor*", analyses the judicial process according to the Albanian customary law. He delves into the main judicial bodies,

34 The informer. Articles 1079 et seq of the Kanun of Lek Dukagjini (KLD)s defines *kapucari* as the person who reveals the author of a crime, whilst retaining anonimity.

35 Articles 1044 et eq of the KLD defines *porota* as persons who warranted, by testifying under oath, that the accused did not commit a violation of the KLD norms.

and the important role of the Chiefs and Elders of the tribe in initiating the assemblies and trial procedures. He elaborates the provisions contributing to the regime of the preliminary investigation, the procedures of elders' meetings *(mbledhjeve të pleqësisë)* and the decision-making mandate they upheld.

In the second and third chapters of this publication, **Omari, Luan** delves into the Albanian League of Prizren and its acts regarding the organization of the judiciary, the independent state of Albania in the years 1912–1924, the role of the International Control Commission and the Organic Statute of Albania under Prince Wied.

In the fourth chapter, **Hysi, Grigor** examines the efforts to build an Albanian democratic state in the years 1920–1924 and expands on the Statute of Lushnja.

Brozi, Zef highlights the characteristics of the revolution of June 1924 and the government of Fan Noli.

Gjilani, Feti explores "The state and law during Zog's regime" (*Shteti dhe e drejta gjatë regjimit të Zogut*), focusing on the Fundamental Statutes, the division of powers and the development of the law during the rule of King Zog.

Puto, Arben analyses the organization of the Albanian state following the Albanian League of Prizren until the declaration of Independence. He reviews the fundamental acts approved by the League of Prizren on 18 June, 1878, known as Book of Decisions (*Kararname*), which provided the program of the League, as well as the *Talimati* ordinance that regulated the organization of the administration and of the army.

The series were republished as integral editions, with the following references.

64. **Omari, Luan. Luarasi, Aleks.** (Sci. Ed.). Historia e Shtetit dhe e së Drejtës në Shqipëri. Tiranë, 2001. BK: S 212 E 31
65. **Omari, Luan. Luarasi, Aleks.** (Sci. Ed.). Historia e Shtetit dhe e së Drejtës në Shqipëri. Tiranë, 2005. BK: S 234 C 52
66. **Omari, Luan. Luarasi, Aleks.** (Sci. Ed.). Historia e Shtetit dhe e së Drejtës në Shqipëri. Tiranë, 2007. BK: S 266 E 5

67. **Begolli, Valbona.** Pozita e Gruas në Kosovë me një Vështrim të Posaçëm në të Drejtën Zakonore. 'Rilindja'. Prishtinë, 1984. BK: S 168 F1

"The position of the woman in Kosova with a special regard for the customary law" explores the evolution of women's rights and obligations in Kosova, according to customary and positive law. The author discusses the organization and features of the extended family and the small family units. She notes that the extended family was based on joint ownership of adult males over the means of production, whereas the small family was based on private property managed by the man of the house. The rights and obligations of the woman were treated as part of the entirety of the legal relations of the small family, either in her father's family, or after marriage, in her husband's family. The work is structured in three parts. The first deals with the organization of the patriarchal family and the position of the woman in it, including the personal and property relations of the spouses, according to the *kanun* of Lek Dukagjin. Of interest in this part is the analysis of the woman's right of inheritance in her father's and her husband's family, as well as her right to dispose of property through a will. In the second part, the author delineates the rights of women according to the Yugoslav law, applicable in Kosova at the time of the publication. The author delves into the evolution of the legislation for the protection of women's rights in work relations from 1918–1941. In the third part, the author describes the historical evolution of women's positions in Kosova from 1946 until the time of publication.

68. **Biçoku, Nazmi.** E Drejta e Trashëgimisë e RPSH. Universiteti i Tiranës. Tiranë, 1984. BK: S 46 F 29. 'SHBLU', Tiranë, 1988. BK: S 103 G 43
69. **Biçoku, Nazmi.** E Drejta e Trashëgimisë e Republikës së Shqipërisë. 'Onufri'. Tiranë, 1997. BK: S 91 F 87
70. **Biçoku, Nazmi.** E Drejta e Trashëgimisë e Republikës së Shqipërisë. 'Albapaper'. Tiranë, 2011. BK: S 365 E 64

The different editions of "The law of inheritance" explore the evolution of Albanian inheritance law. Beginning with the applicable legislation after Albania's proclamation of independence from the Ottoman Empire in 1912, the text then traces the reminiscence of the Ottoman law, the introduction of a new regime by the Civil Code of 1929 and its application until the first years after the Second World War. It analyses the regime of inheritance under the Decree of 1954, and later in the provisions of the Civil Code of 1981. The 2011 reprint includes the author's interpretation of the new regime introduced by the Civil Code adopted in 1994, illustrated by some decisions of the Civil College of the Supreme Court *(Kolegji Civil i Gjykatës së Lartë).*

71. **Fishta, Iliaz. Toçi, Veniamin.** Ekonomia e Shqipërisë në Vitet e Para të Ndërtimit Socialist: 1944–1948. Akademia e Shkencave e RPSSH. Tiranë, 1984. BK: S 40 E 50; AQSh: F/1.s 3; BASH

The monograph "The economy of Albania in the first years of the socialist making 1944–1948" provides an insight into the communist-style nationalization of banks, the extraordinary tax on war profits, the reform of the monetary and credit systems, the tax system and the agrarian reform, undertaken during the mentioned time period. The book also analyzes some of the main economic agreements between Albania and Yugoslavia during this period, such as the one equalizing the Albanian and Yugoslav currencies, customs unification, the agreement for the creation of import and export joint stock companies, and the joint stock company formed for the creation of a joint Albanian-Yugoslav bank at the beginning of 1947.

72. **Halili, Ragip.** Sanksionet Penale sipas të Drejtës Zakonore në Kosovë. Enti i Teksteve dhe i Mjeteve Mësimore i Krahinës Socialiste Autonome të Kosovës. Prishtinë, 1985. BK: S 167 27 E

"The penal sanctions according to the customary law of Kosova", written when Kosova was part of former Yugoslavia, offers a study on the penal punishments according to the customary law applicable in Kosova, and their reflection on the country's political and legal systems. The first part of the study analyzes criminal sanctions as protective social measures, their development in a historical context, and the public or state approach towards these sanctions in different social orders, from the slave-owning societies to the self-governing socialist system in Kosova. In the second part, the author delves into types of criminal sanctions according to the customary law applied in Kosova, categorizing them into death sentences, blood vendetta, expulsion from the village, boycott, property punishments (blood payment or reconciliation by means of rewards, monetary fines, confiscation or destruction of property) and other sub categories. This part also notes the procedures and competent bodies for enacting and executing criminal sanctions, the means for collection of evidence and enforcement of the criminal punishments according to customary law. The third part weighs on the consequences of criminal sanctions of the customary law and the necessary measures to prevent their application.

73. **Elezi, Ismet.** Aparati Administrativ Shtetëror në RPS të Shqipërisë. Shtypshkronja 'Mihal Duri'. Tiranë, 1987. BK: S 89 F 56; BFDUT

This book examines, from a historical viewpoint, the creation of the administrative apparatus by the anti-fascist national-liberation army during the Second World War and the creation of the administrative apparatus of communist state afterward. The study provides an overview of the governing structure during the communist regime, the main governing bodies and their competences, as well as the main legal acts that provided the foundation of the communist regime.

74. **Doçi, Muharrem. Samsuri, Perikli.** Marrëdhëniet Valutore Ndërkombëtare të RPSSH. '8 Nëntori'. Tiranë, 1987. BK: S 176 T 2

The study of the international currency relations of Albania focuses on trade exchanges between the Albanian-style socialist government and third parties, the system of payment in export-import contracts in foreign trades and the determination of foreign exchange terms and conditions. It analyzes forms of direct payments, barter payments, the currency defined in contracts, hedging measures against currency risks, as well as the framework for internal payment transactions and bank loans for state-owned enterprises which operated in foreign trade.

75. **Malltezi, Luan.** Qytetet e Bregdetit Shqiptar gjatë Sundimit Venedikas. Aspekte të Jetës së Tyre. Akademia e Shkencave e RPS të Shqipërisë. Instituti i Historisë. Tiranë, 1988. BK: S 89 20 G

This book reflects from an historical viewpoint the important legal elements of governance and administration of Albanian cities after the Venetian conquest, during the centenarian period from the 13th to the 14th century. During this period the medieval Albanian cities developed as autonomous units regulated by statutes, which recognized their legal capacity and defined the separation of powers between the governing bodies of the city as well as their relations with other cities. The study highlights the main governing bodies of the towns and their respective competences. The book contains a summary in French and a glossary of terms.

76. **Pulaha, Selami.** Pronësia Feudale në Tokat Shqiptare (Shek. XV–XVI). Akademia e Shkencave e RPSSH. Instituti i Historisë. Tiranë, 1988. BK: S 80 59 F

"The feudal proprietorship in Albanian lands" analyzes the different forms of feudal land ownership after the occupation of Albanian lands by the Ottoman Empire. The book is divided into three parts; the first, titled "Ottoman Feudal Ownership of Land" (*Pronësia feudale osmane mbi tokën*) analyzes the expropriation of the Albanian feudal class, the new categories of property and their respective feudal dues. The second part—"The Feudal Dependence of the Raja Villagers" *(Varësia feudale e fshatarësisë raja)*—analyzes the rights of the *sipahi* (sahib-I Arz) and the feudal dependency of the *raja* peasant, his obligation not to abandon the land, and various applicable taxes. The third part deals with the class structure of the Albanian society, the conditions of the Albanian *raja* peasantry, the military class (*askeri tayifesi*), the free peasantry in the self-governing provinces of the mountainous regions of the North Albania and the peasantry of the southern provinces, in Kurvelesh and other coastal areas. In this part, the author also delves into the rights and obligations of the Albanian cities under the model of the Ottoman fief and the role played by the Sipahis. The book relies on a vast bibliography and documents drawn mainly from the Turkish archives. At the end there is a summary in French.

77. **Fishta, Iliaz.** Ndërhyrja e Kapitalit të Huaj dhe Pasojat e saj Skllavëruese për Shqipërinë (1931–1936). Akademia e Shkencave e RPSSH. Tiranë, 1989. BK: S 147 C 1; BASH

The monography titled "The intervention of foreign capital and its enslaving consequences for Albania (1931–1936)", explores important aspects of Italian-Albanian relations shortly before the occupation of Albania by Italy in 1939. It focuses specifically on the control gained by Italy over the monetary and credit systems of Albania, through the SVEA loan (1925), as well as through a series of concessions that included the exploitation of oil resources in Kuçova, the olive oil industry, agriculture and other important sectors of the economy. The author finds that these measures enabled Italy to penetrate and effectively occupy Albania before the formal act of invasion on April 7, 1939.

78. **Baboçi, Sinan.** Organizimi i Drejtësisë në RPSH. Fakulteti i Shkencave Politike dhe Juridike, Universiteti i Tiranës. 'SHBLU'. Tiranë, 1989. BK: S 177 C 53

The work provides an extensive overview of the Albanian justice system during communism, the role of the "People's Courts" (*Gjykatave Popullore*) established according to Marxist-Stalinist doctrine, and the subordination of the courts to the guiding principle of the dictatorship of the proletariat.

79. **Ilia, Frano.** Kanuni i Skanderbegut. 'La Rosa'. Milot / Brescia, 1993. BK: S 197 A 4

The customary code known as the Kanun of Skanderbeg was collected by Father Frano Ilia, who lived as a priest in the area where this *kanun* was applied. As explained by the author in the introduction, the Kanun of Skanderbeg *(Kanun i Skënderbeut)* bears some distinctive characteristics, despite its many similarities to the Kanun of Lek Dukagjin. He notes that although the *kanun* is also known as the Kanun of Kurbin *(Kanuni i Kurbinit)*, the author titled it the Kanun of Skanderbeg because the latter had approved some of the *kanun* laws applicable in the provinces that were under his principate. The *kanun* is organized in seven parts. The introduction of the *kanun* defines the geographical area of its jurisdiction, as well as the bodies that were competent to issue binding norms. The first part of the *kanun* regulates family relations, engagement, betrothal, arranged marriages and other institutions of this domain. The second part focuses on the house and the determination of property boundaries, as well as the important role of the elders *(pleqve)* as a decision-making and judicial body. The third part regulates rights and obligations in trade practices, and particular restrictions for the sale of common ownership properties, such as land, water resources, and domestic animals. The fourth part provides the regime of rights and obligations of the Bayrak (*Bajrak),* the role and competencies of the eldership *(pleqësisë)* in delivering binding decisions and changing the rules of the *kanun*. The fifth part establishes the legal framework for punishments, the role of the bailiffs *(gjobtarëve)*, as well as the importance of the institution of *besa* and its subcategories according to this *kanun*. The sixth part includes provisions on crimes *(fajet)* against life, property and honor. The rights of the Catholic Church and its protection, the role of the elders *(pleqve)* of the church, as well as the punishments for sins against the Church are regulated in the seventh part.

80. **Elezi, Ismet.** E Drejta Zakonore e Labërisë në Planin Krahasues. 'SHBLU'. Tiranë, 1994. BK: S 86 F 5
81. **Elezi, Ismet.** Kanuni i Labërisë. Second Edition. 'Toena'. Tiranë, 2006. BK: S 261 B 50. BFDUT; BFHFUT

"The customary law of Labëria on a comparative perspective" explores the customary law applicable in the area of Labëria, and the features of this law spanning from the second half of the 19th century until beginning of the 20th century. The author delves extensively into the regime of the customary law of Labëria regarding family relations. Particular attention is given to the regime of inheritance in the area of Kurvelesh and Himara. The analysis covers the coexistence of this *kanun* first with the Ottoman legislation, and then with the legislation of the Albanian state (1912–1939); the decisions of the Assembly of Men *(kuvendi i burrave)*; and the various covenants (*besëlidhjet*) on important issues. This text also reviews the "Decrees of Idriz Suli" *(Shartet e Idriz Sulit)*, which were interprovincial decisions for reforming the customary law of Labëria in matters regarding property relations, family relations, as well as aspects of the criminal law regime. A comparative analysis is drawn with the Kanun of Lek Dukagjin and the Kanun of Skanderbeg. In this text, the *kanun* of Labëria is divided into 10 parts, with 50 chapters and 883 articles. In this codification of the *kanun* the author uses the Albanian literary language, although in some passages the author clarifies that he preferred to maintain the dialect of Labëria in order to be as faithful as possible to the original expressions. The dialect terms are explained in a dictionary at the end of the work.

82. **Fishta, Iljaz. Kareco, Theodhor.** Prona Private në Shqipëri. 1924–1944. 'Dituria'. Tiranë, 1996. BK: S 191 A 51

"Private property in Albania. 1924–1944" offers documented statistics on the development of private property in Albania throughout a 20-year period, coinciding with the government of Ahmet Zog and the Second World War. It provides data on private enterprises, and especially joint stock companies that operated in strategic economic sectors where the growth of foreign investments is noticeable, especially in the oil exploration and mining industries. In addition to information on shareholders, profits and dividend distribution, the authors also provide statistics on the cartels created in Albania, the development of the Albanian banking system, documents on the economic, customs and currency union between Albania and Italy, and Italian investments in Albania. The book´s preface is in Albanian and Italian.

83. **Ndreçi, Plasari. Malltezi, Luan.** Marrëdhëniet Shqiptaro-Jugosllave, 1945–1948. Drejtoria e Përgjithshme e Arkivave. Tiranë, 1996. BK: S 117 E 63; AQSH: A/1. s 8

The archival documents from the funds of the Albanian Labour Party, international agreements, public political speeches and judicial documents compiled in this book describe the relations between Albania and Yugoslavia during the period 1945–1948, the beginnings of economic integration and the ambitions for the union of the two countries in a Balkan federation. Of interest to lawyers are the bilateral agreement provided in the book, such as the friendship treaties between the two countries, agreements on economic collaboration and the creation of joint economic enterprises, cooperation in the military domain and international relations, and agreements aiming at the financial unification.

84. **Stavileci, Esat. Reka, Blerim. Bajrami, Arsim.** Kosova: Political, Constitutional and International Law Arguments. Kosova Law Review (Special Edition). Prishtinë, 1996. English Edition. BK: PP 323.1 (Sta)

The publication contains different writings of the authors, who analyze the right to self-determination of Kosovo in the framework of public international law. The work is organized in two parts. The first part is divided into three chapters. In the first chapter titled "Political dimension of the question of Kosovo", Esat Stavileci highlights in a historical-legal context the arguments in support of Kosovo's independence. In the second chapter titled "The right of self-determination as an international legal-dimension of Kosovo problem" Blerim Reka dwells on the Serbian documents on the annexation of Kosova and on the evolution of the principle of self-determination, before and after the Bujan Conference. The author also shows the selective application of the Constitution of the Federal Republic of Yugoslavia, from 1974, as well as the implementation of the '*uti possidetis*' principle in defining the borders of Kosova. In the third chapter, entitled 'Constitutional legal dimensions of the question of Kosova', Arsim Bajrami elaborates the legal position of Kosova under the Constitution of 1974 in relation to the federal state, the violation of the rights and of the subjectivity of Kosova and the constitutional declaration of July 2, 1990. The second part of the publication compiles extracts from various writings of these authors.

85. **Bezhani, Nafiz.** Proçesi i Shekullit. 'Eurorilindja'. Tiranë, 1996. BK: S 152 T 49; BHF

The history of the murders of April 2, 1991 in Shkodra, is presented under the lens of official communications between the governing bodies of the district of Shkodra. Of interest is the legal analysis of the investigation process and its shortcomings; the author was also the victims' legal counsel.

86. **Meçi, Xhemal.** Kanuni i Lek Dukagjinit. Varianti i Pukës. 'Çabej'. Tiranë, 1997. BK: S 21 54 B

The book offers an analysis of the characteristics of the Kanun of Lek Dukagjin (KLD) applied in Puka region. The author offers an introduction on the ancient civilizations of the zone and notes that after becoming one of the main provinces of the principality of Dukagjin, the area was subject to the KLD. This legal regime was enriched with local elements, becoming a special version of the *kanun* distinct from the general version. The author stresses that the Puka version of KLD is based on the model of governing autonomy, which has distinguished the province of Puka for centuries. The work is structured in two parts, the part of the *kanun* and the part of its practices. In the first part, divided into three subchapters, the author reflects the social order based on the family, the basic principles of the *kanun*, the governing bodies and institutions regulated by the Kanun of Puka, where the importance of the assembly *(kuvendi)* comes to the fore. Also of interest is the analysis of the institution of *vetëgjyqësia,*[36] the importance of mediation and reconciliation, as well as the role of religious institutions—the church and mosque. The second chapter focuses on provisions regulating the economic order, obligations, private property, property boundaries, rules for the division of the property, inheritance and various agricultural activities. The third chapter is organized in two parts: (i) the general part, which provides the regime of sanctions for crimes (*mbrapshtinat)* against life, health, killing of animals, and damages to property, and (ii) the special part, which depicts practical enforcement cases of this regime in the region of Puka. The paper has a preface in Albanian and French by Mark Tirta, as well as a glossary of terms.

87. **Quku, Sabri.** Kanuni i Lek Dukagjinit. (Në Profilin Juridik). Muzeu Historik. Shkodër, 1997. BK: S 65 V 146; AQSH: F/1.s 3

This study is a reprint of the author's graduating thesis at the University of Turin in 1937, entitled *Le consuetudini delle montagne Albanesi nella legislacione di Lek*

36 Taking justice in its own hand – an institute of Albanian customary law.

Dukagjini (The Customs of the Albanian Mountains in the Kanun of Lek Dukagjin). The work analyzes from a legal point of view the Kanun of Lek Dukagjin collected by Gjeçovi, while also taking into consideration the law of Jibal (*xhibal*), which the author claims was created as a result of the legal activity exercised by the Turkish administration, to supervise the implementation of the KLD in the areas where the Ottoman system had not penetrated. The author highlights the legal value of the *kanun*, its binding effect, the punishments provided in the *kanun*, the role the elders (*pleqësia*), of the assembly (*kuvendi*), of the trial assistant (*ndihmësit*), of the house of Gjomarkaj, the heads of the tribe, the importance of the church, and the protection it enjoyed according to the *kanun*. Further, the author provides a brief overview of some *kanun* institutes, such as the marriage, damages, murder, blood feud, the role of the Jibal Commission, as well as the institutes of the *kanun* that influenced the Albanian Criminal Code of 1928.

88. **Gjeloshi, Nikë.** Kosova në Udhëkryq '89: Humbja e Subjektivitetit dhe Përpjekjet për Pavarësi. 'Velar'. Gorle, 1997. BK: S 151 G 83

"Kosova in a crossroad '89: the loss of subjectivity and its efforts for independence" draws the reader's attention to the constitutional changes of Serbia, focusing especially on the work of the parliamentary commissions and the proposed constitutional amendments—which had a negative impact on the status of Kosovo. Amongst them, the author highlights amendment no. 46, which *de facto* reduced the power and competences of the assemblies of the autonomous provinces in favor of the Assembly of Serbia. He notes that the proposed constitutional amendments represented a regress to the constitutional arrangements of 1963 and that they were met with strong opposition from Albanians. The author analyzes the constitutional declaration of July 2, 1990, the Constitution of September 7, 1990, the declaration of the Albanian political parties and the referendum of September 1991.

89. **Haxhi, Paskal.** Regjimi Juridik i Tokës në Shqipëri. Vështrim Historik. 'Albin'. Tiranë, 1998. BK: S 116 26 G

"The legal regime of land in Albania" presents chronologically the historical development of land ownership structures in Albania, with a particular focus on agricultural land. Beginning with a depicption of the model of communal tribal property according to customary law, the author then explores the changes brought about by the Ottoman *Tanzimat* reform, the legal regime of the land after Albania's independence in 1912, the agrarian reform during the reign of King Zog, the agrarian reform of 1945 after the installation of communism, the abrogation of private property and the creation of cooperatives, and the fundamental changes after the collapse of the Albanian socialist system in 1990. The work relies on a series of legal acts that established the regimes on agricultural land in different periods, including the changes to this legal framework after the fall of the communist regime and the reinstitution of private property.

90. **Elezi, Ismet.** Zhvillimi Historik i Legjislacionit Penal në Shqipëri. 'Albin'. Tiranë, 1997. BK: S 120 65 E

"The Historical development of the criminal legislation in Albania" is structured in three parts. In the first part, the author analyzes the regime of the penal sphere implemented in Albanian territories, from ancient times until the creation of the independent Albanian state in 1912. The analysis highlights the Albanian customary criminal law and its coexistence with the regimes of positive law. In the second part he delves into the criminal legislation applicable in Albania from the proclamation of independence (1912), until the end of the Second World War. He notes several of the most important legal acts adopted during this period, including the Albanian Penal Code, of January 1, 1928. The author further explores several decisions of the Court of Dictation *(Gjykatës së Diktimit)* rendered in accordance with the newly adopted Penal Code of 1928, which consisted of the amendments introduced by the Italian authorities after Albania's occupation from Italy; these include the decree of the General Viceroy of the Emperor in Albania *(Mëkëmbësi i Përgjithshëm i Perandorit në Shqipëri)*, no. 288, dated 31.12.1939 *On crimes against the state personalit.* In this part, the author also analyzes the penal norms approved by *the National-Liberation Councils of the Albanian Communist Party*, based on the resolutions of the Conference of Peza of September 16, 1942, which were declared applicable in the liberated areas of Albania. The third part of the publication includes references to the penal legislation of the totalitarian regime that was installed in Albania after the Second World War. It focuses on major acts adopted during the years 1944–1952. This part also discusses the changes that marked the criminal legislation after the change of the political system and the restoration of political pluralism in 1990. The analysis is illustrated with Albanian jurisprudence.

91. **Luarasi, Aleks.** Aktet Juridike për Historinë e Shtetit dhe e së Drejtës në Shqipëri. Part I. 'Luarasi'. Tiranë, 1998. BK: S 45 E 83.
92. **Luarasi, Aleks.** Aktet Juridike për Historinë e Shtetit dhe e së Drejtës në Shqipëri. Part I. Second Edition. 'SHBLU', 2001. BK: S 87 F 85

In the first volume of the book "Legal acts on the history of state and law in Albania", the author presents legal research and acts pertaining to the state and legal order, from ancient times until the League of Prizren (June 10, 1978). The book deals with aspects of the law that applied in the province of Illyria after the Roman occupation, which consisted of feudal principates of the 12th–15th centuries, as well as the organization of Albanian cities during the Middle Ages. A separate chapter is dedicated to the legal organization of the independent state of Albania under the leadership of Skanderbeg. The author also analyses Ottoman institutions and their regime in the Albanian territory. The first volume concludes with the acts of the League of Prizren, whose decisions—known as *Kararname*—are presented in full.

93. **Luarasi, Aleks.** Aktet Juridike për Historinë e Shtetit dhe e së Drejtës në Shqipëri. Part II. 'Luarasi'. Tiranë, 1999. BK: S 199 R 24

The second volume offers the fundamental legal acts that were adopted from Albania's independence in 1912 until its occupation on April 7, 1939. These acts regulated or affected different aspects of the emerging Albanian state: the organization and functioning of the judiciary; the gendarmerie and the public administration under Ismail Qemali's government; the final decision of the Conference of Ambassadors in London of July 29, 1913—which left more than half of the Albanian autochthonous territories outside of the country's official borders; the Organic Statute of Albania of April 10, 1914, which is the first Constitution after the declaration of independence and was imposed by the International Control Commission; the Statute and decisions of the Congress of Lushnje, as well as the Extended Statute of Lushnja (1922). Attention is also given to the main documents of the government of Fan Noli and the ensuing governments, as well as the legal reforms during the period of consolidation of the Albanian state until the Second World War, the Fundamental Statute of the Republic of Albania of 1925, the Fundamental Statute of the Kingdom of Albania (1928), the Criminal Code (1928), the Civil Code (1929) and the Commercial Code (1932).

94. **Luarasi, Aleks.** Shteti dhe e Drejta Shqiptare në Epokën e Skënderbeut. 'Luarasi'. Tiranë, 1998. BK: S 196 F 81

In "The Albanian state and law in the era of Skanderbeg" the author has expanded on his doctoral thesis, presented in 1981. The analysis begins from the 12th century principate of Arbër and the feudal formations that preceded the state of Skanderbeg. A special chapter is dedicated to the organization of the state apparatus and the legal regime during the rule of Skanderbeg, as well as his relations with other countries, and the signature of international agreements during his rule. The study also analyzes other Albanian principalities of the 14th and early 15th centuries, as well as the Albanian towns of this time and their legal and political organization.

95. **Anastasi, Aurela.** Institucionet Politike dhe e Drejta Kushtetuese në Shqipëri (1912–1939). Monografi. 'Luarasi'. Tiranë, 1998. BFDUT

96. **Anastasi, Aurela.** Institucionet Politike dhe e Drejta Kushtetuese në Shqipëri (1912–1939). Monografi. Second Edition. 'Luarasi'. Tiranë, 2002. BFDUT

The monograph "The political institutions and the constitutional law in Albania" is dedicated to the history of the institution development during the state-forming years, covering a period from Albania's independence (1912) until Albania's occupation by Italy (1939). It analyzes public institutions between 1912–1914, the Basis of the Law of the High Council *(Bazat e Kanunores së Këshillit të Lartë)*—an act of a constitutional nature, also known as the "Statute of Lushnja", approved by a representative body of a national character, as well as the Extended Statute of Lushnja *(Statutit i Lushnjës i Zgjeruar)*. The discussion expands on the historical developments that brought Ahmet Zog to power, the proclamation of the Republic in 1925, the relationship between different power components and the relationship between the state and religious communities. The second edition of 2002 elaborates more in-depth on aspects of governance during the period of monarchy.

97. **Meta, Beqir.** Politika Tatimore e Shtetit Shqiptar: 1925–1939. Akademia e Shkencave të Shqipërisë, Institutit të Historisë. Tiranë, 1999. BK: S 196 D 21. BHF; BKSH

The monograph "The fiscal policy of the Albanian State: 1925–1939" analyzes the policies and tax legislation imposed by the newly emerging Albanian state, after the proclamation of independence; it is based on archival documents published for the first time, as well as on Albanian and foreign historiography. The study focuses on key historical periods, namely, the period of the Republic (1925–1928), the Monarchy (1928–1939) and the economic crisis between 1929–1935. It provides readers with a list of the financial legal acts and bylaws adopted in the mentioned period, chronological arrayed and their respective references in the official journal. The study is of interest to researchers of history of law, economic and trade law.

98. **Elezi, Ismet.** Mendimi Juridik Shqiptar. 'Albin'. Tiranë, 1999. BK: S31 D 181
99. **Elezi, Ismet. Elezi, Ela.** Zhvillimi Historik i Mendimit Teoriko – Juridik Shqiptar: Para Krijimit të Shtetit të Pavarur Shqiptar, 1912–2009. 'Erik'. Tiranë, 2010. BK: S 353 A 5; BFDUT

In this work, the authors explore the main currents of legal thought developed by Albanian authors. Starting from the Illyrian period, the text focuses on important historical moments, such as the national renaissance, the declaration of independence, the years of monarchy, the period of communism (1945–1990) and the developments of the Albanian doctrine between 1991–2009. The researchers give special attention to the *kanuns* of the Secret Committee of the Manastir (also known as "The Committee for the Freedom of Albania"); the positions of several well-known Albanian thinkers of the period of the Ottoman occupation, including the Frashëri brothers, Zef Jubani, Jani Vreto; prominent Albanian jurists of this period, such as Nexhip P. Alpani—author of the book *Albanians in the Ottoman Empire (Shqiptarët në Perandorinë Osmane)*; and Mustafa Bej Korçari who drafted a report-memorandum presented to Sultan Murat IV in 1631, on the reformation of the Ottoman state. It proceeds to review the contributions of numerous Albanian lawyers who contributed to the reforming of the legal system in the period from the declaration of independence until the end of the Second World War, the contribution of legal scholars between 1945–1990, represented by various authors and their work in "The History of the State and Law in Albania" *(Historia e Shtetit dhe e së Drejtës në Shqipëri)*, the study of Andrea Sahatiçi on the history of Albanian law and other noted contributions. The book gives due consideration to the development of the theoretical-legal thought in Kosova, the notable works of Sokol Dobrashi, Syrja Pupovci, Ragip Halili, Ismet Salihu, Valbona Begolli, Hilmi Ismaili, Bardhyl Caushi and others. The work also includes cases from the jurisprudence of the Albanian Constitutional Court and the unifying decisions of the United Colleges of the High Court *(Kolegjeve të Bashkuara të Gjykatës së Lartë)* between 2000–2009.

100. **Hasani, Enver.** Shpërbërja e Jugosllavisë dhe Kosova. Aspekte Politiko-Juridike. Instituti Shqiptar për Studime Ndërkombëtare. Tiranë, 2000. BK: S 200 E71

"The dissolution of Yugoslavia and Kosova. Legal – political aspects" provides an overview of the developments in the legal opinion of the international community regarding the process of dissolution of Yugoslavia and the recognition of the new countries that emerged from this process. The author discusses the legal opinion of the Badinter Commission on Yugoslavia and its influence on the resolution of the conflict, the dispute regarding the borders and the principle of *c.d. Uti Possidetis* that was taken into consideration by the international community for the resolution of conflicts in Yugoslavia. The author analyzes Kosovo's right to self-governance under the rules of international law, the agreements on the normalization of relations, the *Dayton Agreement* and the status of Kosovo.

101. **Duka, Ferit.** Berati në Kohën Osmane. (Shek. XVI–XVIII). Akademia e Shkencave e Republikës së Shqipërisë. Monografi. 'Toena'. Tiranë, 2001. BK: S 195 T 79

"Berat during the Ottoman times (16th–18th century)" explores the governance of the city of Berat, the military hierarchy and the role of powerful Albanian feudal families, who, due to the *timar* mechanisms of the Ottoman system, were integrated into the ranks of the Ottoman ruling class. The author presents the history and origin of some feudal families such as the Skuraj and Muzakaj, their influence on governance and representation of the city in relation with third parties. Of interest is the analysis of the organization of craftsmanship in guilds *(esnaf)*, and the highlighting of the most important *esnafs*, such as the leather processing, silk processing, and stone works. The author notes that the development of craftsmanship and the production of goods influenced the expansion of trade in the city of Berat, and as a result the increase in the number of guilds. The author delves into the internal organization of guilds *(esnafeve)* and their governing bodies. Of interest are also the analysis of the *kanunname* that regulated the relations between buyers and sellers, those pertaining to relations between traders and the Ottoman government, as well as the controlling structures of the market, such as the market inspector *(muhtesibit)* appointed by the Ottoman administration. Additionally, the publication offers insights into the types of taxes, the fiscal status of the citizens of Berat, and the significant role of the state taxes, such as the poll tax *(taksa për kokë - xhizja)*, or taxes levied by the judicial administration (Sharia). The author notes that the Sharia registers of Berat reflect the spreading of the practice of concessions of tax collections, while also establishing a supervisory system to prevent abuse and corruption. The work was based upon numerous documents extracted from the archives of Albanian and Turkish institutions.

102. **Uruçi, Dashamir.** Kosova dhe e Drejta e Vetëvendosjes. 'Shtjefni'. Shkodër, 2001. BK: S 57 G 183

In this publication the author focuses on the right of self-determination of Kosovo, in accordance with the international acts as well as with the framework of the 1974 Constitution of the Federal Republic of Yugoslavia on this issue.

103. **Bajrami, Arsim.** E Drejta e Kosovës në Tranzicion (E Drejta Kushtetuese). The Kosova Law in Transition. Universiteti i Prishtinës, Fakulteti Juridik. Prishtinë, 2001. BK: Al 28 43 C

The publication explores the evolution of the history of the state of Kosova from a legal point of view. The author analyzes (i) the legal position of Kosova as an essential element of federalism in the constitutional-legal system of former Yugoslavia in the period 1945–1974; (ii) the change in Kosova's position with the Constitution of 1974; (iii) the impact of the Rambouillet Conference on the international legal plane; (iv) UNSC Resolution no. 1244 and (v) Kosova's international administration. The publication contains a complete set of legal acts as well as a short summary in English.

104. **Hoxha, Izet.** Marrëdhëniet Juridike në Kanunin e Lek Dukagjinit. 'Albin'. Tiranë, 2002. BFDUT

The author focuses on "The legal relationships in the Kanun of Lek Dukagjin", highlighting the legal value of the norms of customary law and the importance of studying the evolution of the Albanian customary law over the centuries. He analyses the basic features of the system of norms contained in the *kanun*, their origin, and their territorial validity. He further delves into the essence of the legal norms, the socio-economic structure of the *kanun*, the origin of the KLD and the links between state legislation and canonical norms, where the autonomy of the latter has emerged evidently throughout centuries.

105. **Meçi, Xhemal.** Kanuni i Lek Dukagjinit. Në Variantin e Mirëditës. 'Geer'. Tiranë, 2002. BK: S 167 80 F

This book analyses the version of the Kanun of Lek Dukagjin (KLD) applied in Mirëdita, and the key roles of the Gjomarkaj family, the Captain and the Chiefs (*Kapidani dhe Krerët*). The author notes that unlike other areas of the north that followed the KLD, in Mirëdita the right of the Elder of the Village *(Plakut të Katundit)* was a hereditary function. The book is structured in three parts. The first part depicts the organization of the family and society, the basic principles of the *kanun*, the governing and leading institutes such as the assembly (*kuvendi*), the elders (*pleqtë*), the grand-elders (*strapleqtë*), the youths (*djalëria*, the commoners), the bayraktar (*bajraktari*), the village (*katundi*), the province (*krahina*) and the House of Gjomarku (*Gjomarku*). Further, the author presents the roles of the institutes for the prevention of *vetëgjyqësia*, the body of Elders (*pleqtë*) and the role of the Church. The second part deals with the economic organization according to the KLD of Mirëdita, the modalities for the division of property, the rules for defining property boundaries, the division of the family in young units, the inheritance, as well as the norms on obligations. In the third part, the author analyzes the criminal law, focusing further within its two subdivisions: the general and the special parts. The last sections of the book include explanatory notes, various examples of *kanun* case law, as well as a glossary of terms.

106. **Hoxha, Shefqet.** Instituti i Kuvendit në Lumë. Punim Etnologjiko-Historik. 'Geer'. Tiranë, 2002. BK S 125 S 80

"The Institute of Assembly in Luma" provides information on the functioning and powers of the Assembly (*Kuvendi*) as a self-governing body according to Albanian customary law, focusing specifically on its characteristics according to the Kanun of Luma. It further presents a series of decisions taken by the elders of Luma in the Assembly, during a period that extends from 1823 until 1967.

107. **Drejtoria e Përgjithshme e Arkivave.** Kodikët e Shqipërisë. Tiranë, 2003. BK: S 207A 24.[37]

Published in 2003, the Codices of Albania is devised as a catalog of 100 of the codices written in the Albanian territories since the 6th century, which are found in what is known as 'fund 488 of the Central State Archive'.[38] The publication contains the descriptive passes of 100 codices, prepared by well-known authors of historiography and archival science, accompanied by relevant archival and bibliographic references. Included as well are writings on the importance of these codices as evidence of the history and culture of the Albanian population. It should be noted that the codexes are subject to slight variations in classification of both authors and works, not all of which are part of this bibliography.[39] The codices classified as philological codices are mainly ecclesiastical books—gospels, rules of religious organization, church music anthologies, or stories of church martyrs. The earliest codices included in this publication reflect a content especially closely related to the divine message and the functioning of the church. The authors point out that churches and monasteries were the centers of writing, but also the center of gravity of civic life, and that ecclesiastical law has regulated the regime of these communities alongside customary and civic law.[40] The codices that had initially served to write the divine message evolved over time, in the secular world, where they were put to the function of order and justice—not only in the public domain, but also in the private one. The codices included in this edition prove the expansion of their scope and role. From the beginning of the 16th century, some codices, classified as nomocanons, reflect norms which, although classified as religious-moral norms, provide the code of conduct that should be respected by the believers under the relevant ecclesiastical jurisdiction. Rules illustrating this function include those establishing the characteristics that a judge was expected to demonstrate, the conduct of the judge and the exercise of his activity, the definition and the meaning of unlawfulness, justice and application of

---

37 In the National Library, as well as in the Library of the General Directorate of Archives, the publication is catalogued as follows: Sinani, Shaban. Kodikët e Shqipërisë. Drejtoria e Përgjithshme e Arkivave. Tiranë, 2003. AQSH: I/1 s. 6.

38 Sinani, Kodikët, p.14.

39 Popa, Theofan. Dorëshkrimet Kishtare Mesjetare të Shqipërisë, tek Kodikët e Shqipërisë, ibid, p. 199–206. Sinani, Shaban. Kodikët Kronografikë të Shqipërisë – Shkrime dhe Dorëshkrime prej Rilindjes Europiane deri në Rilindjen Kombëtare. 'Naimi'. Tiranë, 2014. Chapter I; The author suggests improvements on the methodology of classification of the codices.

40 Sinani, Kodikët, p.12, see also p. 207.

the law, the role of unwritten customs of the church and the cities, obligations of both parties in case of betrothal, the regime of inheritance, adoptions and care of minors.[41] Gradually, some later codices took on the features of registers, recording data on gifts to the church in land, money and valuables. The information recorded on a Codex of Korça of the 19th century, classified as Codex no. 99, cover a wide area and includes amongst its data the rules and decisions of the guilds of these areas, facts on the history of schools and charitable associations.[42] The Codex of Fier, which dates to the first half of the 19th century, testifies to an established practice in this community of registering the betrothal contracts, in the form of written legal acts, signed by witnesses.[43] The publication does not provide the transcript of the codices, but their summary pass. Yet, it serves as a very valuable starting point for legal scholars in finding bibliographic references on the codices and the study of this little-explored regulatory framework.

108. **Fishta, Iljaz. Ziu, Mihal.** Historia e Ekonomisë së Shqipërisë (1944–1960). 'Dita'. Tiranë, 2004. BK: S 217 E 31

In this work, the authors analyze the history of Albania's economy during the 20-year period after the Second World War and the establishment of communism. The period was marked by the adoption of a series of legal acts which radically transformed the economic and ownership structure, leading to the installation of a centralized socialist economy and the elimination of private property. The analyses commence with Albania's economic situation from its independence until 1924 and the government of Fan Noli, and continue by reviewing the economic developments between 1924–1939 under the rule of Ahmet Zog and the Italian invasion of Albania. Among other important points, it provides information regarding several of the concessionary and joint stock companies that operated in the Albanian market, as well as the penetration of Italian capital into the country's economy. The authors proceed by addressing the country's main economic developments under the Italian,

41 Ibid. See for example the pass no. 60, of the codices of Berat, p.148, pass no. 66, codice of Beratit, which is considered to date on 1613, p.152, codice no. 86, of Elbasan, which dates around the mid-16th century, p.166, codice no. 97, of Gjirokastra (1562), p. 175, codice no. 99, of Korça (1676), p. 177 et seq.

42 Ibid. p. 195–196. Contains notes from 1847, on the rules of the bakers' guild of Korça and the punishments for those who violate the rules, decisions of the guild of gunsmiths, decision of the butchers' guild. In addition to testamentary acts, acts of sale, purchase and inheritance, it recordes that Voskopoja had guilds of ironworkers, goldsmiths, bakers, butchers. It also provides data on the history of the first school for girls in the area, in the Greek language (1856–1857), the creation of charitable associations which did not discriminate on religious basis (Brotherhood for the Poor, 1870).

43 The codices no. 100, ibid.

and later, the German occupation between 1939–1944. The history of the legal acts of the period 1944–1960 notes several important moments, such as the decisions of the First Plenum of the Central Committee of the Communist Party *(Pleniumi I i Komitetit Qendror të Partisë Komuniste)*, in February 1946, which paved the way for the confiscation of private property and the preparation of the agrarian reform in Albania, as well as the transformation of commercial relations, their centralization, and the orientation of the foreign trade towards other countries of the socialist camp.

109. **Reinkowski, Maurus.** Die Dinge der Ordnung. Eine Vergliuchende Untersuchung uber die Osmanische Reformpolitik im 19 Jahrhunderrt. Sudosteeuraisce Arbeiten. 'Oldenbourg'. München, 2005. German Edition. BK: BA 28 4 B.

The author analyzes Ottoman law, with specific attention to the characteristics of the Tanzimat Reform, analyzing the differences between its implementation in the center of the Empire and in peripheral areas, such as in cities like Shkodra, Mirëdita and the areas of northern Albania. The paper focuses on the coexistence of Albanian customary law with Ottoman law, and the integration of the latter into Albanian customs and customary law, such as *besa*. The work contains a rich bibliography of various studies on Ottoman law.

110. **Shabani, Sinan. Firatli, H. Erkan. Atmaca, Tayfun.** Fermanlar. Të Shkruash Historinë me Tolerancë. 'Arbëria'. Tiranë, 2005. AQSh: A. s. 2

This catalog contains about 60 legal acts—*fermans, berate, buyuruldu (*order*)*, ordinances and proclamations—of the high Ottoman administration that shed light on different aspects of Ottoman governance in the Albanian territories. The legal instruments addressed various matters, such as the status of the churches and private property issues. The edition is published in three languages: Albanian, Turkish and English. At the end, there is a glossary of terms in Albanian and Turkish.

111. **Hobdari, Florjan. Jorganxhi, Alba.** Debati Kushtetues. Diskutimet në Komisionin Parlamentar për Hartimin e Projekt-Kushtetutës Mars-Shtator 1998. Vol. I. 'R.S.H. 2015 shpk'. Tiranë, 2006. BKSH
112. **Hobdari, Florjan. Jorganxhi, Alba.** Debati Kushtetues. Diskutimet në Komisionin Parlamentar për Hartimin e Projekt-Kushtetutës Mars-Shtator 1998. Vol. II. 'R.S.H. 2015 shpk'. Tiranë, 2006. BKSH

The two-volume work "The constitutional debate" presents in full the parliamentary debates related to the approval of the Albanian Constitution of 1998. Additionally, the volumes include legal acts undertaken during the process of approval of the

Constitution, such as the decision of the Parliament (*Kuvendi i Shqipërisë*) no. 339, dated 03.09.1997, and the decision no. 393, dated 21.10.1998, "On the adoption of the Constitution of the Republic of Albania by public referendum". Of interest are also the comments of the Commission of Venice on the proposed constitutional changes.

113. **Leci, Elmaz.** Krime në Kohën e Komunizmit. Instituti i Problemeve të Sigurisë dhe Mbrojtjes. Tiranë, 2007. BKSH

"Crimes during communism" explores in five chapters the different mechanisms that the communist regime, established after the Second World War, used to implement the restrictive reforms in the political and economic domains, which included extreme persecution of political opponents and the elimination of private property. The fifth chapter delves into the events that led to the departure of the American mission from Albania, the measures taken by the Presidium of the People's Assembly (*Presidiumi i Kuvendit Popullor*) to limit the activity of the so-called '*kulaks*'[44] by implementing the extraordinary tax on profits, the undertaking of the agrarian reform, and the consolidation of the class struggle. Illustration is provided, for instance with the ordinance no. 55, dated 31.X. 1950, which served as a basis for imposing a discriminatory two-tier tax system for '*kulaks*'. The work is based on archival documents collected from the National Archives.

114. **Sinani, A. Petrit.** Historia e Avokatisë Shqiptare 1912–1967. Dhoma Kombëtare e Avokatisë të Republikës së Shqipërisë. 'Medaur'. Tiranë, 2007. BK: S 281 F 4

In this work, the author reflects in chronological order the evolution of the profession of the private attorney in Albania and its regulatory framework, as of the declaration of independence in 1912 until 2005. The publication provides references to all the laws and by-laws that have served to regulate the legal profession during the ninety-year time period.

115. **Valentini, Giuseppe.** Il Diritto delle Comunità nella Tradizone Giuridica Albanese. Vallecchi Editore. Firenze, 1956. BK: AL 38 C 8. BIHGJL

---

44 *Kulak* was the term used by the communist system to define opponents of the economic reforms undertaken in the countryside. In the legal act in question, the term referred to the rich peasantry, which was perceived as hostile towards these reforms. Over time the term *kulak* gained political importance and even poor peasants who refused to hand over the little property they had were also considered *kulaks*. The classification in the *kulak* category was accompanied by social ostracizing, restriction of civil and economic rights and possibly other punishments.

116. **Valentini, Giuseppe.** E Drejta e Komuniteteve në Traditën Juridike Shqiptare. Albanian Edition and Prepared by Kulla, Ndriçim and Krisafi, Ksenofon. 'Plejad'. Tiranë. 2007. BK: S 274 D 58

"The law of the community in the Albanian legal tradition" provides researchers with a *corpus* of various legal documents from ancient, medieval and modern times, through which Valentini analyses the organization of the *community*, as a communion broader than the family, with a key role in Albanian customary law; the *community* carries in it features of public law institutions. The materials included in the 2007 edition are selected from the works of Valentini, Corpus I, Corpus II and Corpus III.

117. **Valentini, Giuseppe.** Statuti Personal në Shqipëri në Epokën e Skënderbeut. Prepared for Publication by Kulla, Ndriçim and Krisafi, Ksenofon. 'Plejad'. Tiranë, 2007. BK: S 275 F 19

The editors summarize a part of the notes written by Giuseppe Valentini in the archives of the Republic of Venice, which focuses on the concept of the personal law in Albanian customary law, during the rule of Skanderbeg. Valentini notes that, based on the data collected and the systematic interpretation of the provisions of the Albanian customary law, the rights of a natural person were more limited than those of the community or tribe to which he belonged. The author analyzes the division of the Albanian society into classes and their respective rights, highlighting the peculiarities of the lords' regime (*zotërinjëve*), despite the fact that all legal regimes of the time were based upon the family unit. The book discusses the rights and privileges of the natural person in Albanian cities, the way in which the Venetian law was applied in the Albanian territory, the administrative judicial division, and the procedural administration of the civil and criminal justice.

118. **Pepo, Petraq. Pela, Mihallaq.** Kanunorë të Shoqërive Shqiptare: 1870–1936. Vol. 1. Drejtoria e Përgjithshme e Arkivave. 'Ada'. Tiranë, 2007. AQSH: I/1 s. 6

This publication by the General Directorate of State Archives *(Drejtoria e Përgjithshme e Arkivave)* is a compilation of the charters, their amendments and other main acts of Albanian companies, associations and corporations (guilds) created during the period of 1870–1936. From these acts, 60 statutes belong to the period between 1870–1912, while 163 statutes pertain to subjects created in the years 1913–1936. The work provides the complete statutes of legal persons created for the purpose of defending and preserving the territory of the Albanian state, of conducting patriotic activities, of contributing in institutional building, in the preservation of the language, promotion of education, women's rights, unions of employees, professionals, artisans and craftsmen, as well as charitable organizations helping the needy and building infrastructure in service of these communities. The book also reflects the statutes of religious communities and those of some religious organizations in Albania. The text provides a map of the distribution of these entities in various cities and villages in Albania, as well as abroad: in the USA, Romania, Italy, Bulgaria, Egypt, Turkey, Greece; countries where there was an active Albanian diaspora and where about 66 of such associations were present. The full text of the statute is accompanied by brief comments from the publisher regarding the archival references of the acts, notes on the date of the association's registration, as well as its various amendments that may not have been included in the publication.

119. **Mandro-Balili, Arta.** Pashallëqet Feudale Shqiptare nën Këndvështrimin e Shtetit dhe të së Drejtës. Rasti i Pashallëkut të Shkodrës dhe Pashallëkut të Janinës. Monografi. 'Mediaprint'. Tiranë, 2008. BK: S. 306 C59

The monograph "The Albanian feudal pashaliks from viewpoint of the state and the law. The case of the pashaliks of Shkodra and Ioannina", provides an in-depth analysis on the legal nature of the Albanian *pashaliks* after the fall of the feudal state under the leadership of Skanderbeg. The book is organized in four chapters. The first analyzes the historical circumstances in which the Albanian *pashaliks* of Shkodra and Ioannina were created, focusing on the changes regarding land ownership, as well as class and military factors. The second chapter addresses the administrative organization of the Pashalik of Shkodra, where the administrative structure of the state was built upon a family-run model, inherited through generations. The third chapter deals with the Pashalik of Ioannina, the features of its organization, and the concentration of power in the hands of Ali Pasha. The fourth chapter is dedicated to the legal system implemented in the aforementioned *pashaliks*, as distinctive from Ottoman law. It highlights the decisions of Albanian Pashas, whose efforts to respect the customary law impacted the development of special features of positive law in these *pashaliks*. Another unique characteristic noted by the author is the body of rights guaranteed to the church in the Albanian *pashaliks*, and the various privileges of the Christian population, which developed features distinctive from those of the Ottoman Empire. The work is based on sources from Albanian, Italian and French archives.

120. **Krisafi, Ksenofon.** Në Kërkim të Arit. Historia e Arit Shqiptar të Rrëmbyer Gjatë Luftës së Dytë Botërore. Monografi. 'Dita 2000'. Tiranë, 2009. BK: S 301 E 5

"In search of Albanian gold. The history of albanian gold forfeited during the Second World War" dissects from a legal perspective one of the complex issues in the history of Albanian diplomacy. The gold, owned by the Albanian National Bank, was taken by the Italian fascist, and later the Nazi, authorities. The book describes Albania's efforts to return the gold, and the application filed for this purpose in 1947, to the Tripartite Commission for the Return of Monetary Gold; this commission was created by the USA, United Kingdom and France, and was tasked with examining, dividing and returning the amount of gold that German forces had looted during the war. The research presents the negotiations in different periods and interprets documents pertaining to this issue, including the decision of the International Court of Justice on the incident of the Corfu Channel and the impact of this event on the agreement of the Tripartite Commission to transfer Albanian gold to United Kingdom.

121. **Krisafi, Ksenofon.** Diplomaci pas Lufte. Negociatat me Italinë dhe Gjermaninë për Dëmet e Luftës në Shqipëri. 'Dita 2000'. Tiranë, 2009. BK: S 323 D 18

The book presents Albanian diplomacy during the Cold War period and the efforts to negotiate war reparations with Italy and Germany. The work reflects the author's personal experience as a member of groups tasked with diplomatic negotiations during the years 1975–1987. The work is based on archival documents, especially from the archive of the Ministry of Foreign Affair. The analysis spans from the demands for compensation presented by Albania during the Peace Conference of 1919–1920, and continues with the reparations after the Second World War, the peace treaty with Italy, the Italian–Albanian negotiations, the decision to return the gold of the Albanian National Bank, Albania's demands and reparation claims against Germany, the decrees on ending the state of war with Germany and the Albanian–German talks held during the 1980s. An interesting point is the legal framework that preceded the negotiations between the countries, as well as the agreements reached.

122. **Ahmeti, Musa. Lala, Etleva.** Statutet dhe Urdhëresat e Kapitullit të Kishës Katedrale të Drishtit. Statuta Et Ordinationes Capituli Ecclesiae Cathedralis Drivastiensis. 'Ombra GVG'. Tiranë, 2009. BK: S 309 A 125

"The statute and ordinances of the chapter of the Drishti Cathedral" is another important legal source that, alongside with the Statutes of Shkodra, has drawn the attention of many researchers. Prominent Albanologist Milan Sufflay was the first to identify the existence of the Statutes of Drishti, based on a citation in the catalog of Karl Wilhelm Hiersemann of Leipzig (Germany) in 1915. The manuscript on the statutes and ordinances of Drishti was published for the first time by '*Arhiva za Arbanasku starinu, jezik i etnologiju*' in Belgrade in 1927; only in 1972 was a short summary published in the Albanian language in the magazine "Gjurmime Albanologjike", Series of Historical Sciences, in Prishtina.[45] Researchers and translators Ahmeti and Lala brought the full text of the statutes translated from Latin into Albanian in 2009. The publication contains the complete text of the statutes and ordinances of the Chapter of the Cathedral Church of Drishti, in Albanian and Latin. It explains the time and the historical context of the creation of the manuscript, its content, the geographical location of the Drishti Cathedral and the history of discovery of the manuscript. The editors point out that although the manuscript was written by the Canon regular of Tivar, Simon Dromasus, in January 1468, it refers to the official variant of 1464 and that from archival data it appears that the statute was drawn up in 1456, with the authorization of Pope Callistus III.[46] It has been proposed that rather than standing as a typical act of regulating the status and governance of the cities of this period, the statues is rather the fundamental act of regulating a religious entity and that this entire *corpus* of laws remains within the regulatory framework of the cathedral chapter as an expression of ecclesiastical law.[47] Ahmeti and Lala point out that the church has always influenced civic life, exemplified in this case by the statute's regimen on acts that were considered harmful to the individual and society as a whole. Drishti was under the administration of the Cathedral, where the canon regulars also exercised civic duties such as the notary functions or tax collector. On the other hand, part of the norms contained in the statute were based on old customs and served as models for the statutes of other cities.[48] The statutes are divided into books, organized into chapters which regulate various domains in detail. The authors point out that the statutes are accompanied by additions and various amendments that attest to the ability of the norms to adapt to the developments throughout the ages. The cathedral was the center of power and its statute determined the election of the ruling hierarchy—the archbishop, the ecclesiastical prince, the rector, the procuratorate—their duties and powers. The statute provided rules on how elders should be respected, as well as the corresponding punishments for offenders.[49] It also defines the rules for how canon regulars, archdeacons and archbishops perform religious services, the rules

45 Ahmeti, Musa. Lala, Etleva. Statutet dhe Urdhëresat e Kapitullit të Kishës Katedrale të Drishtit. Statuta Et Ordinationes Capituli Ecclesiae Cathedralis Drivastiensis. 'Ombra GVG'. Tiranë, 2009, p. 10.

46 Ahmeti, Lala, Statutet, p.19.

47 Malaj, Edmond. Kanonikët Mesjetarë të Kapitullit të Katedrales së Drishtit sipas Statuteve të saj. (The Canonicals of the Cathedral of Drivasto Second their Statutes). Journal 'Studime Historike'. Tiranë, 2015, p. 7–26.

48 Ahmeti, Lala, Statutet, p. 21–29.

49 Ibid. p. 27.

for the use of the seal, privileges and official documents as well as the consequences in cases of non-compliance with these rules. The statute determined that in the absence of a specific statutory regime for a case, "*...will be proceeded according to justice and honesty*",[50] hence demonstrating its ability to adapt.

123. **Duka, Ferit.** Shekujt Osmanë në Hapësirën Shqiptare (Studime dhe Dokumenta). 'UET Press'. Tiranë, 2009. BK: Al 36 35 F

The historical study titled "The Ottoman centuries in the Albanian space (studies and documents)"contains important data regarding the socio-economic and legal changes of Albanian cities under the occupation of the Ottoman Empire. The publication raises a number of interesting issues from the legal perspective, from which we note:

- The acts on the administrative division of Albania under the rule of the Ottoman Empire;
- The division into special categories of the population, based on whether or not the inhabitants were eligible for drafting in the military service for the benefit of the Ottoman state;
- The implementation of the *timar* system in the Albanian cities that were part of the Sanjak of Albania (*Sancak-i Arvanya*), also known as the Vilayet of Albania (*Vilayet-i Arvanya*);
- Data from the detailed Registry of the Sanjak of Delvina (1551), which also included the village of Himara;
- Data on the *kazas* of Ajdonat and Mazrak in Çameria during the second half of the 16th century;
- The Ottoman Registry "On Properties and Population Records for the Sanjak of Vlora" from the registry of 1520 and the registry of 1583, where there is data on the city of Gjirokastra and the province of Dropulli.

The paper also reflects the efforts to revive the Albanian National Movement of the League of Peja (1882–1899).

124. **Meçollari, Artur.** Incidenti i Kanalit të Korfuzit: Drejtësi e Anuar. 'Tripik'. Vlorë, 2009. BK: S 304 G 24

"The incident of Corfu: biased justice" is the focus of the book, whose author has held the position of a second rank captain and specialist in the Albanian Naval Forces. The work analyzes the 1949 decision of the International Court of Justice (ICJ), on

50 The Statute and Ordinances of the Chapter of the Drishti Cathedral, Chapter XXXV, p. 161.

the incident of Corfu, from a historical and legal perspective. The paper refers to the decision of the ICJ and delves into archival documents of the Albanian ports, kept at the Archive of the Ministry of Defense, Navy Section (Arkivi i Ministrisë së Mbrojtjes, Seksioni i Marinës). Based on the data, the author develops his analysis in a technical context to answer the question whether the Corfu Channel is an international strait from a legal perspective.

125. **Valentini, Giuseppe.** Studime dhe Tekste Juridike II. Edited by Kulla, Ndriçim and Thomollari, Dritan. (Seria Valentini). Shtëpia Botuese '55'. Tiranë, 2010. BK: S 358 E 21

This compilation focuses on public law, the elaboration of the concept of criminal justice in the Albanian *kanun*, as well as the organization of the tribe and the *bayrak*. In addition to Valentini's analysis on the coexistence of religion with the rules of the *kanun* and the exchange of norms between them, mainly in family law, it also includes several articles by foreign researchers who analyze the concept of the nation and the importance of customary law among Albanians.

126. **Nadin, Lucia.** Statutet e Shkodrës në Gjysmën e Parë të Shekullit XIV. (Me Shtesat deri më 1469). Second Edition. 'Onufri'. Tiranë, 2010. Italian and Albanian Edition. BK: Al 23 A 32. BK: S 355 5 B

In 1997, researcher Lucia Nadin discovered in the library of the Correr Museum in Venice the text of the Statutes of Shkodra, based on the data found in *"Bibliografia degli statuti dei comuni del 'Italia superior"* drawn up by Leone Fontana in 1907, where the "Statute of Shkodra" was briefly mentioned among the codes of the *'Cicogna'* collection. [51] The statutes were published for the first time in Italy in 2002 by the publishing house 'Viella', and republished again in 2010. Here reference is made to the second edition, written in Italian and Albanian languages.

The statute of the city of Shkodra consists of 268 original chapters and 11 more added in the period between 1392–1479.[52] The content of the statute testifies to the legal tradition of Albanian cities during this period. The statute and its articles regulate in detail every aspect of city life, in terms of civil, commercial, criminal and public law. The statute's provisions in the private law domain regulate aspects of family relations, inheritance, and other legal relationships with third parties. In the economic sphere it contained rules to regulate different activities, such as those for

51 Nadin, Lucia. Statutet e Shkodrës në Gjysmën e Parë të Shekullit XIV. (Me Shtesat deri më 1469). (Sec. Ed.). 'Onufri'. Tiranë, 2010, p. 10.

52 Ibid. p. 118.

building constructions and the respective permissions, planting trees, constructing irrigation channels, various trades that were allowed to be practiced in the city and in the countryside, as well as the modalities of their practice.[53] The criminal legal norms specifically defined the rules for the territorial application of the law, the conditions of criminal liability, the consequences of cooperating in criminal offenses, criminal acts against life, property, economic relations, customs, as well as criminal offenses committed by high officials, judges and notaries, while exercising their public functions.[54] The statute provides the regime for governing the city, the election of council members and other subordinates, the roles of judges, notaries and arbitrators elected and sworn under oath, as well as other public functions regulated in the statute. It also contains procedural legal norms for the conduct of the trial, the collection of evidence, the role of the defense attorney and other similar aspects. The statute also provides a regime on guarantees and rights of foreigners to settle in the city of Shkodra.[55]

The work is accompanied by an analysis of the statute from Nadin, as well as studies by Giovan Battista Pellegrini, Oliver Jens Schmitt and Gherardo Ortalli on the Statute of Shkodra and its importance.

127. **Goci, Haxhi.** Kanuni i Krahinës së Bendës. Mbledhur dhe Përgatitur nga Goci, Haxhi në vitet 1960–1985. 'Ombra GVG'. Tiranë, 2010. BK: S 343 B 41

"The Kanun of Benda" is a compilation of customary norms applied in the region of Benda, a *bayrak* located in the territory of the Principate of Arbër (Kastriot), which corresponds to the eastern and south-eastern areas of Kruja.[56] The *kanun* is organized in three parts, each divided into several chapters. The first part, divided into three chapters, contains legal norms on the household, its members, their rights and obligations, as well as institutes of family law such as brotherhood, sisterhood and godparenthood. The second chapter details the norms dedicated to the tribe, the *bayrak,* its borders and their constituent elements. The third chapter is dedicated to customs in the event of birth, marriage and death. Likewise the *kanuns*, the institution of the family and family relations, are at the very core of the regime of the Benda Kanun. In the second part, divided into two chapters, the *kanun* codifies the norms on ownership and inheritance, where the types of property division because of inheritance are of particular interest. The second chapter arrays the rules governing trade and commerce, along with rules regarding contractual obligations,

53 Ibid., p. 300–324.

54 Ibid., p. 358–374.

55 Ibid., p. 324–344; 374–382.

56 Goci, Haxhi. Kanuni i Krahinës së Bendës. Collected and Annotated by Goci, Haxhi during 1960–1985. 'Ombra'. Tiranë, 2010, 5 f.

contract of suretyship (*dorzanisë*), pledge *(pengut)*, mandate *(porosinë)*, and other specific obligations. The third part, divided into seven chapters, offers the regime on damages, offenses and their categories, the pertinent types of punishments for each violation, the rights and obligations of the guest, the governance of the village and the *bayrak*, the division of power between the elders of the tribe and their auxiliary bodies. The sixth chapter defines the rules on the provision of justice by the assembly of elders, the customs on the eldership, the pledge, the word in error *(fjala në ngatërresë)*, the deniers *(mohuesit)*, the oath *(beja)*, the fraudulent oath *(beja e gënjeshtërt)* and *parota*. The seventh and last chapter summarizes rules on honor, the institution of reconciliation and its instruments—such as the guarantor (*dorëzanët*) and the trustees *(besëtarët)*.

128. **Frashëri, Kristo.** Monedha, Krediti dhe Banka në Shqipëri gjatë Shekujve. Vështrim i Shkurtër me një Shtojcë Dokumentare. Monografi. UMSH. 'Toena'. Tiranë, 2011. BK: S 374 47 C

The history of the beginnings of currency, credit and banking systems in Albania are presented in this monograph structured in two parts. In the first part, the author depicts the credit activity and coins in antiquity, where an important place is occupied by the drachmas minted by Illyrian kings, and their evolution during the Roman rule, as well as coins and credit during the rule of Skanderbeg in the 15th century. Further, the author delves into the establishment of the Ottoman Imperial Bank (1863), the activity of its branches in the Albanian vilayets of Shkodra, Skopje, Manastir and Ioannina, as well as on the Agrarian Bank (*Ziraat Bankasi*) established in 1888. The latter penetrated Albanian territories by opening branches in every *sanjak* center (prefecture) and by establishing cash desks in every *kaza* center, providing loans on the agricultural sector towards mortgage over the land. Of interest to researchers are the chapters dedicated to the efforts of establishing a National Bank of Albania after the independence, which were finalized on the 15th of March, 1925. The author reflects on its activity, the types of coins issued by the Bank of Albania, the developments under the fascist and Nazi occupation, the establishment of the Albanian National Bank (ANB) by the Presidency of the Anti-Fascist National Liberation Council on January 13, 1945. The ANB was granted exclusive rights to issue currency and banknotes, with the limitation that the value of banknotes could not exceed the triple value of the gold and currency. The author analyzes the activity of the ANB during the years of the communist regime until the radical reforming of the banking system in 1992, after the restoration of market economy in the country. The second part analyzes legal acts and by-laws on the functioning of the banking system, such as the agreement on the National Bank of Albania of October 4, 1913; the Agreement on the National Bank of Albania of March 15, 1925; the law on the Agricultural Bank of Albania of 1936; the decision of the temporary executive committee for the regulation of relations between the Albanian government and the Bank of Albania dated October 19, 1943; the law on the Bank of Albania, dated May 4, 1992; as well as other acts in this domain.

129. **Bardhoshi, Nebi.** Gurtë e Kufinit. Kanuni, Pronësia, Strukturimi Social. 'UET Press'. Tiranë, 2011. BK: S 379 F 22

The work provides an intertwined anthropological and legal analysis of the customary law of the Has region, with a particular interest in the right of ownership. It focuses on the identification of differences in the customary property norms of the areas of Has, within and outside the state border of Albania. The paper is divided into four chapters. The first reflects an anthropological approach to private property and its coexistence with state property. The author focuses on traditional legal terminology, legal norms, and figures of legal authority. The second chapter delves on the elements of the family and property according to customary law, the forms of acquiring ownership and the division of land. In the third chapter, the author explores the concept of the village in a historical context and the ownership of rural land, common property according to the *kanun*, the ways of creating ownership and the forms of dividing common property during the period of 1945–1991. The fourth chapter is dedicated to the property regimes in the bordering area of Has, and the differences between the norms applied within the border of Albania, from those applied across the border, in Kosovë. At the end of the paper there is a glossary of terms and explanatory notes on the book.

130. **Kuri, Vilson.** Tradita dhe e Drejta Zakonore Shqiptare. 'Dajti 2000'. Elbasan, 2011. BK: S 375 B 7

"Tradition and the Albanian customary law" delves into the role of the Albanian customary law in preserving tradition and national identity. The second part of the paper provides a legal analysis of Albanian customary law, its sources and the various *kanuns* implemented in the country. The author draws a comparison between the Albanian customary law and the Hellenic and Roman customary laws, and the limitation of the application of Ottoman law in the self-governing regions of the Albanian mountains. The paper also discusses the main elements of the statute of the city of Shkodra, the Kanun of Lek Dukagjin, the Kanun of Skanderbeg and the Kanun of Labëria.

131. **Egro, Dritan.** Ligji Osman ndër Shqiptarët e Mesjetës së Vonë. Gjysma e Dytë e Shekullit të XV – Fillim Shekulli XVII. Qendra e Studimeve Albanologjike. Instituti i Historisë. Tiranë, 2012. BK: S 402 A 13

The book analyzes the impact of Ottoman laws in Albanian territories during the second half of the 15th to the beginning of the 17th century. The author focuses on the administrative organization and the application of the *timar* system in Albanian territories, based on the legal regimen of the respective *kannuname(s)*. The author notes that from a legal point of view, these type of *kanunname* regulated the relationship between the *timariot*, in the capacity of the Sultan's representative in governing a territorial area, and the *raja*, in the capacity of the taxpayer. Through this act, the Ottoman central administration aimed at supervising the exercise of power by the *timariot*, and preventing abuses or unjust benefits.[57] The publication is organized in 3 parts. The first part focuses on two general *kanunname* of the Ottoman Empire, adopted during the reign of Sultan Mehmet II, which determined the central and provincial organization of the empire.[58] The second part contains the *kanunname*(s) of the *sanjaks* inhabited by the Albanian population, such as the Sanjak of Shkodra, the Vilayet of Montenegro, the Sanjak of Prizren, the Vilayet of Vushtria, the Sanjaks of Skopje, Ohrid, Elbasan, Manastir, Vlora, Delvina, Tërhalla, Lepantos and Eubes.[59] In the third part there are several imperial *fermans* and *berate*(s), that address particular matters, which often served as precedents for solving similar disputes.[60] The author cites as an example the *ferman* on the collection of *haraç* contributions (a type of land taxation also known as *kharaj*), in the areas of Zagoria and Përmet, and notes that this *ferman* was used as a model legal act for collection of *haraç* tributes throughout the Balkans. The acts presented in this publication are of interest to scholars of the history of public law, as well as those of civil and criminal law.

132. **Saraçi, Alvin.** Konfiskimi i Pronës dhe Grabitja e Arit në Vitet 1944 – 1955. Instituti i Studimit të Krimeve dhe Pasojave të Komunizimit. 'West Print'. Tiranë, 2012. BK: S 404 G 21

"The confiscation of property and the robbery of Gold during 1944–1955" explores the process and legal means used for eliminating private property and the confiscation of gold after the installation of communism in Albania. The paper brings to attention specific legal acts that were used in this process, such as law no. 40, dated January 14, 1945 and titled "General provisions on confiscation of private assets"; tax laws of 1945–1946; the law against speculation and economic sabotage of May

57 Egro, Dritan. Ligji Osman ndër Shqiptarët e Mesjetës së Vonë. Gjysma e Dytë e Shekullit të XV – Fillim Shekulli XVII. Botim i Qendrës së Studimeve Albanologjike. Instituti i Historisë. Tiranë, 2012, p. 70.

58 Ibid., p. 45.

59 Ibid.

60 Ibid.

18, 1945; law no. 373, of December 12, 1945 "On the pursuit of prohibited trade, speculation and economic sabotage" that was aimed at restricting trade; and the law of January 14, 1945 on the organization and operation of military courts. The work is divided into five chapters. The first deals with the legal framework adopted immediately after the end of the Second World War, which enabled the confiscation of the private assets of large Albanian and foreign entrepreneurs. In the second chapter, the author expands on the confiscations of private assets of German and Italian citizens. The third chapter provides an overview of the economic policies towards traders and entrepreneurs, where the extraordinary tax and its effects stand out. In the fourth chapter, the author analyzes the transformation of the economy from private to state-controlled, the nationalizations and economic centralization in the period 1946–1948. In the last chapter, the author delves into the confiscation of gold and silver from the merchants and the middle class.

133. **Malltezi, Argita.** Koncesionet në Shqipëri. Nga e Drejta Private në të Drejtën Publike. Monografi. Shkolla e Magjistraturës. 'Mediaprint'. Tiranë, 2013. BK: S 412 B 9; BFHFUT

"Concessions in Albania. From private to public law" focuses on the Albanian regulatory framework on public private partnership and concessions. The first chapter focuses on the history of the legal regime of these instruments in Albania. It offers examples of concessions granted by the High Gate, during the Ottoman rule, the regulatory framework and the concession contracts adopted after Albania's independence until the brink of the Second World War (1912–1939).

134. **Konomi, Rezana.** Rendi Etnojuridik. Nga Statutet tek Kanunet. Monografi. 'Kristalina K-H'. Tiranë, 2013. BK: S 410 B 21

"The ethno – legal order. From statutes to kanuns" analyzes the unwritten customary laws in a historical context, the main features of the Kanun of Lek Dukagjini compared to the Kanun of Skanderbeg, and the survival of customary law alongside different regimes of positive law. The author proceeds with an in-depth analysis of the phenomenon of blood vendetta, and the respective *kanun's* regimen. The analysis expands on the blood vendetta regime according to the statutes of the medieval cities of Shkodra and Drishti.

135. **Baze, Ermal.** Një Qytet me Statute. Shkodra në Gjysmën e Parë të Shekullit XIV. 'Muzgu'. Tiranë, 2013. BK: S 394 94 A

"A city with Statutes. Shkodra in the first half of the 14th century" cited below in this biliography, is the author's doctoral thesis structured in five chapters. In the first chapters, the author delves into the importance of the discovery of the Statute of Shkodra, its role during the Venetian rule of the city, as well as the territorial jurisdiction and institutional organization of the city of Shkodra in the first half of the 14th century. Further, in the third chapter, the author analyzes the economic and commercial organization of the city, the practice of crafts and small commercial enterprises. The fourth chapter deals with the social and religious organizations. In the last chapter, the author conducts a comparative analysis of the statute of the city of Shkodra with other statutes of the Balkan Peninsula – the Codex of Stefan Dušan, the Statutes of Budva and the Kanun of Lek Dukagjin.

136. **Krisafi, Ksenofon.** Organizimi Politik në Trojet Shqiptare. Monografi. 'UET Press'. Tiranë, 2014. BK: S 441 D 25

The monograph analyzes from a legal point of view the important stages of development of the history of the Albanian state, from the state organization in Illyria to the most recent developments in Albanian territories. The author considers the various positions on the origins of the Albanian justice system and highlights that a native Albanian judicial system has evolved and been applied independently and in parallel to the Ottoman judicial system. The author explores the activity of the Ottoman courts, the legislation upon which they operated in the Albanian territories and the termination of jurisdiction of these courts in Albania. He draws attention to the program of the Albanian League of Prizren, which determined that only judges who knew the language of the country would be appointed in the courts of the Albanian *Vilajet*. The legal position of Albania during the period from the Conference of Ambassadors in London until the end of the First World War, the competences of the International Control Commission, the detailed project for the organization of all branches of the Albanian administration, the conditional international recognition of Albania, its neutrality and the decision of the Conference of Ambassadors of Paris, are also examined in depth. The review extends to more recent events, in which the author analyzes the constitution of the Republic of Kosova, as well as the debate on the issue of the Albanian maritime border with Greece and the respective decision of the Constitutional Court of Albania (2010).

137. **Pepa, Eugen.** Il Pensiero Giuridico sul Diritto Consuetudinario Albanese. 'Intergrafika'. Tiranë, 2015. Italian Edition. BK: S 452 C 21

The Italian edition examines the development of Albanian legal thought in its customary law and the influence of historical events. The analysis spans the Albanian customary law from the Illyrian period and its relationship to Roman law, through to Byzantine law and its development in the confederate state of Arbëria, where the codification of the first civil statutes began to emerge. It then proceeds with the evolution of the customary law during the Ottoman occupation. The author points out the common principles of the various *kanuns* implemented in Albania, such as the concept of honor, *besa*, and blood vendetta. The attitude of the Albanian society towards the *kanun* is highlighted, further analyzing the reasons which favored its revival in some areas of Albania during the years of political transition from the dictatorial regime to pluralism.

138. **Castelleti, Giuseppe.** Normat Zakonore dhe Jeta Shoqërore në Kanunin e Lek Dukagjinit. Studi Albanesi. 'Ombra GVG'. Tiranë, 2012. BK: S 396 E 34

The book is a translation of the 1933 Italian publication, titled *Consuetudini e vita sociale nelle montagne albanesi secondo il Kanun di Lek Dukagjini.*[61] The author praises the Albanian customary law as a genuine legal and constitutional system, that reflects the values of Albanian society within a certain period of time. The paper focuses on the KLD and its role in imparting the legal thinking of ancient times, which either in the absence of written documents, or lost due to various historical circumstances, has survived by being transmitted verbally. The efforts for the codification of the Albanian customary law have been continuous, among which the author mentions a Turkish bill on the codification of the Albanian customary law from the second half of the 19th century. In his analysis, the author underlines the fact that the norms reflected in the *kanun* are not a rigid code, and given their rather dynamic nature, they have been adapted to epochal developments, while it is the *kanun* itself that determines the procedures for amending its provisions.

139. **Vilari, Salvatore.** Normat Zakonore Juridike të Shqipërisë. Kanuni i Lek Dukagjinit. 'Ombra GVG'. Tiranë, 2012. BK: S 396 E 37

The book is the Albanian edition of the title *Le consuetudini giuridiche dell'Albania,* originally published in Italy in 1940.[62] The author, an associate professor of colonial law at the Royal University of Rome, provides an analytical perspective on the customary norms of Northern Albania. The *kanun* is analyzed as the law of the tribe, whereby the author provides details regarding the particularities of the Albanian tribe and its organization. While the author relied on the works of other important authors of the time, he also had the opportunity to conduct research directly in the areas where the *kanun* was applied, where he collected evidence on the applicable

61 Castelleti, Giuseppe. Consuetudini e Vita Sociale nelle Montagne Albanesi Secondo il Kanun di Lek Dukagjini. Studi Albanesi. Vol. 3–4. Roma, 1933, p. 4.

62 Vilari, Salvatore. Le Consuetudini Giuridiche dell'Albania. Societa Editrice 'Del Libro Italiano'. Roma, 2012, p. 4.

norms from his meeting with the chiefs and highlanders.[63] These meetings enabled the researcher to become acquainted with other customary norms created after the first publication of the *kanun*, or norms known and implemented only within a certain *bayrak* or tribe. The author further interprets specific criminal material and procedural norms.

140. **Hoxha, Shefqet.** E Drejta Dokësore në Lumë (Kanuni i Lumës). 'Geer'. Tiranë, 2013. BK: S 420 A 4; BFD

The book explores the Kanun of Luma, as a rather moderate variation of the KLD, and analyses the influence of the Ottoman occupation on the regime of customary law. The book is structured in four parts which provide the norms of the Kanun of Luma and the author's interpretation of these norms, illustrated by the case law of the community representative *kanun* bodies. The first part is dedicated to the social structure and relations according to this *kanun*, family law, the rights and obligations of each family member, the institution of marriage, personal honor, the honor of the house, the honor of the community, hospitality, *besa* and its subtypes, as well as the equality of (the blood of) people.[64] The author analyzes in detail the institutions of public law according to *the Kanun of Luma,* the role of the Assembly (*kuvendi)* and its subtypes such as the assembly of brotherhood (*kuvendi i vllazërisë*), the assembly of bayrak (*kuvendi i bajrakut*), the assembly of the soil (*kuvendi i dheut*), the way of summoning and conducting their meetings, the powers and the competence for each of them. The text further addresses the provisions of the *kanun* that regulate criminal law, the institution of *vetëgjyqësia,*[65] and the mediation for the reconciliation of blood vendettas. The second part is dedicated to the economic order and property relations, and includes the rules for determining property boundaries, types of property, division of property, ways of acquiring ownership and the inheritance regimen, norms regulating various important activities, types of obligations and ways of ensuring their fulfilment, agreements and trade practices, the types of damages and the method for calculating their compensation. The third part includes the punitive provisions of the *kanun*, bodies that were competent for providing punishments, and the role of the executioners (*gjobtarët*). Part four

63 Vilari, Salvatore. Normat Zakonore Juridike të Shqipërisë. Kanuni i Lek Dukagjinit. 'Ombra GVG'. Tiranë, 2012, p. 10.

64 The *kanun* provided equal regimen of people of the same gender, regardless of their or disabilities or social rank. For instance, despite of the fact that a household's power was indicated by the number of men that were able to use weapons, the KLD (§886 – §893) the customary law regarded the life of a person with physical or mental disabilities, having the same value as that of other men.

65 Taking the law in its own hand – an institute regulated by the Albanian customary law (*kanun*).

analyzes the main offenses provided for by the Kanun of Luma, illustrated with case law of their enforcement. The paper has a glossary of terms at the end.

141. **Bjanku, Florian.** Çështja e Pronave në Shqipëri. 'Gurten'. Tiranë, 2013. BUSH.

The protection of the right of ownership still remains a problem in Albania. In this publication, the author provides a comparative historical overview of the protection of property rights in Central and Eastern Europe countries after the fall of communism, and the impact of the European Convention on Human Rights in this regime. The third part focuses specifically on the historical development of this branch of law in Albania. The paper provides data on the Ottoman cadastral records, land legislation after the declaration of independence, the regime on private ownership during the communist period, and the drastic changes pursuant to the reforms after the fall communism in 1990, until 2011. The publication refers to the legal framework, as well as to the jurisprudence of the Constitutional Court of the Republic of Albania over the period 1994–2010.

142. **Hoxhaj, Entela.** E Drejta Kushtetuese e Krahasuar. Monografi. 'Gurten'. Tiranë, 2013. BUSH

The monograph "Comparative constitutional law", based on the author's doctoral thesis, analyzes in a comparative context the evolution of the constitutional jurisprudence of the continental European countries and Albania. The first chapter delves into the evolution of the constitutional law in Albania and references to the constitutional provisions of Albania in the period 1912–1944, the constitutional provisions and amendments adopted during the communist dictatorship in the period 1944–1991, as well as the constitutional changes in Albania after the return of pluralism in the 1990s.

143. **Krisafi, Ksenofon.** Për Tokën dhe Detin e Shqipërisë. Qasje Juridiko-Ndërkombëtare. 'UET Press'. Tiranë, 2014. BK: S 441 D 22

"On the Albanian land and sea. An international legal approach" explores two agreements: the agreement signed between Esat Toptani and Nikolla Pashic in 1914, and another signed in 1915 between King Ahmet Zog and Nikolla Pashic. Both acts, although not legally enforceable, preceded the further fragmentation of Albanian territories. The author analyzes these two acts in light of the negotiations on maritime water borders between Albania and Greece. The author also delves into the Greek law on the state of war with Albania, within the context of international public law. The work offers an analysis of the decision of the International Court of Justice regarding the independence of Kosovo.

144. **Malaj, Edmond.** Drishti. Historia dhe Fizionomia e një Qyteti Mesjetar Shqiptar. Qendra e Studimeve Albanologjike. Instituti i Historisë. Tiranë, 2015. BFHF; AQSH: A/1.s7

The main focus of the publication is the history of the development of Drishti, its church statutes and organization, economic development, trade, the various crafts practiced in the city and the types of coins that were used. The book is structured in two parts. The first focuses on the contributing factors that led to the development of the political, socio-cultural and economic history of Drishti, the traces of ancient regimes, from the Illyrian-Roman period to the Serbian rule, the rule of the Balsha, the Venetian period and the Turkish occupation of Drishti. The analysis extends to the organizational structure of Drishti, the role and powers of its principal authorities, such as the rector, castellan, judges, notary, tax collectors and other officials, ethnic composition, noble families and other limited rights' citizens, such as the simple inhabitants, Arbers, Slavs and foreigners. Aspects of the city's economy, trade and crafts are also dealt with. The second part explores the ecclesiastical history of the diocese of Drishti in the Middle Ages, the ecclesiastical monuments and the clergy, the interpretations of the canonical regime and life in this community. The book provides references of archival documents published for the first time.

145. **Omari, Luan.** Kushtetuta e Republikës së Kosovës në një Vështim Krahasues. 'Dudaj'. Tiranë, 2009. BK: S 322 G 19

This edition, with a new title and two added parts: (i) 'Rruga drejt pavarësisë' (The road to independence) and (ii) 'Mbi zbatimin e Kushtetutës dhe rishikimin e saj' (On the Constitution and its revision), has been reprinted with the coordinates as follow.

146. **Omari, Luan.** Për Kosovën e Djeshme dhe të Sotme. Vështrim Juridik-Kushtetues. Dudaj. Tiranë, 2016. n.c.

This work analyzes the provisions of the Constitution of Kosovo from a comparative historical perspective. Within the historical context, the author interprets Kosova's legal and constitutional position as a former autonomous province in the Yugoslav Federation, according to the framework of the first constitution of the People's Federal Republic of Yugoslavia, as well as the positions of Yugoslav and Albanian communist leaders regarding the matter of Kosovo. Further, the work addresses the transitional status of Kosova until its independence in 2008. The interpretation discusses the necessity of the revision of the constitution of the Republic of Kosovo.

147. **Martini, Xhafer.** Kanuni i Maleve të Dibrës. 'Arbëria'. Tiranë, 2003. BK: S 209 D 11
148. **Martini, Xhafer.** Kanuni i maleve të Dibrës. 'Emal'. Tiranë, 2007. BK: S 267 F 32
149. **Martini, Xhafer.** Kanuni i Dibrës. Trashëgimi Etnojuridike. 'M-B'. Tiranë, 2016. BK: S 492 B 32

The Kanun of Dibra explores the *kanun* applicable in the area of Dibra. The author points out that the Kanun of Dibra is characterized by its tolerance and self-restraint in matters of blood vendetta, which is applied alongside with *besa*, mediation, reconciliation, and the support of the religious institutions. In this edition, the compilation of the Kanun of Dibra is divided into 29 chapters, 27 of which compile legal norms, whilst the last two chapters summarize typical expressions of the area and various narratives with canonical content. The first two chapters codify provisions that regulate matters pertaining to the functioning of the household, the role of the master and the mistress of the house, the role of other family and household members, the regime on the cattle and other animals. The third and fourth chapters are dedicated to blood ties and include institutions such as brotherhood, blood brotherhood and godfatherhood, tribe, borders, meadows, stables and other constituent components of common property. Chapters five and six regulate the regime of the assembly of the mountains, the chiefs of the mountains and the famous institute of the Chambers of Dibra (*Odat e Dibrës*), which were forums of debate, but also of education for the younger generations, regulated under strict norms.[66] The seventh chapter, entitled 'Economy', is dedicated to the *kanun's* regime on the

66 *Oda*, in literal translation means chamber. The Chamber of Men (*oda e burrave*) was an institution well known throughout the aorthern Albanian area, Dibra's chambers being amongst the most famous of them. They were forums of gathering of the tribe's men, although guests were commonly welcomed regardless of the area. The Chamber convened during evenings and was used as a place of socialization, and an informal forum for discussion of community issues. Besides the current affairs, it included singings and story telling about heroes and the wars that had warranted the tribe's and the country's survival. For this reason, although it was a forum of men, children were allowed to stay, without the right to speak, as a way of teaching them how to hold chambers, honor and preside over their conduct and resolve community issues. It was a forum in which theoretically anyone that met the basic criteria (such as age, gender, etc.) could participate and speak, upon condition that the rigorous rules of chamber communication were respected. Verbal offenses could lead to extreme consequences, as the insult to the honor of any of the participant entailed the pertinent consequences provided in the *kanun*. Thus, although no one could be refused participation without due reason (such as previous breaches of the rules) active participation in the chamber orations favored individuals characterized by strength of arguments and composure. These norms were strictly safeguarded by the host—the house master, who was responsible for safeguarding the honor of his guests and ensuring that the order of the orations as well as their content were carried out according to the *kanun's* rules and did not offend any of the participants. The organization of

bazaar and its types, shops and the organization of inns. The ensuing chapters, up to the 12th, regulate institutions of family law such as engagement, marriage, the status of the wife, death, blood vengeance, the regime for ambush, executor *(dorësi)*, abduction of wife, types of murder, carrying a rifle, blood forgiveness, reconciliation and *the giving of the cartridge*. Other chapters regulate the regime on the production of food, status of the friend, the institution of *ndorja,*[67] mediation, the role of the elderly, the rules of *besa* and oath, and the regime on inheritance. Chapter 21 and the consecutive chapters regulate several types of civil-commercial legal relationships, such as downpayments, conditional purchase, stolen property, transactions on land, sale of weapons, rules for granting loans, pawning, *qefili,*[68] hunting animals, and fishing. Chapter twenty-five is dedicated to the status and the protection of the messenger. The twenty-sixth chapter, entitled "The *Kanun* Against Evil", contains the punishments for crimes, the regime on aiding and abetting, the rules on theft and its types, robbery, the damages, consequences and punishment for harsh words and fines. Chapter twenty-seven is dedicated to the regime of the mentally ill persons.

150. **Likmeta, Engjëll.** Mbrojtja Penale e së Drejtës së Pronës. Një Vështrim Historiko-Juridik. Monografi. 'ASD –Studio'. Tiranë, 2016. BFDUT.

In this monograph, the author explores in a historical context the evolution of the legal mechanisms for protection of property under the Albanian criminal legislation. The work is organized in five chapters. The first describes the rules of Albanian customary law, the *kanuns* that operated in different areas of Albania. The second chapter analyzes how the charters of the medieval cities of Durrës and Shkodra protected the right of ownership by means of penal instruments. This chapter also discusses the protection of ownership in the statutes and ordinances of the Chapter of the Drishti Cathedral. The third chapter delves into a comparative analysis of the regime of penal protection of property under the governance of different empires that have ruled Albania. The fourth chapter reflects the legal regime during the reign of King Zog. In the last chapter, the author analyzes the criminal legal protection of property rights in a chronological context, from 1939 until the adjustments made with the Criminal Code of 1977.

---

chambers required a suitable premise and entailed expenses for providing food for guests. Therefore, chambers were usually organized by prominent households, with good incomes.

67 According to the Kanun of Dibra, '*ndorja* [ndoria]', is the institute of providing warranties to someone who faces threats on his life or honor.

68 *Qefili* was a middleman who vouched on behalf of the buyer, in cases when the latter could pay the price of the merchandise instantly, and requested to pay it latter, in accordance with the conditions agreed upon by the parties.

151. **Hobdari, Danja.** Regjimi Juridik i Pronës dhe Trashëgimisë në Shqipëri (1912–1939). 'Naimi'. Tiranë, 2017. BK: S 518 A 38

The work studies from a historical viewpoint the development of property and inheritance rights in Albania, during a period spanning from Albania's independence until its occupation by Italy at the beginning of the Second World War. It provides readers with an analysis of the agrarian reform of king Zog, as well as the novelties brought by the Civil Code of 1929, the laws and the decrees approved in the period 1925–1934, with a special focus on the provisions governing the regime on inheritance. Part of the expose is also the impact on property rights of the bilateral relations between Albania and Turkey, Albania and Greece, and Albania and Italy.

152. **Caka, Eduart.** (Prepared and Edited). Regjistri i Sanxhakut të Arvanidit i Vitit 1431. The Turkish Edition Prepared by Inalcik, Halil. Translated from Turkish by Janina, Mykerem. Akademia e Studimeve Albanologjike. Tiranë, 2017. BK: S 540 C 1; BIHGJL

In commemoration of the 550th anniversary of the death of the Albanian National Hero Gjergj Kastrioti-Skënderbeu, the Academy for Albanology Studies undertook the re-publication of several cadastral registers (*defters*) of the Ottoman administration in the occupied Albanian territories that attest to the implementation of *timar* in Albania. These works are structured in 4 volumes and include the Arvanid Register *(defter)* of 1431, the Register of Përmet and Korça of 1431, the Register of Dibra of 1467, and the Shkodra Register of 1485. In the first volume, the editor analyzes the historical context in which the register of Sanjak of Arvanid was drawn up in 1431. He notes that the Register, known as *Sûret-i defter-i sancak-i Arvanid,* was first prepared for publication by Halil Inalxhik and was published for the first time in Ankara in 1954. This register was translated into Albanian by Mykerem Janina in the 1960s and was published for the first time together with the Registry of the Sanjak of Shkodra (1485) by Selami Pulaha, cited above in this bibliography. The register of the Sanjak of Arvanid is dedicated to the registration of *timar* and taxes for each timar in a wide area spanning from central Albania, around Kruja, to the South, in Thesproti and Gjirokastër. The cadastral register includes *timars* belonging to the different ranks of beneficiaries, providing the rank and name of the owner of the *timar*, the villages that were part of the said *timar*, detailed information about the houses, the bachelors, the widows and the amount of tax that was levied by each of them. The registry provides data also about the timars of Skanderbeg. Other interesting information pertains to the implementation of the timar system in the vilayet of Kanina, the vilayet of Tomorinca, Skrapar, and area of Sopot.

153. **Caka, Eduart.** (Sci. Ed.). Defteri i Regjistrimit të Përmetit dhe Korçës i Vitit 1431. Translated from the Ottoman language by Buharaja, Vexhi. Akademia e Studimeve Albanologjike. Tiranë, 2018. BK: S 540 C 4; BFHFUT; BIHGJL[69]

The official Registry *(defter)* of Përmet and Korça of year 1431, as the author notes, is considered one of the earliest registers drawn up by the Ottoman administration. It reveals that the *timar* was given not only to representatives of the army (*pashas, sipahis* and guards of fortresses), but also judges, *imams*, priests, secretaries, stablemen. The book is divided into three parts, presenting the characteristics of the registry and its elements, as well as the historical context in which this registry was drafted. The second part is a paper written by the orientalist Vexhi Buharaja. A facsimile photo of the original registry, in the Ottoman language, is presented in the third part. *Timars* are arranged according to Arabic numerals, while symbols, accompanied by Roman numerals, are reflected according to the chronological criterion. The paper is accompanied by a glossary of Ottoman terms to assist researchers in understanding the criteria of registration and its content.

154. **Bala (Pajo), Valbona.** Rrugëtim Kushtetues. Sfidat, Arritjet, Perspektiva e Gjykatës Kushtetuese. 'Geer'. Tiranë, 2018. BKSH

"The constitutional journey. Challenges, achievements and perspectives of the Constitutional Court" analyzes the main institutions regulated in the Albanian constitution and the relations between them, the main constitutional principles, as well as the influence of European jurisprudential traditions on the Albanian Constitutional Court. The history of the development of constitutional law is unraveled in the ensuing chapters, and comprises a discussion on the most restrictive Constitution of 1976, the developments of constitutional justice after the restoration of pluralism in Albania, and all of its milestones, such as the law *'On the main constitutional provisions' (Për dispozitat kryesore kushtetuese) of 1991,* the Constitution of 1998, and later amendments, including the justice reform of 2016.

155. **Shabani, Sinan.** Antropologji Entojuridike. Studime në Antropologji Kulturore. Part II. 'Naimi'. Tiranë, 2019. BK: S. 551 B 37

---

69 Defteri i Regjistrimit të Përmetit dhe Korçës, Translated by Buharaja, Vexhi can be found at the State Central Archive (Arkivi Qendror i Shtetit). Akademia e Studimeve Albanologjike. ASA. Tiranë, 1969. AQSH: A/1.s1.

This volume is the second part of a series of anthropological studies authored by Shaban Sinani,[70] in which he analyzes from an ethno-legal point of view the development of Albanian legal thought. It focuses on the ecclesiastical law and its development in Albania, where church rules, also known as the religious codices, played an important role in the medieval life of the country. The author explores the statutes of the Albanian cities, while opening way for further discussion on whether these statutes are a legacy of the Venetian tradition, or a product of local culture and legal thought. Of interest is the analysis of the ecclesiastical codes implemented in Albania and the influence of the Ottoman law in these codes.

156. **Caka, Eduart.** (Ed.). Defteri i Hollësishëm për Zonat e Dibrës i Vitit 1467. Translated from the Ottoman language by Buharaja, Vexhi. Akademia e Studimeve Albanologjike. Tiranë, 2019. BK: S 566 B 20. BIHGJL

The official Registry (*defter*) for the area of Dibra of the year 1467 is drawn up according to a detailed model and contains records on the *timars* of the *vilayets* of the upper and lower Dibra, the *vilayet* of Golloborda, the *vilayet* of Çermenika, the *vilayet* of Mati, the *zeamet* of Reka, and the *nahija* of Benda. This official Registry was first published in 1968 by Selami Pulaha, as part of the book *Albanian-Turkish War in the 15th Century: Ottoman Sources* (Lufta Shqiptaro-Turke në shekullin e VX-të: burime osmane), cited above in this bibliography. The 2019 edition is structured in three parts. The first part discusses the historical context in which this official Registry (*defter*) was drafted, highlighting the fact that it coincides with the time of the rule of Skanderbeg and his war against the Ottomans. It notes that the registry data indicate that in 1467 a significant part of the Albanian territory—the northeastern areas up to the walls of Kruja—were placed under the *timar* system, while Kruja was still protected by Skanderbeg. The second part is dedicated to the Albanian version of the book, where the author highlights the notes of Vexhi Buharaja, the translator from Ottoman, which clarify the meaning of Ottoman terms, as well as Pulaha's notes, extracted from the first edition. The third part contains facsimile images of the original registry, in the Ottoman language. The publication contains also a glossary of terms.

157. **Meta, Beqir. Mema, Albana. Verli, Mariglen. Barjaba, Kosta.** Akte të Parlamentit Shqiptar 1920–1924. Akademia e Studimeve Albanologjike, Instituti i

70 Other publications from the same serie are: Sinani, Shaban. Anthropology of Identity: Studies in Cultural Anthropology. Part I. 'Naimi'. Tiranë, 2018. BK: 531 D 29. Sinani, Shaban. Anthropology of Religion: Studies in Cultural Anthropology. Part III. 'Naimi', Tiranë, 2021. BK: S 613 A 34.

Historisë, Drejtoria e Përgjithshme e Arkivave. Kuvendi i Shqipërisë. Tiranë, 2019. BK: S. 564 A 5; BKSH

Published within the framework of the 100th anniversary of the Congress of Lushnja (1920), this book offers an extensive compilation of materials and legal acts adopted by the Albanian parliaments during the period between 1920–1924. The legal framework created by these acts aimed at establishing a constitutional framework to regulate the functioning of the state apparatus. The series of acts include various economic and fiscal laws, concessionary contracts, laws that regulated the functioning of the administration, and amendments to the civil and criminal legislations. These acts are accompanied by the pertinent archival references from the archival fund "Parlamenti no. 146", which is kept at the Central State Archive.

158. **Kalaja, Florian. Fullani, Arjana.** Gjykimi në Gjykatën e Lartë. 'UET Press'. Tiranë, 2019. BFHFUT

"The adjudication at the Supreme Court" focuses on the interpretation of trial procedings before the Supreme Court, according to the legislation currently in force. In its first part it delves extensively into the evolution of this legal recourse since the Independence of Albania. The historical analysis follows the progress of the jurisdiction of the Court of Dictation, according to the constitutional and organic acts adopted in 1912 after the declaration of independence, until 2016. The first chapter deals with the regulatory framework after the declaration of independence until the end of the Second World War. The authors include the regime of the Court of Dictation according to the Law of the Jury (1913), the Organic Statute (1914), the Statute of Lushnja, other constitutional acts approved under the governance of king Zog, organic laws and procedural codes of this period. The second chapter, which deals with the regulatory legislation of the Supreme Court during communism (1945–1991), includes the regime of the constitutions adopted in this period, the codes of criminal and civil procedures, special laws for the military trials, as well as the judiciary organic laws. Chapters three to five analyse the legal changes that have affected the jurisdiction and trial procedures in the Supreme Court after the fall of the dictatorship, during the period of 1991 to 2016.

159. **Caka, Eduart.** Vakëfet dhe Impakti i tyre Social në Shqipërinë e Periudhës Osmane. Akademia e Studimeve Albanologjike. Tiranë, 2021. BK: Al 52 E 35; BIHGJL

"The waqfs and their social impact in Albania during the Ottoman era" offers a legal interpretation of the main constituent elements of these charity foundations, their organization and functioning in Albania, as well as the influence of large *waqfs* of viziers and pashas in the infrastructure and architectural objects. The study is structured in three parts. In the first part, the author presents opinions from various sources on the origin of *waqf* and its constituent elements, illustrated with judicial decisions rendered by *waqf* organizations for resolving internal conflicts. The second part discusses the emergence of *waqfs* of the military officials, pashas, great viziers of Albanian origin and other Albanian nobility during the 16th–19th centuries. The third part touches upon the impact of the Christian charities in the Albanian society and economy, as well as the self-governing of some Christian communities, known as the milet system.

160. **Rizvanolli, Masar.** Vendosja e Sistemit të Timarit në Kosovë në Gjysmën e Dytë të Shekullit të XV. Instituti i Historisë 'Ali Hadri'. Prishtinë, 2021. BIHGJL

This monograph analyzes the *timar* reform and its implementation in Kosova's Vilayet of Vëlku, Sanjaks of Vuçiterin, Skopje, Prizren, Shkodra and Dukagjin. The study is structured in six chapters. The author analyzes from a territorial perspective the history of Kosova and the gradual establishment of the Ottoman rule in it, focusing on the administrative organization of Kosova in the 15th century. He then explores the administrative and judicial organization depending on the territorial division made according to the *timar* reform, the way the *timar* system was implemented and its constituent elements, the class division created by this system, class relations and their respective fiscal obligations, types of feudal rent and the different types of taxes applicable. Among other things, in the last chapter, the author analyzes the causes that led to the downfall of the *timar* system. The work is of interest to scholars of commercial and medieval law.

161. **Kulla, Ndriçim.** Shqipëria, një Histori e Mentalitetit Juridik. 'Plejad'. Tiranë, 2022. n.c.

In "Albania, a history of legal mentality" the author, a well-known publicist and researcher in the field, analyzes the formation of the Albanian legal thought and its development over the centuries. He points out that despite the attention paid to the study of Albanian customary law, this is not the only source of law in Albanian territories. The author delves into the role of statutes of the Albanian medieval cities where the *arbër* law was developed, preserving some of its distinctive characteristics from the Byzantine law. In this context, an interesting point is the author's analysis of the statute of the Cathedral of Drishti, an act with characteristics of positive and customary law. He also interprets data on the development of cities, considering the example of the University of Durrës, where the Albanian legal opinion of the time was formed. The paper provides an interesting analysis of the characteristics of Albanian *kanun* law and its developments under the influence of historical factors, as well as comparative aspects with the law of guilds *(esnafëve)* and nomocanons *(nomokanonet)*.

162. **Shkurtaj, Gelanda.** Doke dhe Tradita, një Histori e Shkurtër e Gjakmarrjes ndër Kanunet Shqiptare. 'Toena'. Tiranë, 2022. BK: Ar 211 B 41[71]

The author explores the institution of blood vendetta in Albanian customary law, following a comparative approach between the KLD, the Kanun of Labëria, the Kanun of Benda and the Kanun of Luma. She also highlight the historical events that affected the application of this institute during the anti-fascist national-liberation (1939–1944), during the first years after liberation and the installation of the communist system, and finally the state interventions in preventing blood vendetta after the fall of dictatorship in 1990. Another interesting point of the book is the analysis of the Albanian judicial practices between 1991–1998 on the institution of blood vendetta.

163. **Kalaja, Florjan.** Lirimi me Kusht. 'Enja'. Tiranë, 2022. BFDUT

"The conditional release" provides a detailed analysis of the criminal law institute of parole and its implementation in Albania. The first chapter of the publication is dedicated to the historical evolution of this institution, from its regulation in the Criminal Code of the Ottoman Empire to its regulation in the Criminal Code, currently in force. The interpretation is illustrated with jurisprudential approaches on this matter.

164. **Skënderaj, Klodian.** Ekzekutimi i Vendimeve Penale. 'Morava'. Tiranë, 2023. BFDUT

In over 500 pages, the book thoroughly explores aspects of the Albanian material and procedural law that compose the regime of the implementation of the penal decisions. We draw the attention of legal history researchers, into the first chapter of the book, which is dedicated to the evolution of the legislation in this field, from times of the reign of King Zog. The author offers a brief look at the laws adopted in this period, which is known for the abrogation of the Ottoman Empire legislation, which applied in Albania, as well as for the adoption of a contemporary legal framework, according to the European models. Further, the chapter offers four other subheadings that delve more extensively with the legislation applicable

71 The author's PhD theses, with the same title, can be found at the National Library. BK: OS 33D 30.

in this domain during, respectively, the period 1945–1953, 1954–1979, 1979–1990, as well as the legislation after the fall of the communist system in 1990.

Part 2:
Publications of a Philosophical, Historical, Diplomatic or Anthropological Nature

The second part contains publications of a philosophical, historical, diplomatic or anthropological nature, which delve at least in part into the history of a particular legal regime.

Many of the publications included in this part constitute key sources for further publications and analysis in the legal field. We mention as illustration the "Selected Sources of the History of Albania", published by the Academy of Sciences in the years 1961–1965; the studies on the chartered medieval Albanian cities; the works on the incident of the Corfu channel; and the explanation of the notions of the tribe, *bayrak*, family or other elements of customary law which have been fully addressed by anthropological studies cited in this section.

This section also contains works that provide texts of the legal acts accompanied by historical analysis, as for instance the publications on the League of Prizren.

***

165. Kosova Vilajet-i Salnames-I, n.p. Edited in Year (1304), 1888. Osman Edition. BK: AL 8 A 29

The photocopy of the 1888 (1304) Annuary of the province of Kosova in the Ottoman language can be found in the National Library.

166. **Bourcart, Jacques.** L'Albanie et les Albanais. 'Bossard'. Paris, 1921. French Edition. BK: PP 9 Bou

This work provides an overview of the history, geography and ethnography of Albania, from its origins to the declaration of independence from the Ottoman Empire and the ensuing international administration. In the second chapter, dedicated to the formation of the Albanian state, the author dwells on the role of the French military in the administration of the Albanian border with Greece, and on the legal status of Korça and other Albanian territories administered by the French during the period 1916–1920, amongst other international administrations.

167. **Godart, Justin.** L'Albanie en 1921. Preface de d'Estoumelles de Constant. Les Presses Universitaires de France. Paris, 1922. French Edition. BK: 81 T 42

Justin Godart[1] developed a special connection to Albania, thanks to his mission as a diplomat there. In this French edition of his work, he provides detailed information on the economic and political situation of Albania at the end of the 1920s. The report provides statistics and an accurate reflection on the situation of Albania during the Ottoman rule, on the state organization of Albania after its independence, as well as into the relations of Albania to Italy, Greece and Yugoslavia. The author highlights national unity, despite the diversity of religious beliefs, and offers an overview of the organization and the legal framework of the religious communities. The paper sheds light on the historical-political context that preceded the Treaty of London of 1913 and the Balkan wars. Chapter 9 focuses on the relations between Albania and the League of Nations and the debate on the legal status of Albania before the Plenary Assembly of the League of Nations.

168. **Godart, Justin.** L'Albanie en 1922. L'Enquete de la Societe des Nations. Introduction de d'Estoumelles de Constant. Bulletin Trimestriel, dr. l. La Fleche (Sarthe), 1922. French Edition. BK: 81 T 30

This French edition of the series of Godart's publications on Albania provides readers with an insight into the various topics of the General Report presented to the Council of the League of Nations by the Commission of Inquiry (*Rapport général présenté au Conseil de la Société des Nations par la Commision d'Enquête*). The author also supplements the first edition with other important information, which mainly refers to the economic situation in Albania, including the applicable types of taxes, customs duties, monopolies, as well as aspects of Albania's foreign trade exchanges with other countries.

169. **Šufflay, Milan.** Serbët dhe Shqiptarët (Original Title: Srbi i Arbanasi). With introduction of Stanoviq, Stanoje; Translated from Slavish to Albanian by Fekeçi, Zef and Gurakuqi, Karl. Drejtoria e Përgjithshme e Arsimit. Shtypshkronja 'Mbrothësija' Kristo P. Luarasi. Tiranë, 1926. BK: S 12 C 143
170. **Šufflay, Milan.** Historia e Shqiptarëve të Veriut. Serbët dhe Shqiptarët. 'Rilindja'. Translated by Fekeçi, Zef and Gurakuqi, Karl. Annotated by Cana, Zekeria. Prishtinë, 1968. BK: S 92 G 16.

---

1 Godart was a member of the 'International Comission of Inquiry to Study the Recent Balkan Wars' tasked to present a report on the legal status and situation in Albania for the Plenary Assembly of the League of Nations, which concluded with the acceptance of Albania in this organization on December 17, 1920. For more information see Akhund, Nadine. The Two Carnegie Reports: From the Balkan Expedition of 1913 to the Albanian Trip of 1921. A Comparative Approaches. Balkanologie. Revue d'études pluridisciplinaires Vol. XIV, n° 1–2 | 2012 in https://journals.openedition.org/balkanologie/2365 [last access 15.11.2023].

171. **Šufflay, Milan.** Serbët dhe Shqiptarët: Historia e Shqiptarëve të Veriut. Translated by Fekeçi, Zef. Gurakuqi, Karl. Cana, Zekeria. Prepared for Publication by Bargjini, Ibrahimi Ilir. Tiranë, 2001. BK: S 89 S 82
172. **Šufflay, Milan.** Serbët dhe Shqiptarët. Translated form the Original by Çipuri, Hasan. 'Toena'. Tiranë, 2004. BK: S 224 F 44
173. **Šufflay, Milan.** Serbët dhe Arbërit. Simbioza e tyre në Mesjetë (Original Title in Serbo-Croatish: Srbi i Arbanasi. Njihova Simbioza u Srednjem Vijeku). Translated and Annoted by Ndreca, Arben. 'Rradhonjtë e Shejzave'. Tiranë, 2022. n.c.

"Serbs and Albanians" is a reference book in the field of Albanology, history and politics. The work sheds light on the history of the Arbërs, from antiquity until the Middle Ages, based on archival data collected by the prominent Croatian researcher and Albanologist, Milan Šufflay. The book highlights the tribal structure of Arbër society inherited unchanged from the time of the Illyrians. According to Šufflay, a key role within the structure of the tribe was that of the chief (*prijësi)*, tasked with guaranteeing the survival of the tribe. In order to meet the tribe's needs, the chief (*prijësi)* had the right to broker agreements with other parties, such as the Serbs, Angevins and Venetians. Another aspect underscored by the author is the fact that the Arbër tribes, despite being divided in terms of religion as a result of lengthy Ottoman occupation, always maintained good relations with each other. This was strikingly evident in the face of wars that threatened their existence. The book also explores the types of ancient cities that survived throughout the centuries, their fortification systems, and the various events that marked their history; the self-governance of cities along the Adriatic shores based on their statutes, the coexistence of Greek and Latin notaries in these cities and their roles, as well as the various taxes levied on neighboring communities. The author delves into the influence of the church on the tribal organization, the interaction of the clergy with the chairman (the first elder—*plakun e parë*) and the council of elders (*këshillin e pleqve)*, as well as the interaction of the Arbër tribes with the Croatian and Serbian ones. In the end, the author reflects on the features of the high nobility, which he views as a genuine state nucleus.

174. **Çelebi, Evliya.** Shqipnija para dy Shekujsh (Original Title: Evlija Çelebi Sejjahatnamesi). Translated from Turkish by Vuçiterni, Salih. 'Shkodra'. Tiranë, 1930. BK S 315 E 17
175. **Çelebi, Evliya.** Shqipëria 350 Vjet më Parë. Prepared for Publication by Rrumbullaku, Filip. Second Edition. 'Horizonti'. Tiranë, 2000. BK: S 201 E 49

The famous traveler and chronicler of the time of the Ottoman Empire, Evlija Çelebi, travelled several times in different parts of Albanian territories. Memories of his several journeys through Albanian lands at different points in time between the years 1660–1670 provide information on the country's history, culture, trade, social life, Albanian customs and traditions, dating from almost four centuries ago. In terms of law, the book is not a scientific study. Nonetheless, it provides data that can lead researchers to further investigation. The book illustrates various aspects of the application of Albanian customary law, and offers examples of various concession contracts on Albanian natural resources concluded by the High Gate with commercial companies of Western Europe, the exploitation of other natural resources, as well as the various taxes applied.

176. **Pasko, Dhimitër.** Tri problema në Lidhje me Bankën Kombëtare. (Me disa Anekse). "Shqipëria e re". 'Albania'. Konstancë, 1932. BK: S 54 R 84

"Three problems with respect to the Bank of Albania" researches from a historical perspective the issue of the absence of small currency denominations issued by the National Bank, from the period of the Ottoman occupation until after the First World War, as well as the crisis of the korona and of the lek, which damaged the Albanian economy. The author also analyzes several of the problems related to the functioning of the National Bank, under a comparative approach with the central banks of other countries, and delves into the relationship between the National Bank and the Albanian state. The text contains two annexes. The first reflects a summary of the report of Albert Calmes, *La situation economique et financiare de l'Albanie*, presented to the Economic and Financial Section of the League of Nations, in Geneva, in 1922 (Doc. A. 195). The author uses this report as part of his arguments on the need for the reformation of the banking system in Albania. The second annex is dedicated to the author's specific proposals for the amendment of some provisions of the organic law of the National Bank.

177. **Williams, George Fred.** The Skypetars. 'Harper's Weekly'. Boston, 1919. English Edition. BK: PP 908 wil
178. **Williams, George Fred.** Shqiptarët. 'Dielli'. Tiranë, 1934. BK S 53 T 59
179. **Williams, George Fred.** Shqiptarët-Albanians. 'Argeta-LMG'. Tiranë, 1999. BK: S 197 F 43

In 1914 Williams was the representative (minister) of the United States of America in Greece and Montenegro, as well as an observer of the International Commission of Control in Durrës.[2] The translator, Shaban Balla, translated several articles published by the author, presenting his views on the state of Albania at the time.

2 Williams, George Fred. Shqiptarët-Albanians. 'Argeta-LMG'. Tiranë, 1999, p. 1.

In his writings, the author delves into the Albanian custom of blood vendetta, the limitations on the implementation of Turkish legislation, the position of Albanian woman, and the causes that led to the fall of the government of Prince Wied (Wilhelm Friedrich Heinrich Princ zu Wied) and the fragmentation of Albania.

180. **Belegu, Xhafer.** Lidhja e Prizrenit e Veprimet e sajë (1878–1881). 'Kristo Luarasi'. Tiranë, 1939. BK: S 19 B 5

"The League of Prizren and its activity (1878–1881)" is a study of an historical nature, which provides a series of important documents on the League of Prizren and its activity regarding the unification of the Albanian lands. Among the documents we note (i) the Memorandum of the representatives of the city of Shkodra addressed to Lord Beaconsfield, the prime minister and the chief delegates of United Kingdom at the Congress of Berlin; (ii) the first decision of the League of Prizren, dated June 18th, 1878, that recognized only the government of the Ottoman Empire and the sovereignty of the Sultan; (iii) other acts, telegrams or correspondence on issues of the Congress of Berli. The compendium of decisions, known as 'Karare', were initially published in Turkish. According to the author, these decisions were published for the first time in the book the "League of Prizren", published by Kristo Dako, in 1922 in Bucharest.

181. **Hasluck, Margaret.** The Unwritten Law in Albania. 'J. H. Hutton'. Cambridge at the University Press. Cambridge, 1954. English Edition. BK: Al 22 F 12
182. **Hasluck, Margaret.** E Drejta e Pa shkrojtur (Zakonore) në Shqipëri. University Press. Cambridge, 1954. BK: A 115 A 35

The book focuses on the Albanian customary law, as well as aspects of Albanian ethnography. The author illustrates the correct interpretation of the institutes of *kanun* with details of the daily life of the Albanian people who were governed by the *kanun's* regime. She analyzes the Albanian family and its primary role in rural communities, cooperation amongst tribe members, the role of the head of the family and the separation of brothers. She further focuses on the institutions of customary law pertaining to the public domain, such as the role of the elderly (*pleqësia*), the *bayraktar* and the delivery of justice. Another aspect explored is the section on the institution of *besa* and the pertinent sanctions for non-compliance.

183. **Shkodra, Zija.** Procesi i Shthurrjes së Feudalizmit dhe i Lindjes së Marrëdhënieve Kapitaliste në Shqipëri gjatë Shekullit të XIX. Ministria e Arësimit dhe Kulturës. Tiranë, 1957. BK: S 66 63 R

"The disintegration of feudalism and the emergence of the capitalist relations in Albania during the 19th century" analyzes the political and economic causes that led to the weakening of the rule of the Ottoman Empire, and the collapse of feudalism and the tax system in Albanian territories. The author notes that in the second half of the 19th century, as agricultural production developed, it became evident that the land law of the Ottoman Empire of 1858, as well as the law on the sale of state property and the regime on *waqf* (*vakëfit*) (1875), were inadequate to meet the developments of the time, whilst the model of Ottoman feudalism was gradually disintegrating. The reforms undertaken by the Ottoman Empire, which led to the elimination of the military feudal caste, created favorable conditions for new feudal lords to amass plots of land. The increase in the production of goods in other areas of the economy, the development of sea and land trade, as well as the destruction of the old administrative organization of the Ottoman Empire, further affected the demise of feudalism. The author also notes that the guilds (*esnafet*) which had flourished in the 18th century entered a general crisis by the second half of the 19th century. This situation gradually paved the way for the introduction of the capitalist model, which in Albania was introduced in the form of simple cooperation and manufacturing.

184. **Shkodra, Zija.** Shqipnia në Kohën e Tanzimatit. Ministria e Arsimit dhe Kulturës. Tiranë, 1959. BK: S 23 E 11

"Albania in the times of Tanzimat" focuses on the situation in Albania before the Tanzimat Reform, and the resistance that the Ottomans encountered for almost half a century in the implementation of this reform in Albania. The work analyzes from an historical perspective the different stages of the installation of the Tanzimat in Albania and the characteristics of the implementation of this reform in different Albanian territories, and offers an overview of the armed resistance during the years 1831–1875.

185. **Zamputi, Injac. Naci, Stavri. Shkodra, Zija.** Burime të Zgjedhura për Historinë e Shqipërisë. Vol. III. Shqipëria nën Sundimin Feudal-Ushtarak Ottoman (1506–1839). Universiteti i Tiranës. Instituti i Historisë dhe i Gjuhësisë. Tiranë, 1961. BK: S 42 E 7; BIHGJL

The third volume contains a series of normative acts adopted by the Ottoman administration and applied in the Albanian territories, collected from the archives of Albanian and Turkish institutions. They include the registers (*sicils*) of the religious courts (*seriye*) that functioned in the Albanian territory, such as the registry of the cities of Berat and Elbasan, as well as other acts regarding the categories of kannuname, fermans, waqfia, and registers of merchants and artisans. The publication reflects in full the kanunname of Skopje, Thessaloniki, Elbasan, Shkodra, Vlora and Ohrid, which regulated the rights and obligations in Albanian lands, according to the Turkish administrative division. The list also includes the kanun of the Sipahis to the province of Rumelia, applicable in the Albanian territories that were part of this province, as well as the kanun of Tërhalla. These documents reflect the implementation of the Ottoman military feudal system and its subsequent disintegration in the period, otherwise known as the feudal anarchy of the 18th century. They shed light on interesting aspects, such as the structure of land ownership, the position of sipahi feudal lords and their relationship with the peasantry, the organization and commercial development of cities, the strengthening of guilds (*esnafe*), market regulatory mechanisms, and competition in the wharf trade between Durrës and Ragusa. The work refers to court decisions given mainly for defaults on debts and on tithes (*të dhjetës*). Some of the documents refer to resistance against the establishment of the timar system by the inhabitants of the mountainous areas of Albania, and their efforts to establish alliances with various European states for the coordination of their action against the Ottoman Empire. Acts that attest to the organization of the Albanian Pashaliks are also part of the compilation. The aforementioned sources are structured in three chapters, divided in sub-chapters according to the topic. The first chapter is dedicated to the position of the Albanians against the Ottoman Empire during the 15th–17th centuries and includes various legal acts—kanunname, fermans, ordinances, feudal properties (timar, mylq, waqfs)—which depict aspects of the process of Islamization of Albanian villages, trade and crafts in Albanian cities, and the conflicts related to the jurisdiction between the Orthodox patriarch of Peja and the Catholic archbishop of Tivar in 1558. The second chapter provides sources on the fall of the timar regime, the taxes of the feudal lords on farmers, the violent acquisition of lands by the feudal lords, the feudal disobedience to the sultan's fermans, the regulation of trade and the various privileges possessed by merchants, the development of guilds and some testamentary acts. The last chapter reflects acts dedicated to the Pashalik of Shkodra under the rule of Kara Mahmut, the Pashalik of Tepelena under the rule of Ali Pasha Tepelena, and the acts that show the oppression of these pashaliks by the Ottoman Empire. At the end, there is a glossary of terms. The publication is an important reference for the law applicable in Albanian lands during the mentioned time frame.

186. **Frashëri, Sami.** Shqipëria ç'ka Qënë, ç'Është e ç'do të Bëhetë. 'Naim Frashëri'. Tiranë, 1962. BK: Al 26 F 7; BFHF

Published for the first time in Bucharest in 1899, this book is considered a cornerstone of Albanian legal thought and philosophy of national renaissance, in the period of the crumbling of the Ottoman Empire and the national uprisings in Albania. The author reflects on the origin of the Albanians, their connection with the Pelasgians and delves into the political and economic situation of Albania. He further elaborates his vision for how the independent Albanian state should be organized, based on a republican model, and on the principles of the separation and balance of powers. He suggests that the leadership of the state should be undertaken by a "Council of Elders" consisting of fifteen members, who would have the power to elect the prime minister and the government and would serve as a mechanism to limit their individual power. The government elected by the elders should be separate from the legislative power, which would be exercised by the parliament. The author also expands on the role and power of the local administration. The book has been reprinted several times in Albania and can now be accessed digitally on the website of the National Library.[3]

187. **Prendi, Frano. Ceka, Hasan. Islami, Selim. Skënder, Anamali.** Burime të Zgjedhura për Historinë e Shqipërisë, Ilirët dhe Iliria tek Autorët Antikë. Vol. I. Tiranë, 1965. BK: S 64 B 2
188. **Prendi, Frano. Ceka, Hasan. Islami, Selim. Skënder, Anamali.** Burime të Zgjedhura për Historinë e Shqipërisë, Ilirët dhe Iliria tek Autorët Antikë. Vol. I. Second Edition. 'Toena'. Tiranë, 2002. BK: S 205 E 22

The Institute of History, in this three-volume publication titled "Selected sources on the history of Albania", provides a compilation of sources and documents on the topic. The first volume is based on early Hellenic literary sources, including the poems of Homer and Hesiod, which provide information about Illyrians and Illyria. It also includes references from Roman and later Byzantine authors, who describe the creation of an early class-based society and the birth of the first formations of a state, the administrative organization of Illyria, as well as the Roman slave-owning system in the east. The sources are arranged in chronological order, according to the time when the authors lived, and are accompanied by explanatory comments, as well as a glossary of terms.

189. **Buda, Aleks. Zamputi, Injac. Frashëri, Kristo. Pepo, Petraq.** Burime të Zgjedhura për Historinë e Shqipërisë, Shek. VIII-XV. Vol. II. Universiteti i Tiranës, Instituti i Historisë dhe i Gjuhësisë. Tiranë, 1962. BK S 45 C 30; BIHGJL

The materials and documents published in the second volume rely on three different categories of sources: (i) medieval sources from the time's chronographic literature (Byzantine, Latin, Italian, Slavic and Turkish), (ii) archival sources in Greek, Slavic, Latin, Italian and Turkish published by different researchers, as well as (iii) sources

3 https://www.bksh.al/details/39150 [last access 15.11.2023].

from medieval inscriptions found in the territory of Albania. Among the legal acts included in this volume, we note the agrarian law of the 8th–9th centuries, the tax statute of the 10th–11th centuries, the land registration of the Sanjak of Albania in the period 1431–1432. Each chapter begins with an introduction explaining the contents of the document from a historical and critical perspective. At the end, the work has a glossary of terms.

190. **Naçi, Stavri.** Pashallëku i Shkodrës nën Sundimin e Bushatllinjëve në Gjysmën e Dytë të Shekullit të XVIII (1757–1796). Universiteti Shtetëror i Tiranës. Instituti i Historisë dhe Gjuhësisë. Tiranë, 1964. BK: S 47 A 92

"The Pashalik of Shkodra under the rule of Bushatli during the second half of the 18th century (1757–1796)" provides valuable information regarding the history of law, research on the administrative situation of the Sanjak of Shkodra before the ascension of the Bushatli dynasty to power, as well as the crisis of the Ottoman military feudal system in the Albanian lands. The author deals with the formation of the Pashalik of Shkodra under the rule of Mehmet Bushatli Pasha during the years 1757–1775, severance of *pashalik* territories as a result of various wars, its revival under the rule of Kara Mahmud Bushatli Pasha, the uprisings for independence during years 1786–1787, as well as the creation of the Albanian feudal state of this *pashalik* during the years 1788–1796. The author notes that the weakening of the Turkish administration affected the economic development of Albanian cities, with special attention to Shkodra and Ulcinj (Ulqin), and closely exmaines the consequences of the feudal anarchy in the Sanjak of Shkodra. The publication contains a summary in French.

191. **Naci, Stavri.** Shqipëria e Veriut në Shekullin XVIII (1706–1756). Vol. I. Letra të Zëvendës Konsujve Venedikas të Shkodrës. Universiteti Shtetëror i Tiranës. Instituti i Historisë dhe Gjuhësisë. Tiranë, 1967. BK: S 22 A 16

"Northern Albania in the 18th century (1706–1756)", 1st volume, offers a compilation of archival documents published in Italian and Albanian, collected mainly from the State Archives of Venice. These documents provide important information on the history, trade and daily life of the city of Shkodra during the period of 1706–1756. A part of the documents are letters addressed to the "Five Wise Men of Trade in Venice" (*Pesë të urtëve të tregtisë në Venedik*), reflecting the process of transition from state feudal ownership of land, known as the *timar* system, to that of private feudal ownership of the fiefs and the divestment of the peasantry from property rights. The author highlights the strengthening of the fiefdom system, the fiscal policies that were implemented, the devaluation of the Turkish currency and the impact of the outdated Ottoman agrarian legislation. The work notes the effect that the new structure of land ownership and agrarian relations had on market relations, bringing the fiefs' lords closer to the market, and consequently to the merchant and artisan classes. The correspondence shows that after the signing of the Treaty of Karlovac in 1699 merchants from other European countries, including representatives from France, England, Holland and Austria, began to show increasing interest on the city of Shkodra, thereby undermining the monopoly that the Republic of Venice had preserved for a long time.

192. **Rahimi, Shukri.** Vilajeti i Kosovës më 1878–1912. Enti i Teksteve dhe i Mjeteve Mësimore të Krahinës Socialiste Autonome të Kosovës. Prishtinë, 1969. BK: S 78 D 9

The scholar analyzes the economic and political developments of the province of Kosova (*vilayet* of Kosova) in the last years of the rule of the Ottoman Empire, until the declaration of independence of Albania (1878–1912). The research is based on documents collected in the Diplomatic Archive of the Secretariat for Foreign Affairs of Yugoslavia, the State Archive of Bosnia-Herzegovina, the State Archive of Macedonia and the Provincial Archive of Prishtina. The first chapter in particular (Social-economic and cultural conditions until 1908) discusses the formation of the administrative unit of the Vilayet of Kosova, its feudal relations, fief ownership and *waqfs*. The author delves into the dues levied on the peasantry,[4] as well as the development of crafts and trade in the cities of this *vilayet*.[5]

193. **Shkodra, Zija.** Esnafet Shqiptare (Shekujt XV–XX). Akademia e Shkencave RP e Shqipërisë. Instituti i Historisë. Monografi. Tiranë, 1973. BK: S 105 B 13

"The Albanian Guilds (15th–20th centuries)" explores the organization of Albanian cities during the five centuries of Ottoman occupation, focusing mainly on the activities of crafts and trade, and the organization of guilds (*esnafe*), also known as corporations or trade guilds. These entities, which in terms of purpose and organization did not differ from other European guilds, and were associations of a professional nature. Endowed with legal personality, their object was the regulation of the exercise of professions in the domain defined in the statute. The author analyzes the historical events and conditions that influenced the revival of Albanian guilds (*esnafe*) during the 15th–17th centuries, the class structure, craft production, as well as the importance of bazaars and fairs that characterized the organization of

4 Rahimi, Shukri. Vilajeti i Kosovës më 1878–1912. Enti i Teksteve dhe i Mjeteve Mësimore të Krahinës Socialiste Autonome të Kosovës. Prishtinë, 1969, p. 31.

5 Ibid., p. 35.

trade in Albanian cities. The book, structured in four chapters, is based on archival documents collected in Albania, Turkey and other countries. It includes the registers of the Albanian town courts, the internal by-law of the guild of Elbasan—published here for the first time—and the charter of another guild in Elbasan, *Esnafi i Tabakëve*, of 1657. The second chapter delves into the functioning of the guilds based on their rules, the internal conflict resolution mechanisms, the role of the guild leader, the criteria of taxation and social differentiation between the apprentice (*çiraku*), the journeyman (*kallfa*), and the master. The third chapter is dedicated to the influence of guilds in the political and social sphere. In the fourth chapter, the author analyzes the causes that influenced the disintegration of the guilds, depicting an overview of the Albanian market in the 18th century, the decline of guilds in the 19th–20th centuries, and the penetration of foreign capital which contributed to the bankruptcy of old crafts and Albanian handicrafts. The work contains a summary in French.

194. **Naçi, Stavri.** Shqipëria e Veriut në Shek. XVIII (1757–1802). Vol. II. Letra të Zëvendës Konsujve Venedikas të Shkodrës. Universiteti Shtetëror i Tiranës. Instituti i Historisë dhe i Gjuhësisë. Tiranë, 1975. BK: S 104 50 C

The second volume of "The Northern Albania in the 18th century" documents the commercial development of the Sanjak of Shkodra, during the feudal anarchy of the years 1757–1802. The author highlights the weakening of the role of the *timar* and the strengthening of the local feudal (fief) lords, the uprisings against the Ottoman Empire, the forging of allies between the local feudal lords around the Bushatli house, and their struggle to turn a large number of *timar* lands into fiefdoms. This new system of land ownership was accompanied by the imposition of feudal rent on a value of one-third of total production, which the author notes to be at least three times higher than the tithes of the *sipahi*. The correspondences referenced in the book show that during the wars with Russia and Austria in the second half of the 18th century the High Gate recruited numerous contingents of soldiers from the Sanjak of Shkodra, mainly from the mountainous areas, who accepted conscription due to poverty. The publication contains a short glossary of terms.

195. **Bozhori, Koço. Liço, Filip.** Burime Tregimtare Bizantine për Historinë e Shqipërisë. Shek. X–XV. Akademia e Shkencave e RPSH. Instituti i Historisë. Tiranë, 1975. BK: S 124 27 C

The publication reflects a series of narrative and documentary Byzantine sources by authors of the 10th–15th centuries, about Albania and Albanians. The chronologically ordered writings reflect a long period of Albania's history under the rule of the Byzantine Empire. Besides documents of historical, political, and ecclesiastical nature, these sources also include administrative acts and correspondence of state and ecclesiastical institutions with relevance for Albanian territories and Albanians. Among these are references to the administrative division into themes, taxes and duties which the inhabitants of the western provinces of the Byzantine Empire were obligated to pay. The published documents are translated into Albanian and in some cases accompanied with notes that clarify parts of the text or specify events and dates.

196. **Çami, Muin. Luga (Bejtja), Hidajete.** (Prepared) Lufta e Popullit Shqiptar për Çlirimin Kombëtar: 1918–1920. (Collection of Documents). Written in Collaboration with Andoni, Dhimitër. Shuteriqi, Mediha. Rexha, Zekeria. Akademia e Shkencave, Instituti i Historisë dhe Drejtoria e Përgjithshme e Arkivave të Shtetit. Tiranë, 1976. BK: S 368 17 C

"The war of Albanian people for national liberation: 1918–1920" provides a compilation of documents that help to understand the events that preceded the Congress of Lushnja of January 21st–31st, 1920, and the war for the liberation of Vlora, which began on January 28th, 1920, and lasted until the armed uprising, of June 4th, 1920. The book highlights the efforts of the Congress of Lushnja, which culminated in the adoption of a series of documents that were instrumental in consolidating Albania's independence, the contest of the Anglo-Franco-Italian agreement on the Albanian borders and the war against Italy. The documents, arranged in chronological order, provide important information with respect to the diplomatic exchanges between the Albanian state and the Great Powers, as well as on the legal acts adopted by the Congress of Lushnja and the bodies created by it.

197. **Pollo Stefanaq. Pulaha, Selami.** Akte të Rilindjes Kombëtare Shqiptare 1878–1912. Akademia e Shkencave të RPS të Shqipërisë. Tiranë, 1978. BKSH.

The publication provides a chronology of a number of fundamental programmatic acts of the Renaissance national movement. In addition to memoranda, calls for protest, press releases and diplomatic communications of the Albanian national movement against Turkey, the publication includes the program and the decisions of the Albanian League of Prizren. It also describes relations with neighboring countries and the Great Powers of time.

198. **Puto, Arben.** Pavarësia Shqiptare dhe Diplomacia e Fuqive të Mëdha 1912–1914. '8 Nëntori'. Tiranë, 1978. BK: S 299 E 1; BFHFUT

A lawyer and author in the field of the public law and history of law, Arben Puto focuses his analysis on the diplomatic efforts of the Albanian national movement and the diplomacy of the Great Powers. He examines the first years after Albania's independence through the perspective of international public law, while also considering the historical events of the time. The reader should bear in mind that the text was written in a time period where the propaganda of the party-state was mandatory.

199. **Prifti, Kristaq.** Lidhja Shqiptare e Prizrenit në Dokumentet Osmane 1878–1881. Akademia e Shkencave e RPS të Shqipërisë. Instituti i Historisë. Tiranë, 1978. BK: S 136 10 B

In "The Albanian League of Prizren in the Ottoman documents (1878–1881)", the author highlights the importance of the Albanian League of Prizren as one of the most important movements of the Albanian national renaissance. He further describes the struggle to preserve the territorial integrity of Albania after the signing of the Turkish-Russian Treaty of Saint Stephen in 1878, which determined the fragmentation of the Albanian territory. This work published for the first time documents collected in the Turkish Archives of the Prime Minister's Office and the Ministry of Foreign Affairs, as well as in the Central State Archives of Albania. Among these documents are included acts, decisions and correspondence of the Ottoman civil and military administration, organized in the following order: (i) decisions of the council of ministers of the High Gate and imperial orders; (ii) the correspondence of the High Gate with the governors and commanders of the Ottoman military forces in Albania; (iii) correspondence and reports of the Ministry of the Interior, the Ministry of War and other central departments; (iv) reports of ministers and others high Turkish officials sent to Albania; (v) reports and letters of the prefects and deputy prefects from different Albanian provinces; (vi) decisions and reports of the Military Court of Prizren. The documents shed light on the activity of the Albanian League of Prizren for the national unification of all the Albanian provinces and the formation of an autonomous Albanian national state under the Ottoman Empire.

200. **Rexha, Iljaz.** Lidhja e Prizrenit në Dokumente Osmane. Arkivi i Kosovës. Prishtinë, 1978. Edited in Albanian, Serbian and English. BK: S 68 33 D.

"The League of Prizren in Ottoman documents. (Translation and commentary of the documents)" is a publication of the Archives of Kosova. The work contains documents from the archive of the Prime Minister of Turkey. The structure of presentation of documents reflects three main moments in the evolution of the Albanian League of Prizren: (i) the preparations and establishment of the League of Prizren in the period March–June 1978; (ii) The League' military organization in forging a resistance against the decisions of the Congress of Berlin, the conflicts with the High Gate, the efforts for union and independence, the military organization; (iii) the battles against the High Gate and the loss of support in the international arena.[6] The documents highlight the efforts to unite Albanians, regardless of their religious beliefs, and the role played by the conservative feudal elite in maintaining the *status quo* of the High Gate.

201. **Zamputi, Injac.** Dokumente për Historinë e Shqipërisë. 1479–1506. Part I. Akademia e Shkencave të RPS të Shqipërisë. Instituti i Historisë. Tiranë, 1979. BK: S 149 30 B

The first part of the series of 15th century documents on the history of Albania (1479–1499) was first published in 1967, in tribute to the five hundredth anniversary of the death of Skanderbeg. The first edition was supplemented with new documents in a second volume, pertaining to the period 1499–1506. The first part includes administrative acts such as decisions, letters, and ordinances. The notes of M. Sanuto, an official historian of Venice, are published in the second part. These notes, although kept as a diary, refer to specific administrative acts. The documents refer to various important issues of the time, such as the construction of a shipyard in the delta of Vjosa river that would serve for the construction of the Ottoman imperial fleet, which was opposed by Venice and Spain, or the differentiated treatment of social classes after the conquest of Shkodra by the Ottoman Empire in 1479. All documents are in their original language and translated into Albanian. The work includes an introduction in Albanian and French, and a glossary of terms.

202. **Ducellier, Alain.** La Façade Maritime de l'Albanie au Moyen Age. Durazzo et Valona du XIe au XVe Siècle. Institute for Balkan Studies. Thessaloniki (Greece), 1981. BK: AL 10 B 5

Ducellier's text is considered a reference work by history researchers and is an important source for the history of law. The work provides an analysis of the maritime commerce in the Albanian coastal cities, as well as the social, geopolitical and economic transformations of these territories during the 11th–15th centuries, which are of interest to the researchers in the field of commercial and public law. The work is based on archival documents from the main archives of Venice and Dubrovnik, including Byzantine and Italian sources, as well as a rich bibliography. The first part of the book analyzes the social and economic structure during Byzantine rule, the strategic role of the Albanian coastal cities, the legal regime on land applicable in the Albanian territories, the social stratification, the place of Albania in the regional

6 Rexha, Iljaz. Lidhja e Prizrenit në Dokumente Osmane. Arkivi i Kosovës. Prishtinë, 1978, p. 12.

trade, the political position of Albania under the Byzantine rule—with particular emphasis on the Duchy of Durrës—as well as the rise of the autonomist forces. The second part discusses the Venetian conquest of Durrës and its subsequent decline, the commercial routes in the Albanian territories during the 13th century, the growth of Ragusa's influence in the Albanian coastal cities, the foreign kingdoms that ruled these territories—with emphasis on the Angevin conquest—as well as the relations between the church and the state. In the third part, the author dwells on the causes that led to the failure of the Albanian principalities of the 14th century; the clashes between the heads of these principalities; the social and economic features of some of the country's important centers of this period, such as Durrës, Vlora, or Devolli; the establishment of foreign colonies in the Albanian coast; as well as the movement of goods and people from the coastal commercial centers of the Albania.

203. **Hoxha, Teuta.** Ismail Qemali. Përmbledhje Dokumentesh: 1888–1919. '8 Nëntori'. Tiranë, 1982. BHF; BKSH

The publication offers in chronological order the Albanian translation of documents, most of which were originally written in Turkish, that pertain to a narrow period of time before and after the proclamation of Albania's independence. In addition to the records of the meeting for the declaration of Albania's Independence, held in Vlora on November 28th, 1928, the publication includes correspondences between the first Prime Minister of Independent Albania, Ismail Qemali, and representatives of the local administration and foreign chancellors. It also contains a concession signed between the provisional government of Vlora, representatives of the Commercial Bank of Milan and representatives of Wiener Bank in Vienna for the creation of the National Bank of Albania.

204. **Mile, K. Ligor.** Çështje të Historisë Agrare Shqiptare. Fundi i Shekullit XVIII – Vitet 70 të Shekullit XIX. Akademia e Shkencave të RPS të Shqipërisë. Instituti i Historisë. 'Shtypshkronja e Re'. Tiranë, 1984. BK: S 34 D 7

The author explores the agrarian evolution of the Albanian village under the fiefdom system from the end of the 18th century to the end of the 1870s. Although the paper is an historical analysis of the agrarian structure of the Albanian village, it may be of interest to legal researchers. It offers a clear picture and an historical analysis of agrarian relations, their development since the establishment of the feudal-military system of the *timar* (and the fall of the latter), the transition to the new social structure of the fief's village and the penetration of the fiefdom system into the Albanian territory.

205. **Puto, Arben.** La Question Albanaise Dans lex Actes Internationaux de L'Époques Imperialiste (1867–1912). French Edition. '8 Nëntori'. Tiranë, 1985. BFH-FUT
206. **Puto, Arben.** Çështja Shqiptare në Aktet Ndërkombëtare të Periudhës së Imperializimit. Përmbledhje Dokumentash me një Vështim historik. 'Kombinati Poligrafik'. Second Edition. Tiranë, 1987. BK: S 58 F 6

"The Albanian issue in international acts of the period of imperialism" interprets documents pertaining to the Albanian cause during the Balkan wars and the First World War. The publication contains acts of various international institutions regarding the Albanian cause during the period of 1912–1914. Part of the series are the acts of the Conference of Ambassadors in London, those of the Control Commission as well as of the commissions for determining the borders in the north and south of Albania.

207. **Hasani, Sinan.** Kosova. Të Vërtetat e Mashtrimet. 'Rilindja'. Prishtinë, 1986. BK: Al 13 E 22

The book "Kosova. The truths and deceits" analyzes the position of Kosova during the Second World War, the cooperation of the Yugoslav Communist Party with the Albanian Communist Party, as well as the background of the Conference of Bujan. The author refers to historical legal documents which are of interest to researchers of the history of state and law, such as the decisions of the Albanian League of Prizren (1878), the resolution of the First Regular Provincial Conference of the Communist Party of Yugoslavia for Kosova and Metohija (1939) (*Konferenca e Parë e Rregullt Krahinore e Partisë Komuniste të Jugosllavisë për Kosovën e Metohinë*), and the resolution of the Provincial People's Assembly (*Kuvendi Popullor Krahinor*), asserting Kosova's right of self-determination.

The book has been republished and can be found with the following references:

208. **Hasani, Sinan.** Kosova. Të Vërtetat e Mashtrimet. Second Edition. 'Rilindja'. Prishtinë, 1987. BK: Ar 72 F 76

209. **Naçi, Stavri.** Pashallëku i Shkodrës në Vitet e Para të Shekullit XIX (1796–1831). Akademia e Shkencave e RPS të Shqipërisë. Instituti i Historisë. Monografi. Tiranë, 1986. BK: S 52 C 51; BHF

"The Pashalik of Shkodra in the first years of the 19th century (1796–1831)" explores the creation of the self-governed Pashalik of Shkodra under the rule of the Bushatli dynasty. The monograph, divided into six chapters, delves into the most important political events in Northern Albania under the rule of the Bushatli. It analyzes the legal aspects of the organization of this *pashalik*, based on documents extracted from Central State Archives, the archive of the Ministry of Foreign Affairs of France and the archive of the prime-ministry of Turkey. The book also provides information on the establishment of diplomatic relations between the Pashalik of Shkodra and the French empire.

210. **Zamputi, Injac. Malltezi, Luan.** Dokumente Për Historinë e Shqipërisë të Shekullin e XV (1400–1405). Vol. I. Akademia e Shkencave e RPS të Shqipërisë. Instituti i Historisë. Tiranë, 1987. BK: Al 13 29 B

The first volume of the book titled "Documents on the history of Albania in the 15th century" offers archival documents pertaining to the period 1400–1405. The publication is part of a project of the Albanian Institute of History to systematically publish documents on the history of medieval Albania, with sources from Albanian and foreign archives.[7] The book contains documents from funds of the archives of Venice, Ragusa and the Vatican. They are published in their original language and in Albanian and arranged in chronological order, according to acts and events that occurred in the years 1400–1405. The documents reflect the political and economic development of the Albanian territories, especially the Albanian coastal cities under the rule of Venice. They present the self-governance of these cities based on their charters, as well as a series of acts related to customs duties, concession contracts, the granting of special privileges to Albanians for their services and loyalty to Venice, and various wills and testaments. The work contains a preface in Albanian and French and is accompanied by a glossary of terms.

211. **Çami, Muin.** Shqipëria në Marrëdhëniet Ndërkombëtare: 1914–1918. Akademia e Shkencave të Republikës Popullore të Shqipërisë, Instituti i Historisë. Tiranë, 1987. BK: S 96 105 C

This work, primarily of a historic-diplomatic nature, discusses various issues related to acts of international public law and Albania's international relations during 1914–1918. Among the legal acts addressed are the treaty of Italy with the countries of the Entente that recognized the sovereignty of the Italian state over Vlora (1915), the Albanian-French protocol (December 1916), as well as the internationalization of the city of Shkodra. The work, despite the propagandistic tones of the time of its writing, relies on numerous archival materials collected from the Albanian,

7 Zamputi, Injac. Malltezi, Luan. Dokumente për Historinë e Shqipërisë të Shekullin e XV (1400–1405). Vol. I. Akademia e Shkencave e RPS të Shqipërisë. Instituti i Historisë. Tiranë, 1987, p. 3 et seq.

Austrian, Bulgarian, French and Italian archives. At the end there is a summary in French.

212. **Pulaha, Selami. Malltezi Luan. Huta, Përparime.** (Prepared for Publication) Studime për Epokën e Skënderbeut. Akademia e Shkencave e RPSSH. Vol. I. Instituti i Historisë. Tiranë, 1989. BK: S 181 F 58

The publication consists of three volumes, which compile studies of Albanian researchers on the period of Skanderbeg's rule, published in various scientific mediums. The volumes are organized based on the criterion of each topic. The first includes studies dealing with issues of the economic and social development of Albanian territories. Among the works published in this volume, in the context of this bibliography, we note: **Thëngjilli, Petrika.** Some Aspects of the Albanian Nationality in Ottoman Sources of the XV–XVI Century, p. 56–77 ('Studime Historike' no.1, 1981, p.177–193).[8] **Zamputi, Injac.** Autonomies of Albanian Cities of the Principate of Balshaj and the Negative Consequences of the Venetian Occupation – End of the 14th Century – Beginning of the 15th Century, p. 91–111 ('Studime Historike', no. 3, 1980, p. 169–185).[9] **Malltezi, Luan.** On the Monopoly of the Venetian State on Grains in Albania in the XV Century, p. 210–233 ('Studime Historike', no. 1, 1986, p. 129–148).[10] **Pulaha, Selami.** Expropriation of the Albanian Feudal Class from the Land and the Mechanism of its Integration into the Ottoman Feudal Class in the XV Century, p. 252–285 ('Studime Historike', no. 3, 1982, p. 139–165).[11] **Pulaha, Selami.** Contribution to the Study of Settlement of Villages and the Creation of Tribes in Northern Albania in the XV–XVI Century, p. 344–383 ('Studime Historike', no. 1, 1975, p. 75–107; 'Selected Sources for the History of Albania', Vol. II, Tirana, 1962; O. Gorka, Anonymi Desriptio Europea Orientalis, p. 25–29).[12]

213. **Pulaha, Selami. Malltezi Luan. Huta, Përparime.** (Prepared for Publication) Studime për Epokën e Skënderbeut. Akademia e Shkencave e RPSSH. Vol. II. Instituti i Historisë. Tiranë, 1989. BK: S 182 G 2

8 Original Title: Disa Aspekte të Kombësisë Shqiptare në Burimet Osmane të Shekullit XV–XVI.

9 Original Title: Autonomitë e Qyteteve Shqiptare të Principatës së Balshajve dhe Pasojat Negative të Pushtimit Venedikas – Fundi i shekullit të XIV – Fillim i Shekullit të XV.

10 Original Title: Rreth Monopolit të Shtetit Venedikas mbi Drithin në Shqipëri në Shekullin e XV.

11 Original Title: Shpronësimi i Klasës Feudale Shqiptare nga Toka dhe Rrugët e Integrimit të saj në Klasën Feudale Osmane në Shekullin e XV.

12 Original Title: Kontribut për Studimin e Ngulitjes së Katundeve dhe Krijimin e Fiseve në Shqipërinë e Veriut në Shekullin e XV–XVI.

The second volume contains studies on the political history and role of Skanderbeg as leader and founder of the Albanian state. In the context of this bibliography we note: **Biçoku, Kasem.** On the Extension of the Sanjak of Albania and some Issues Related to the Registration of Albanian Lands during the First Decade of the 15th century, p. 389–404 ('Studime Historike', no. 3, 1974, p. 85–98).[13]

214. **Pulaha, Selami. Malltezi Luan. Huta, Përparime.** (Prepared for Publication) Studime për Epokën e Skënderbeut. Akademia e Shkencave e RPSSH. Vol. III. Instituti i Historisë. Tiranë, 1989. BK: S 98 D 25

The third volume compiles writings from different authors, on the issue of international relations between the state of Skanderbeg and other feudal state structures, as well as studies in the customary law in the 15th century. In the context of this bibliography, we note: **Bogdani, Pranvera.** Trends Towards the Unification of the State throughout the Albanian Territories in the Second Half of the 14th Century and at the Beginning of the 15th Century, p. 3–14 ('Konferenca Kombëtare për Formimin e Popullit Shqiptar, të Gjuhës dhe të Kulturës së tij'. Tiranë, 1988, p. 121–131).[14] **Biçoku, Kasem.** The Formation and Empowerment of the Central Government under the Leadership of Scanderbeg, p. 18–27 ('Drejtësia Popullore'. Tiranë, 1973, no. 6, p. 46–58).[15] **Frashëri, Kristo.** Scanderbeg, the Founder of the Medieval Albanian National State, p. 28–32 ('Në Shërbim të Popullit'. Tiranë, 1978, no. 1, p. 20–21).[16] **Luarasi, Aleks.** The Law in the State of Scanderbeg, p. 33–53 ('Drejtësia Popullore'. Tiranë, 1982, no. 1, p. 72–88).[17] **Luarasi, Aleks.** A Political-Legal View on Some Treaties of Skanderbeg, p. 54–71 ('Studime Hitorike', no. 1, 1982, p. 173–188).[18] **Frashëri, Kristo.** On the Kanun of Skanderbeg, p. 94–111 ('Studime Historike', no. 2, 1977, p. 125–138).[19] **Pupovci, Syrja.** Sources for the Study of the Kanun of Lek Dukagjin, p. 112–139 ('Studime Historike', no. 2, 1971, p. 75–94).[20] **Pupovci, Syrja.** The Origins and Name of the Kanun of Lek Dukagjin, p.140–170 ('Studime Historike', no. 1, 1972, p. 103–123)[21] **Hadri, Flamur.** The Albanian Centralist Feu-

---

13 Original Title: Mbi Shtrirjen e Sanxhakut të Shqipërisë dhe disa Çështje lidhur me Regjistrimin e Tokave Shqiptare gjatë Dhjetëvjeçarit të Parë të Shekullit të XV.

14 Original Title: Prirjet drejt Bashkimit Shtetëror të Trojeve Shqiptare në Gjysmën e Dytë të Shekullit XIV dhe në Fillim të Shekullit XV.

15 Original Title: Formimi dhe Forcimi i Pushtetit Qendror nën Udhëheqjen e Gjergj Kastriot Skënderbeut.

16 Original title: Skënderbeu Themelues i Shtetit Kombëtar Shqiptar Mesjetar.

17 Original Title: E Drejta në Shtetin e Skënderbeut.

18 Original Title: Vështrim Politiko-Juridik mbi disa Traktate të Skënderbeut.

19 Original Title: Mbi Kanunin e Skënderbeut.

20 Original Title: Burimet për Studimin e Kanunit të Lek Dukagjinit.

21 Original Title: Origjina dhe Emri i Kanunit të Lek Dukagjinit.

dal State in the Era of Scanderbeg and its International Relations with other States, p. 171–190 ('Gjurmime Albanologjike'. Seria e Shkencave Historike 14–1984, Prishtinë, 1985, p. 55–73).[22] **Drancolli, Jahja.** Relations between Raguza and Durrës from the 9th Century until 1501, p. 241–253 ('Gjurmime Albanologjike'. Prishtinë, 1983, p. 29–52).[23]

215. **Zamputi, Injac.** Dokumente të Shekujve XVI–XVII për Historinë e Shqipërisë (1507–1592). Vol. 1. Botim i Akademisë së Shkencave të RPS të Shqipërisë. Instituti i Historisë. Tiranë, 1989. BK: S 178 S 5

The chronologically ordered documents presented in this volume, although of an historical nature, contain important data on the legal framework through which the history of Albania has progressed during 1507–1592. These reflect the wars and historical events from the time of the death of Skanderbeg, the efforts of Albanians to reinstate their principates, the collegial governance, the consolidation of the institution of the Assembly (*Kuvendi*) and the interprovincial alliances. Many of the cited documents are from the funds of the Albanian National Library, while other documents are collected from foreign archives and libraries. The documents are presented in their original language, and in Albanian.

216. **Zamputi, Injac.** Dokumente të Shekujve XVI–XVII për Historinë e Shqipërisë (1593–1602). Vol. 2. Botim i Akademisë së Shkencave të RPS të Shqipërisë. Instituti i Historisë. Tiranë, 1989. BK: S 186 10 D

The second volume of the series of "Documents on the History of Albania" delves into the development of assemblies (*kuvendet*) during 1593–1602, which focused on the organization of war and coordinated with other countries. The author notes that the Albanian assemblies of this period were composed of the heads of the Albanian provinces, mostly Christian, who aimed at the unification of the entire Albanian population. Several decisions of the Assembly of Dukagjin are highlighted and reflected in chronological order. The documents are presented in their original language and in Albanian.

217. **Zamputi, Injac.** Dokumente të Shekujve XVI–XVII për Historinë e Shqipërisë (1603–1621). Vol. 3. Akademia e Shkencave të RPS të Shqipërisë. Instituti i Historisë. Tiranë, 1989. BK: S 180 17 B

---

22 Original Title: Shteti Feudal Centralist Shqiptar në Epokën e Skënderbeut dhe Marrëdhëniet e tij Ndërkombëtare me Shtete të tjera.

23 Original Title: Marrëdhëniet e Raguzës me Durrësin prej Shekullit të IX deri në Vitin 1501.

The third volume is also dedicated to the documents adopted by the provincial assemblies (*kuvendet*) in the span of almost 20 years (1603–1621), depicted in their efforts to liberate the Albanian territories from the Ottoman occupation. The author highlights particularly the role of several of the Albanian leaders, such as Nikollë Mekjashi and Mark Gjini, who convened some of the most important Albanian assemblies, reflected in this volume through the documents adopted by the assemblies. The documents also testify to their efforts to bring the Albanian cause to the European chancelleries through diplomatic channels. The documents are in their original language and in Albanian.

218. **Injac, Zamputi. Pulaha, Selami.** Dokumente të Shekujve XVI–XVII për Historinë e Shqipërisë. 1675–1699. Vol 4. Botim Akademia e Shkencave të RPS. Instituti i Historisë. Tiranë, 1990. BK: S 165 A 35

The fourth volume includes documents collected from the archives of Venice, Ragusa and Austria, in their original language and in Albanian. The documents focus on the struggles of the Albanians against the Ottoman rule and against the feudal model of *timar*, both in the occupied territories and in the autonomous provinces of the mountainous areas. Documents mainly refer to the areas of Albania's western coastal provinces, to Kosova and to the Dukagjin Plain. The authors note that the materials obtained from the archives of Venice and Ragusa pertaining to the end of the 17th century have been published previously, whilst the documents collected from the Austrian, Kriegsarchiv, Wien, Turkenkrieg fund 1689–1691 are published for the first time. The documents reflect the political and social situation of Albania and its position in terms of international diplomatic relations, mainly with state and military representatives of Austria. They also depict important aspects of the economy, such as documents referring to grain trade with Venice and Ragusa, the import export of goods, and the struggle against the piracy.

219. **Shkodra, Zija.** Qytetet Shqiptare të Rilindjes. '8 Nëntori'. Tiranë, 1990. BK: S 183 U 63

The author analyzes the political and social life of Albanian spanning from the Middle Ages to the period of the national renaissance. The publication argues that artisanship and craftsmanship developed mainly in cities in the internal areas of country, as the coastal cities continued to retain their character of commercial transit piers, oriented towards trade exchange with other countries. The author notes that Albanian crafts flourished with civic life since the 14th century, whilst during the Ottoman occupation craftsmanship decreased, only to recover again later, especially around the mid-18th century. Among the distinguished skills, he highlights leather processing, textile production and metalwork. The third chapter analyses the development of the internal market, weekly bazaars and trade fairs. The book is of interest to researchers of the history of economy and commercial law.

220. **Puto, Arben.** Demokracia e Rrethuar. Qeveria e Fan Nolit në Marrëdhëniet e Jashtme, Qershor – Dhjetor 1924. '8 Nëntori'. Tiranë, 1990. BHF

The book focuses on the revolution of June 24th, 1924 and the international relations of the government led by Fan Noli that then emerged, aiming to provide a complete overview of the complicated diplomatic situation that the Fan Noli government faced. The publication also contains primary sources of documents issued by Prime Minister Fan Noli.

221. **Thëngjilli, Petrika.** Renta Feudale dhe Evoluimi i saj në Viset Shqiptare (XVII–XVIII). Monografi. 'Libri Universitar'. Tiranë, 1990. BK: S 187 R 20

The book explores in detail the historical development of feudal rent in Albanian territories during the 17th–18th centuries and the different categories that benefitted from these revenues. The author notes that initially the rent revenues were divided between the Ottoman central state administration and the Sipahi feudal lords, whereas after the emergence of the new class of feudal lords (*çifligarë*), the rent contribution was distributed amongst the central administration of the High Gate, the Sipahi feudal lords, the new feudal lords (*çifligarë*) and the provincial administration. The author analyzes the differences in the implementation of feudal rent in the areas where the *timar* system was fully implemented and in the self-governing provinces. The book reflects the central tax obligations, such as the poll tax (*xhizja*) which influenced the spread of Islam in the country, the cattle tax and extraordinary taxation. The paper is accompanied by a summary in French and a glossary of terms.

222. **Stavileci, Esat.** Kosova dhe Shqiptarët ndërmjet Kërcënimeve të Brendshme dhe Premtimeve të Jashtme. Qasje Juridiko-Politike. 'Rilindja'. Prishtinë, 1991. BK: S 209 F 26. BFDUT.
223. **Stavileci, Esat.** Kosova and Albanians between Negation (Foreign Rule) and Independence. Shoqata e Pavarur e Juristëve të Kosovës. Prishtinë, 1995. English Edition. BK: Ar 87 G 83

"Kosova and Albanians amidst internal threats and foreign promises" analyzes the issue of the self-determination of the Albanian population of Kosova and the absence of a functioning rule of law under the Yugoslav framework, the consequences of the restrictions on Kosova's autonomy by means of laws adopted by the Serbian

Parliament (March 28th, 1989–March 18th, 1991) in defiance of the basic principles of the Constitution of Yugoslavia of 1974. The legal and historical expose provides a deeper understanding of the course of events leading up to the war in Kosova in 1998, the NATO intervention in 1999 and its independence in 2007.

224. **Reka, Blerim.** Kosova në Dokumentet e Kongresit Amerikan: (1986–1995). 'Rilindja'. Prishtinë, 1995. BK: S 167 F 46

Based on documents collected at the archives of different institutions, and especially at the archive of the American Congress, the author explores from a legal-political point of view the debate on the issue of Kosova's quest for independence during the years 1986–1995.

225. **Kristo, Frashëri.** Lidhja Shqiptare e Prizrenit: 1878–1881. 'Toena'. Tiranë, 1997. BK: S 94 E 32

The monograph "The Albanian League of Prizren: 1878–1881" analyzes one of the most important events in Albanian history. Initially, the work was intended to be published in two volumes, and the first volume was published in 1990 by the Academy of Sciences. The second volume was never published; however, this edition published in 1997 includes the materials of both volumes. In an historical context, the author analyzes important legal acts such as the Treaty of St. Stefan, the Resolution of Dibra of November 1st, 1879, the Berlin Conference and the Reforms Commission, the acts of the Assembly of Dibra held on October 20–23rd, 1880, and the activity of the provisional government of Prizren in January 1881. The work relies on a rich bibliography from Albanian and foreign authors who have dealt with this matter and on archival documents collected in Albanian and foreign archives.

226. **Gashi, Gjergji.** Vatikani dhe Arbëria. (Acta Albaniae Vaticana). 1700 (1622) – 1922. Vol. 1. XVI; XVI/I-II. Dokumente për Historinë e Arbërisë. Dok. Nr. 1-1531. Vol. XVI-1; Treguesi i Dokumentave-Index Materiale. Vol. XVI-II: Monografi. Doc. no. 50; 67 (487). 'Onufri'. Tiranë, 1998. BK: Ar 96 B 35

"The Vatican and Arbëria" focuses on the historical evolution of the Albanian Catholic Church and its relations with the Vatican. The documents on which the publication relies provide important data on the customary law applied mainly in the northern areas. Researchers are presented with the regime of administration of church assets, and with the position of the church regarding some institutions of customary law implemented in Catholic areas, such as extramarital cohabitation, leaving a wife (effectively a divorce), mixed marriages, blood vendetta, theft, and robbery.

227. **Destani, Bejtullah.** Albania and Kosovo. Political and Ethnic Boundaries 1867–1946. Archives Edition Limited. Slough, 1999. English Edition. BK: 949 Alb 65

We draw the attention of researchers of public international law to this book, which discusses the evolution of the events that have influenced the determination of Albania's borders from an historical viewpoint. The publication is rich in documents, such as correspondence, memoranda or reports of various organizations involved in this matter, which were collected by the author at various institutions, especially at the London Public Record Office. These acts, although some are not of a legal nature, reflect (i) the problem of defining the southern border of Albania in 1881 and then in the years 1912–1914; (ii) the activity carried out by the International Commission in the years 1922–1925 for defining the borders of Albania; (iii) the 1937 memorandum of the Foreign Office on the forced expulsion of Albanians from their lands in Kosova, and (iv) the changes that the Albanian border underwent during the years 1941–1946.

228. **Çami, Muin.** Shqiptarët dhe Francezët në Korçë (1916–1920). 'Dituria'. Tiranë, 1999. BK: AL 21 29 F

The publication, based on archival documents collected in Albania and other countries, analyzes from an historical point of view one of the most delicate periods, the years after the declaration of independence of Albania and the efforts to preserve its territorial integrity. The author deals, among other things, with the status of Korça as an autonomous province, its later transition under the governance of Tirana, as well as the Albanian-Greek protocol of Kapshtica. The appendix of the paper provides the complete text of relevant documents on this subject, like (i) the protocol on the autonomous province of Korça, dated December 10th, 1916, according to which the city of Korça and its surroundings formed an autonomous province administered by Albanian officials under the jurisdiction of the French military; (ii) the decision dated February 16th, 1918 for the abrogation of the protocol dated December 10th, 1916; (iii) decision no. 557, dated September 25th, 1919 of the temporary government of Durrës, for the placement of the city of Korça under the administration of an Albanian official; (iv) the decision of the National Assembly of Korça, dated May 26th, 1920, which announced the union of this city with the national government of Tirana; (v) the Albanian-Greek agreement of Kapshtica dated May 28th, 1920.

229. **Plasari, Aurel.** Fenomeni Voskopojë. 'Phoenix'. Tiranë, 2000. BK: S 193 R 65

"The Voskopoje phenomenon" explores extensively the splendor and decline of the city of Voskopoja, and its formation as a Balkan product where Vlachs, Albanians and Greeks lived in harmony. Although it is an historical work, it contains data referring to the organization of the city and the development of the city's corporations (*esnafe*), which are of interest to legal scholars. The data on corporation include the number of corporations that operated in the city, their management structure, the organization of their "court of the peace" with judicial powers determined in their by-laws for the resolution of disputes between merchants. The author dwells on the role and importance of corporations, Venice's relations with Voskopoja, as well as the causes that led to the destruction of this city.

230. **Hoxha, Shefqet.** Bajrakët e Lumës. Punim Etnologjiko-Historik. Tiranë, 2000. BK: S 194 T 108

In this short work titled "The Bayraks of Luma" the author analyses the institution of *bayrak* according to the customary law, especially focusing on the organization of the *bayrak* of Kalisi and the *bayrak* of Luma. Although the work is not of a legal nature, it is helpful in understanding the elements of the institute of *bayrak*, its representative bodies, and their competence in representing the community.

231. **Yamamoto, Kazuhiko.** Struktura Etike e Kanunit. A është ajo Forma Origjinale e Etikës në Shoqërinë Njerëzore. (The Ethical Structure of the *Kanun*: is it the Original Form of Ethics in Human Society?). Translated and Enriched with Notes by Gurakuqi, Romeo. Qendra 'Drejtësi dhe Paqe'. Shkodër, 2001. BK: S 193 U 101

In this bilingual Albanian and English edition, the author offers his analysis on the customary law of the Kanun of Lek Dukagjin (KLD). Through the institutions of KLD and their impact on ethics and social order in northern Albania, the author explores his perspective on the origin of ethics and social order in human societies "without a state structure". The publication includes other articles published by the author on these matters.

232. **Buda, Alex.** Shkrime Historike. Akademia e Shkencave të Shqipërisë. Instituti i Historisë. 'Toena'. Tiranë, 2002. BK: S 205 49 G

The publication contains a number of manuscripts, reports, and articles, prepared over the years, some of which have been previously published. It is organized into four main headings: (i) the birth and development of feudal relations in Albania

(8th–15th centuries); (ii) the struggle of the Albanian people against the Turkish invasion and the role of Skanderbeg; (iii) authors of the national renaissance, pertaining to the period before and after the League of Prizren and (iv) figures of the European Enlightenment and contributors to the period of Albanian independence. The historical study carries valuable information for scholars of medieval law.

Of particular interest in the first part are the author's analysis of the establishment of feudal relations in the Albanian territories, the economic-social differentiation within the peasant community, and the formation and empowerment of the Albanian feudal class. He notes that in the Albanian lands, alongside the customary law, the Byzantine agricultural law (*nomos georgicos*) dating from the 8th century also applied; this was based on the peasant community structure and two forms of ownership: collective property and individual property. Peasant communities had a common property fund consisting of forests, pastures, barren lands as well as water resources, which in Albanian customary law were identified with the term "*kujria*". The private property, known as "*bashtina*", was the main form of ownership and consisted of the territory around the house, including the agricultural lands, vineyards, and gardens.

The author delves into the formation of the Albanian feudal class during the 11th–12th centuries, the strengthening of the church as land owner, and the gradual transition from the peasant community to the largest provincial communities. The book discusses the creation of the first autonomous political formations with their ruling structure, which included the head of the village (*caput catonis, cavo*), the first (*prior*), judge (*judex* or *sundia*), army leader (*voivode*), and ruler (*arhond*).

Of considerable interest is the analysis of the "*pronia*" institute, which as of the 12th century became a widely used form of land ownership. *Pronias* were land estates of different sizes, which were distributed by the central government to individual feudal lords under conditional ownership.[24]

The author further explores the rise of medieval autonomous Albanian cities, from the 13th to the 15th century, when the country fell under the rule of the Ottoman Empire. Highlighting the creation of cities as communities (*communitas, universitas*) and the division of the cities' inhabitants into two main classes—the people (*populares*) and the nobility (*nobiles*)—he illustrates these dynamics with a more in-depth analysis of the Durrës Theme during the 13th century. The discussion expands into the conditions that led to the formation of the Albanian nationality, the creation of the Albanian feudal state and, in particular, the creation of the principality of Arbër.

24 Buda, Alex. Shkrime Historike. Akademia e Shkencave të Shqipërisë. Instituti i Historisë. 'Toena'. Tiranë 2002, p. 39.

233. **Malltezi, Luan. Delvina, Sherif.** Mid'hat Frashëri Ministër Fuqiplotë Athinë (1923–1926). 'Lumo Skëndo'. Tiranë, 2002. BK: S 118 B 53

The book is a compilation of archival diplomatic documents related to the activity of Mid'hat Frashëri, a diplomat and one of the important figures of the post-independence period. Drafted during his diplomatic mission in Greece, the documents are not legal acts, but whilst referring to key historical issues they touch upon important legal elements, such as the right of national identification in the case of the villages in the area of Çamëria, the enjoyment of property rights, the arbitrary expropriation of Albanians in Çamëria, their deportation to Turkey, and proposals for various bilateral agreements with Greece.

234. **Cici, Arben.** Marrëdhëniet Shqiptaro-Italiane në Periudhën midis dy Luftrave Botërore (1920–1934). 'Afërdita'. Tiranë, 2002. BK: S 77 F 48

The author analyzes the bilateral relations between Italy and Albania and the economic penetration of Italy into the Albanian economy, during the period between the two world wars. In the second chapter, the author highlights the bilateral military agreements between the two states during the years 1926–1927, the open rivalry between Italy and Yugoslavia, the privileged position of Italy in relation to Albania and the limitations of the latter in conducting transactions with other countries without the participation of Italy. Also of interest is the analysis of England's economic interests in Albania and the influence on the diplomatic relations between the two countries.

235. **Thëngjilli, Petrika.** Shqiptarët midis Lindjes dhe Perëndimit (1506–1750). 'Toena'. Second Edition. Tiranë, 2004. BFHFUT

"The Albanians between East and West" describes in depth the relation between Albanians and the High Gate, as well as the economic, social and political development of the country during the years 1506–1750. Amongst different issues, the author delves into the registrations undertaken by the Ottoman Empire in Albanian territories, and the agrarian relations in the Albanian lands under the Timar Regime. Of interest to legal scholars is also chapter four which presents court complaints regarding the collection of taxes.

236. **Faveyrial, Jean-Claude.** Histoire de l'Albanie. French Edition. 'Dukagjini'. Pejë, 2001. AL 14 C 58

237. **Faveirial, Zhan Klod.** Historia (më e Vjetër) e Shqipërisë. 'Plejad'. Tiranë, 2004. BK: S 235 D51

This manuscript of a French Catholic missionary, written around 1884 and 1889, explores the history of Albanians from their origin in the Pelasgians, relations with Greece and the various dynasties that have ruled the country, such as the Albanian-Bulgarian kingdom of Preslava, the Albanian-Vlach kingdom of Prespa, and that of Dushan and his governors, until the occupation of the Albanian lands by the Ottomans. Of particular interest is the analysis of the history of the Catholic Church in the Balkans, where special attention is given to the history of the Ohrid Patriarchate of 1394–1767. The author points to the historical events that have affected the religious beliefs in Albania: the influence of the orthodoxy of neighboring countries, followed by the Ottoman influence and conversion to Islam, whilst traditional Albanian Catholicism was preserved mainly in the areas of Northern Albania. Although the work is of an historical nature, it is of interest for researchers of the history of ecclesiastical law.

238. **Xhafa, Bajram. Bello, Hasan.** Bisedimet e Asamblesë Kushtetuese për Çështjen e Shën Naumit dhe Vermoshit. 'Arbëria'. Tiranë, 2006. BIHGJL

This short publication presents in full the discussions of the Constitutional Assembly of 1925, regarding the rather polarizing claims that King Zog transferred territories in Vermosh and St. Naum to neighboring countries. The authors base their interpretation on the discussions of the Constitutional Assembly and the writings of various researchers, to come to the conclusion that there was only an adjustment of the border line and the exchange of territories was carried out according to the rules and practices of international law. The book argues that the assignment of borders had been the exclusive competency of the Great Powers and the border agreement was made in accordance with the constitutional provisions.

239. **Dervishi, Kastriot.** Historia e Shtetit Shqiptar: 1912–2005: Organizimi Shtetëror, Jeta Politike, Ngjarjet Kryesore, të gjithë Ligjvënësit, Ministrat dhe Kryetarët e Shtetit Shqiptar në Historinë 93-Vjeçare të tij. Shtëpia Botuese '55'. Tiranë, 2006. BK: S 258 B 34; AQSH: A 1. s 2

The historical publication has an encyclopedic style and relies on extensive archival sources. Most of the chapters provide valuable archival references on legal acts of Albanian governments, the parliament, the kingdom of Ahmet Zogu, international bilateral and multilateral agreements of Albania and other legal instruments. To illustrate the latter we mention (i) the decision of the Assembly of Vlora dated November 28th–December 7th, 1912; (ii) the Organic Statute of Albania dated April 10th, 1914; (iii) the international status of Albania at the end of 1919; (iv) the role of the International Border Commission in the period March 1922–September 1923; (v) the proclamation of the Albanian Republic on January 21st, 1925 and its Fundamental Statute; (vi) the reforms undertaken in the period 1928–1939; (vii) the 2nd Plenum of the Communist Party in Berat and the rise to power of the communist government in Tirana in 1944; (viii) the proclamation of Albania People's Republic (RPSH) and the Constitution of 1946; (ix) political judicial processes in 1948–1949; (x) the new Constitution of the People's Socialist Republic of Albania in 1976; (xi) the November 6th, 1994 referendum on the Constitution; (xii) the adoption of the new Constitution in 1998; as well as important moments in the process of Albania's membership in the EU and other international organizations.

240. **Plasari, Ndreçi. Malltezi, Luan.** (Prepared for Publication) Enver Hoxha dhe Katër Ditët e Beratit: 23–27 Nëntor 1944: Pleniumi i 2-të i KQ të PKSH, Berat, 23–27 Nëntor, 1944. Second Edition. Shtëpia Botuese '55'. Tiranë, 2007. BK: S 278 E 50

The book has shed light for the first tim on the uncensored materials of the Plenum of the Albanian Communist Party (PKSH), held in Berat on November 23–27, 1944. The Plenum of Berat, which discussed the activity of the PKSH and the means it had employed to come to power, are presented from a completely different perspective from the narrative of the 45 years of the monist regime. The minutes of the plenum and the reports presented occupy the first part of the book. In the other part, various types of documents issued by PKSH bodies or its main figures are presented, such as decisions of important conferences, letters, proceedings and resolutions. In context of this bibliography, we draw the legal scholar's attention to the resolution of the Conference of Peza (September 16th, 1942), which established the capillary organization of the national liberation councils; the proclamation of the Committee for the Rescue of Albania that was established in the Conference of Mukje (August 1943); part of the resolution of the 2nd Conference of the National Liberation in Labinot (September 1943); the decisions of the Congress of Përmet (May 1944), which established the Anti-Fascist National Liberation Council (KANÇ) and designated it as the main legislative and executive body representing the sovereignty of the Albanian people and state; the decision on the creation of the Anti-Fascist National Liberation Committee with all the attributes of a temporary government; the decision to prohibit the entry of King Zog in Albania and to refuse to recognize other governments created abroad; and part of the KANÇ Declaration on the rights of citizens, issued in Berat, on October 23rd, 1944.

241. Vilajeti i Kosovës në Dokumentet Arkivorë Osman. Botim i Drejtorisë së Përgjithshme të Arkivave Shtetërore të Qeverisë së Republikës së Turqisë. Departamenti i Arkivit. Stamboll, 2007. AQSH[25]

"The Vilayet of Kosova in archival Ottoman documents" presents a series of authentic documents which explain the administrative organization as well as the economic and political life in Kosova during the rule of the Ottoman Empire. Among them are the decisions of the League of Prizren (*Lidhjes së Prizrenit*), the establishment of the commercial court in Kosova, the law on the *raja* of the *kaza* of Vuçitern, and other aspects of legal interest.

242. **Nosi, Lef.** Dokument Historike 1912–1914. Botim i Institutit të Historisë. Tiranë, 2007. BK: S 287 G 40

The work is a compilation of historical documents, prepared by one of the signatories of the Act of Independence of Albania. These are mainly correspondences, but the publication also contains the decisions approved by the National Assembly of Vlora (*Kuvendit Kombëtar i Vlorës*) in November 1912, as well as the decisions of the Congress of Durrës (*Kongresit të Durrësit*) in December 1918.

243. **Von Hahn, Johann Georg.** Studime Shqiptare. Instituti i Dialogut dhe Komunikimit. Tiranë, 2007. BK: S 274 C 34

The text is a translation of the publication titled "Albanesische Studien", published by the author in 1854 in Austria. It constitutes a fundamental anthropological study of Albanians as well as an ethnographic picture of their cultural life and social organization under Ottoman rule. Although it is not a publication of a legal nature, in its third part, the author describes in detail the kanun-based customs implemented in the regions of Riza, Elbasan and the Shkodra Highlands, providing very valuable data for customary law researchers.

244. **Frashëri, Kristo.** Shpallja e Pavarësisë së Shqipërisë (28 Nëntor 1912). Akademia e Shkencave të Shqipërisë. 'Kristalina-KH'. Tiranë, 2008. BK: S 305 41 B

The book focuses on the interpretation of the historical events that culminated with Albania's independence in 1912. Of interest to legal scholars is the author's analysis of the Albanian League of Prizren (1878), as well as the subsequent developments

25 Introduction and Table of Contents in Turkish and Albanian. The Documents mainly in Turkish.

that led to the request for independence. The second part reflects the minutes of the Constitutional meeting of November 28th, 1912–December 7, 1912, the decisions taken by the Government of Vlora during the first days after the declaration of independence, as well as the full text of the law approved on November 22nd, 1913 by the Provisional Government of Vlora, to regulate and organize the civil administration in the country, through the model of prefectures and sub-prefectures (*Kanuni i Përtashëm i Administratës Civile Shqiptare).*

245. **Hecquard, Hyacinthe.** Historia dhe Përshkrimi i Shqipërisë së Epërme ose i Gegërisë. 'Plejad'. Tiranë, 2008. BK: S 294 F 36

"The history and description of the Upper Albania, or Gegëria" is a recollection of the author's observations during his mission as the French consul in Shkodra. In addition to the description of the customs and political organization of various provinces in the Albanian mountains, the author highlights the differences in their implementation across different areas of these territories. The author further delves into the history of the Catholic Church and its contribution to the preservation of Albanian customary law. The book is organized in two parts. The first part describes in detail the provinces and tribes of Northern and Central Albania. In the second part, particularly interesting for legal scholars is the focus on various aspects of Albanian customary law, the importance of blood ties to the political organization of the country, and the differentiated tax system that was applied in Shkodra and its surroundings, which varied depending on the province and on the religious belief of individuals of the area.

246. **Eichberg, Federico.** Shiriti i Liktorit dhe Shqiponja e Skënderbeut: Italia dhe Shqipëria 1939–1945. 'Emal'. Tiranë, 2008. BK: S 295 C 49

The author, a researcher at the Centro Militare di Studi Strategici and the S. Pio V Institute of Political Studies, has published numerous articles on Italian-Albanian relations. In this edition, the author analyzes the annexation of Albania by Italy in 1939, as well as the most important political and legal events that followed. The paper further deals with the restoration of diplomatic relations between Albania and Italy, which were concluded with the signing of the peace treaty between the two countries in 1947. Albeit a work mainly oriented towards diplomatic and political relations, it provides analysis of legal acts with administrative, economic and financial characteristics, in the implementation of the union of two independent states: Italy and Albania. The analysis also touches on the consequences of this union in international relations, especially with respect to Greece and Germany.

247. **Šufflay, Milan.** Städte und Burgen Albanies, Hauptsächlich während des Mittelalters, Vien, Leipizg, 1924. BK: AL 5 A 173
248. **Shuflaj, Milan.** Qytetet dhe Kështjellat e Shqipërisë. Kryesisht në Mesjetë. Prepared for Publication by Malltezi, Luan. 'Onufri'. Tiranë, 2009. BK: S 318 D 36

The author explores the emergence of cities and castles in Albania from antiquity until their revival at the beginning of the 1300s. He highlights the preservation of Illyrian elements, despite the Greek and Roman colonization. He further discusses the development of cities under the Byzantine governance model until the 15th century, when Albanian territories were conquered by the Ottoman Empire. In the fifth chapter, titled "Constitution and finances", the researcher analyzes the organization of Albanian cities, which on the one hand preserved the features of the Romano-Byzantine government, while on the other hand developed their own model of self-governance and self-formation. The chapter depicts the role of senior military leaders, judges, and other civil officials in the administration of cities. A special part is dedicated to the role and functions of the governor; which included extensive military, administrative and financial powers. The division of citizens into categories and the various taxes applicable to them are also of interest. In the sixth chapter, the author delves into analysis of the legal acts by which Albanian cities were developed, with the statute being the fundamental mechanism for the division of powers and the governance of the cities. The author highlights earlier references found in acts of the Republic of Venice regarding the Charters of Durrës in 1392, the Charter of Shkodra in 1396, and the Charter of Drishti in 1397, whereas he estimates that these statutes are from an earlier time period. Noting the fact that notarial documents, in addition to the statutes, played an important role in the development of the law of the time, the author draws attention to the fact that the Latin notary prevailed over the Greek one. He delves into the influence that the Italian law schools brought to the governance of the Ragusa and other Italian cities, a model that was also applied in Albanian cities, which as of the 1400s followed a gradual alignment with the Ragusan schools of law. The book follows the chronological order, providing a comparative perspective with the organization of other Balkan cities of the Balkan Peninsula.

249. **Dervishi, Kastriot.** Masakra në Çamëri. Përmbledhje Dokumentesh. Dëshmitë e të Mbijetuarve. Shtëpia Botuese '55'. Tiranë, 2009. BK: S 308 D 42

The book contains documents on the genocide in the Albanian province of Chameria from 1944–1945, collected from the archives of Albanian institutions. Documents from the archive of the Albanian Ministry of Interior Affairs and from the fund of the Directorate of State Security for the year 1945 are published in this book for the first time. These documents shed light on the inquiry of the British military mission in Saranda to the Cham community on April 3rd, 1945, as well as the treatment of the Cham issue in the Archive by the Albanian Labor Party as revealed by the archive funds.

250. **Puto, Arben.** Shqipëria Politike: 1912–1939. 'Toena'. Tiranë, 2009. BK: S 315 B 26; BFHFUT.

The book is an historical publication, which provides a quick insight on the legal developments during the period 1912–1939, focusing on the novelties of the legal framework approved by the Congress of Lushnja (*Kongresi i Lushnjës*, 1920), the new legal framework of the republic of 1925–1928, the transformation of the period of the monarchy (1928–1939), acts of public international law as well as on some of the concessionary agreements of this period. The work relies on archival sources.

251. **Krasniqi, Afrim.** Sistemet Politike në Shqipëri. 1912–2008. Historia e Krijimit, e Funksionimit dhe e Ndryshimit të Sistemeve Politike dhe Qeverisëse. Tiparet Kryesore të Institucioneve Politike, Kushtetutave dhe Modeleve Qeverisëse nga 1912 deri në Ditët e Sotme. 'UFO Press'. Tiranë, 2009. BK: S 306 B 39
252. **Krasniqi, Afrim.** Sistemet Politike në Shqipëri. 1912–2008. 'UFO Press'. Second Edition. Tiranë, 2014. BK: S 433 C 4

The publication draws comparisons between the different political systems implemented in Albania, starting from the creation of the Albanian state until 2008. The author analyzes the organizational model of the principate led by Skanderbeg, the creation of the political system with the declaration of independence, the Kanun of Jury, the Interim Kanun of the Civil Administration (*Kanunin e Përtashëm të Administratës Civile*), the Organic Statute of Albania under the leadership of Prince Wied, the constitutional act of the Extended Statute of Lushnja, the Fundamental Statute of the Republic of Albania of 1925, the Fundamental Statute of the Kingdom of Albania of 1928, the Fundamental Statute of the Albanian Kingdom under the Italian and German occupation, the installation of the communist regime based on the one-party model and the Constitutions of 1947 and 1976, the restoration of the democratic system, the 1991 constitutional model, the new Constitution of 1998 and its amendments until 2008.

253. **Milo, Paskal.** Të Vërtetat e Fshehura. Incidenti i Kanalit të Korfuzit. 'Toena'. Tiranë, 2010. BK: S 354 C 12

The author, who during his career also served as Foreign Minister of Albania, analyzes the incident of the Corfu Channel based on archival sources from Albanian archives; the archives of the Russian Ministry of Foreign Affairs; archives in London, Washington, and Paris; as well as on the decision of the International Court of Justice. The work considers the relations that preceded the agreement on friendship and cooperation signed between Enver Hoxha and Jozif Broz Tito, which also included military cooperation, especially in terms of the defense of Albania's southern borders. The explosion of a British ship passing through these waters on October 22nd, 1946 gave rise to United Kingdom's claims before the International Court of Justice and the signing of preliminary agreements for the trial of the case. The author analyzes Albania's refusal of the jurisdiction of the International Court of Justice (ICJ), the ICJ decision that held Albania responsible for the explosion, as well as the efforts for direct Albanian-British negotiations on the amount of compensation.

254. **Valentini, Giuseppe.** Kontribute për Kronologjinë e Historisë së Shqipërisë (337–395). Seria e Publikimeve "Valentini". 'Plejad'. Tiranë, 2010. BK: S 357 D 5

The publication focusing on the chronology of the Albanian history during the years 337–395 was written by the author in cooperation with the Center of Albanian Studies at the Italian Academy, which entrusted him with the compilation of a collection of documentary fund on the History of Albania. The author also relied on the library and archive of the Saverian College of Shkodra.[26] In the geographical context, the paper considers Thraco-Illyrian territories until the end of the 7th century, until the great Slavic influx, which changed a significant part of the region.[27] Regarding the methodology, the material is divided into columns where the first column lists the official position held by the author of the act; the second column records the events in Thrako-Illyria, followed by the citation of the fund for each item; the third column presents the events outside the region, considered as "diaspora"; whilst the last column is given to other notes and remarks. The author relied on the main fund of the *Codex Theodosianus* and *Codex Justinianus*, referring to the laws passed by the cities of the region, as well as to the official activity of the prefects and other officials who held important positions during this period. Among other funds cited are that of Tillemon, *Histoire des Empereurs*, and *Notitia dignitatium*, one of the richest funds of this period, which is thought to belong to the end of the 4th century and the beginning of the 5th century.[28]

---

26 Valentini, Giuseppe. Kontribute për Kronologjinë e Historisë së Shqipërisë (337–395). Seria e Publikimeve "Valentini". 'Plejad'. Tiranë, 2010, p. 9.

27 Ibid., p. 13.

28 Ibid., p. 16.

255. **Tollja, Xheladin.** Lura, një Rast Unikal. 'Julvin 2'. Tiranë, 2010. BK: S 364 D 17

Within an historical and ethnological context, this short book presents the life and customs of the area of Lura. It provides data on the implementation of customary law in the region, which the author esteems to be characterized by self-governance and religious tolerance. He highlights the bodies that were responsible for guaranteeing the enforcement of customary law: the heads of Lura (*paria e Lurës*), which had an organizational function in case of danger; and the eldership (*pleqësia*), a body of a judicial nature consisting of twelve elders of the tribe. The elders were assisted by a body known as the hammers (*çekiçët)*, with advisory functions. Other institutes of the customary law were *dhetarët*, *esnafët*, *këpucarët*, and *dorëzanët*, with clear duties to protect and apply this law.

256. **Meksi, Aleksandër.** Dhjetor '90. Dokumente dhe Materiale. 'UET Press'. Tiranë, 2010. BK: S 354 21 B

In this publication, the first conservative prime minister of Albania after the fall of communism provides a collection of documents that shed light on the political and governing activities during the collapse of the communist system and the restoration of pluralism in Albania. It offers an overview of the activity of the last government of the communist system, led by Adil Çarçani, the student movement of December 1990, the restoration of political pluralism, the creation of the Democratic Party by order no. 12, dated December 19th, 1990, the first technical governments created during the political transition, as well as the activity of the government led by the author himself as Prime Minister. The work contains a series of documents and legal acts presented in chronological order, including the first statute of the Democratic Party and decree no. 7442, dated December 17th, 1990, "On the creation of political organizations and associations" that opened way for the registration of political parties and organizations that opposed the communist ideology.

257. **Xhufi, Pëllumb.** Shekulli i Voskopojës (1669–1769). Akademia e Shkencave e Shqipërisë. 'Toena'. Tiranë, 2010. BK: S 350 E 12

The publication presents from an historical point of view the illustrious age of economic, social, political and religious development of the city of Voskopoja during 1669–1769. Although the work is an historical study, legal scholars might find of interest the analyses of the Codex of the Monastery of Saint Prodrom, in Greek and Albanian, which according to the author was written in 1779 by the former bishop of Gora, based on the data of an earlier Codex. The codex, written in the form of a diary, describes a series of events from the daily life of the monks in the monastery, and contains notes on relationships between the monastery and the city.

Of interest to legal scholars, for instance, may be the reference to a loan agreement, signed in 1662, between the monks and the residents of the three quartiers of the town. Pursuant to this agreement, the residents of Voskopoja would receive a loan of a given amount from the Monastery, to be divided equally among the three neighborhoods and used for the benefit of the city. The agreement was guaranteed by a surety from certain residents of the city who were valued for their reliability.[29]

258. **Kurti, Donat.** Zakone e Doke Shqiptare. First Edition. 'Botimet Françeskane'. Shkodër, 2010. BK: S 356 B 42

"Albanian customs and mores" analyzes of the evolution of the kanun-based customs and mores of the province of Dukagjin, drawing comparisons with other areas of the North of Albania. The work is a product of the author's many years of research in this area. The comparisons are numbered to facilitate the researcher's identification of the customs and the changes that the norms of the Kanun of Lek Dukagjni have incurred in different areas of the North. The work is organized in 18 chapters, depicting the evolution of the notions of the tribe and Bayrak, the rules of respecting the guest, the structure of the family, economic and social life, as well as the co-existence of different superstitions with the religious norms.

259. **Bufi, Ylli.** Tempulli i Demokracisë. 'Ombra'. Tiranë, 2010. BKSH

The author, a former Prime Minister of Albania (June 5th, 1991–December 10th, 1991) analyzes from an historical perspective the electoral systems implemented in Albania, the role of political parties, the institutional and functional structure of the Albanian parliament, as well as the role of parliamentary committees. Amongst others, in the second chapter, he focuses on the history of parliamentarism in Albania, on the creation of state representative bodies between 1912–1919, the beginning of parliamentary democracy in the years 1920–1924, the activity of the parliament in the years 1925–1939 during the Republic and the reign of King Zog until occupation by Italy, the elimination of parliamentary pluralism throughout the period of communism until the return of democracy in 1991, as well as contemporary developments until the 2010s.

260. **Dervishi, Kastriot.** Kadri Hazbiu, Krimet dhe Vrasja e tij. Dëshmi, Fakte, Plenumet e PPSh-së, Hetuesia dhe Procesi Gjyqësor. Shtëpia Botuese '55'. Tiranë, 2011. BK: S 367 C1; BKSH

---

29 Xhufi, Pëllumb. Shekulli i Voskopojës (1669–1769). Akademia e Shkencave e Shqipërisë. 'Toena'. Tiranë, 2010, p. 398.

In this book, the author deals with the judicial process against Kadri Hazbiu, the longest-serving Minister of Internal Affairs of Albania during the communist period, which ended with his punishment as traitor and the death sentence. The book sheds light to the mechanisms of the dictatorial regime, which subjugated the judicial power to the directives of the Albanian Labor Party and the government. The paper also presents the decisions of the 5th Plenum of the Central Committee, held on October 13–14th, 1982, which ended with the expulsion of the minister from the party, the widely used mechanism of "self-criticism", the indictment filed by the investigators of the time, as well as other moments of the farcical judicial process of the time.

261. **Llukani, Andrea.** Kanonet dhe Statutet e Kishës Ortodokse. 'Trifon Xhagjika'. Tiranë, 2011. BK: S 362 52 E

The publication explores the history of the ecumenical synods of the Orthodox Church, from the first Ecumenical Synod, summoned in 325 by Constantine the Great, to the most recent developments at present times. Although the focus is not the legal analysis of the acts, the book is of interest to legal scholars, as it reflects the main legal acts of the Autocephalous Church of Albania and their transformation over the time. In the tenth chapter, the author delves into the statutes and regulations of the Autocephalous Orthodox Church of Albania. The interpretation relies on the main acts governing the Church in the last century: the decisions taken at the Congress of Përmet and the adoption of the statute of the Orthodox Church in 1922, the developments of the Congress of Korça in 1929, the amendments of the statute and the Regulations of the Church, the legal acts adopted by the Congress of Tirana, held in 1950 and the radical changes that the Orthodox Church's statute underwent due to the state control of those years, the mixed clerical-laymen assembly of Saint Vlash which approved a new statute of the Orthodox Church in 2006. The role of the agreements between the state and religious communities, including the Orthodox Church, and the role of the State Committee of Cults is also given due consideration.

262. **Ismajli, Rexhep. Kraja, Mehmet.** (Ed. in Chief). Kosova: Vështrim Monografik. Akademia e Shkencave dhe e Arteve e Kosovës. Prishtinë, 2011. BK: S 364 A 76

"Kosova: a monographic overview" contains a number of research articles in various fields, which provide information on the historical developments of Kosova. In particular, the third chapter, titled "Political-legal developments", includes the scientific works that deal with important aspects of the history of the state and the law of Kosova. Amongst them we mention: (i) **Stavileci, Esat.** The Political History of the Kosovo Issue, p. 255–262; (ii) **Bajrami, Asim.** The Constitutional History, 263–274;

(iii) **Stavileci, Esat.** The International Administration, p. 275–284; **Bajrami, Arsim.** The Independent Sovereign State, p. 285–300.

263. **Gurakuqi, Romeo.** Principata e Shqipërisë dhe Mbretëria e Greqisë 1913–1914. 'UET Press', Tiranë, 2011. BK: S 356 15 C

Based on documents collected in the archives of Albania, the UK and Austria, the book deals with the relations between Greece and Albania, in the matter of determining the southern borders of Albania after its independence in 1912, and the developments following of the Conference of Ambassadors in London. The author analyzes the activity of the International Control Commission in Albania and the activity of the Commission for Determining the Southern Borders of Albania, which concluded with the Corfu agreement. The book contains a short summary in English.

264. **Nopça, Franc.** Pikëpamjet Fetare, Doket dhe Zakonet e Malcisë së Madhe. Prepared by Zallari, Mihal. Malaj, Edmond. Instituti i Historisë. 'Eneas'. Tiranë, 2012. BK: S 406 E 48

The original study, which can be found in the National Library of Austria, Sign.Ser.Nov.9393, has been published in several articles as well as in the book "Albania, constructions, clothing, dishes and utensils" published in Leipzig (Germany) in 1902.[30] It provides an overview on how the *kanuns*, which constituted the law of the mountains, were applied in practice in terms of hospitality, *besa*, weddings and funerals. It is an ethno-sociological analysis which provides information that is helpful to understand the practical application of the norms of the *kanun*.

265. **Durham, Edith.** Shqipëria e Epërme. Një udhëtim në Shqipërinë e Veriut të vitit 1908. 'AIIS'. Tiranë, 2012. BK: S 400 E 5

The author, a prominent 19th century anthropologist and a traveler to the northern Albania tribes, sheds light on the daily lives and organization of northern Albanians, according to the laws and customs transmitted orally through generations. She offers a masterful analysis of Albanian customary law, mainly the Kanun of Lek Dukagjin, and the influence of Ottoman law.[31] The author emphasizes that the Turkish administration, unable to penetrate the mountainous areas of Albania, allowed

30 Nopça, Franc. Pikëpamjet Fetare, Doket dhe Zakonet e Malcisë së Madhe. Instituti i Historisë. 'Eneas'. Botimet Albanologjike.Tiranë, 2012, p. 1.

31 Durham, Edith. Shqipëria e Epërme. Një Udhëtim në Shqipërinë e Veriut të vitit 1908. Botimet 'AIIS'. Tiranë, 2012, p. 39.

the autonomous application of customary law, which enabled its development and inheritance through generations.

266. **Llukani, Andrea.** Kisha në Diktaturë. 'Trifon Xhagjika'. Tiranë, 2012. BFHFUT

The book explores the history of the Albanian Orthodox Church from 1944 until 1994. Of interest from the legal viewpoint is the discussion of the regulatory regime of this church in different moments during the mentioned timespan. Included are the proceedings of the Third Panorthodox Congress held during February 5th–10th, 1950 in the Orthodox Cathedral of Tirana, which clearly evidences the intervention of the executive power in the internal affairs of the Orthodox Church. It was also the last congress held after the installation of communism in Albania.

267. **Shatri, Muhamet. Shpuza, Gazmend. Verli, Mariglen.** Dokumente Britanike për Çështjen Shqiptare në Konferencën e Ambasadorëve në Londër 1912–1913. Qendra e Studimeve Albanologjike në Institutin e Historisë. 'Toena'. Tiranë, 2012. BFDUT; BK: S 366 B 11

The volume presents documents dedicated to the cause of the Albanian state borders at the Conference of London; although not a legal study, these are drawn from the British archives during the period from October 1912 until August 1913 and are of interest to researchers on this cause.

268. **Šufflay, von Milan.** Situata e Kishës në Shqipërinë Paraturke. Zona e Depërtimit Ortodoks në Digën Katolike. 'Botimet Françeskane'. Shkodër, 2013. BK: 409 38 F

The renowned Albanologist presents his investigation into the history of religious communities and their organization in medieval Albania, highlighting the situation of the Church in Albania before the Ottoman occupation. He analyzes the genesis of the dioceses, the Metropolitan Church of Durrës and the Autocephalous Church of Ohrid, as well as the formation and expansion of the influence of the Metropolis of Tivar in northern Albania. Also of interest is the author's depiction of the properties of the bishopric and their relationship with the papacy.

269. **Elezi, Mehmet.** Hebrenjtë dhe Republika e Kanunit. 'Gjergj Fishta'. Lezhë, 2013. BK: S 421 D 1

"The Hebrews and the Republic of the Kanun" is a philosophical analysis of the Kanun of Lek Dukagjin through dissection of some of his main institutions. It offers jurists the opportunity to understand correctly the dimensions, often misunderstood, of this centuries-old legal corpus. In answering the question of whether the institution of *besa*, according to the *kanun*, was the fundamental reason for the salvation of the Jews in Albania during the Second World War, the author explores in depth the weight of the *kanun* in Albanian legal thought in the forging of the moral fiber and other distinctive features of the Albanian nation, an argument amply supported by illustrative quotations from various foreign researchers. The institution of *besa* is analyzed through the identification of features in common with (as well as differences from) other institutes of the *kanun*, such as the guest (*miku*), *ndorejeta*[32] and *ndorja*,[33] which unfolds the interweaving of the legal dimension with beliefs about the surreal, proving that these foundations, as ancient as timeless legends, have been formed in the Albanian lands since antiquity and have served to consolidate legal and moral principles now firmly embedded in the social DNA of the Albanian people. The *kanun*, according to the author, acted as Noah's ark in preserving the essence of the Albanian nation through centuries. The work explores the protection of human rights in the *kanun*: the equality of blood, freedom of the individual (the *kanun* did not recognize slavery), the inviolability of property, democratic self-government through the participation of community members, and the *kanun's* framework for conflict resolution through negotiations and conciliation. The author examines the institution of the blood feud (the vendetta) by highlighting the *kanun's* clear limitations on this institution (one-on-one/blood for blood/*gjaku për gisht*[34] (blood for finger), as well as the transgressions of these restrictions over time (the extension of the vendetta to every man of the tribe, or to a narrower specified circle), the returns to the canonical framework and the limitation of blood feuds through the decisions of the tribes' assemblies, as well as the damage that the communist regime's approach towards the *kanun* caused in the transmission of the moral values of the society.

The book has been republished and can be found with the following coordinates:

---

32 *Ndorejeta* is an institute which shares some common features with *besa*, but also some distinctions and supernatural components. It is a testament, an unfulfilled promise, which should be kept despite the barriers between the worldly presence and the afterworld, even if it requires a divine intervention: a deceased is allowed to rise from the grave and fulfil his promise to the living, the angel guards his grave whilst he is satisfying his obligations. The institute serves to reinforce the holiness of the promise, which is the essence of the *besa* institute as well.

33 *Ndorja* [*ndoria*] means to take someone under protection, provide him *besa* and the status of the guest. To seek *ndorja* from someone means to seek his protection, his *besa*, to request to be his *guest* (Elezi, p. 39). Elezi, Mehmet. Hebrenjtë dhe Republika e Kanunit. 'Gjergj Fishta'. Lezhë, 2013, p. 39.

34 *Ndorja* [*ndoria*] means to take someone under protection, provide him *besa* and the status of the guest. To seek *ndorja* from someone means to seek his protection, his *besa*, to request to be his *guest* Elezi, Hebrenjtë, p. 39.

270. **Elezi, Mehmet.** Hebrenjtë dhe Republika e Kanunit. 'Gjergj Fishta'. Lezhë, 2019. BK: S 555 F 11

We suggest readers refer to the second edition, which has thoroughly expanded on two key issues: *gjaku për gisht* and the status of women under the Kanun. Gjaku për gisht, which literally translates as blood feud to the finger, is one of the fundamental principles of the kanun which aimed at restricting the blood feud only to the person who had committed a killing. The author delves into the reasons why some tribes lapsed from the strict application of this principle, extending the killings for revenge to any man of the tribe, and the dramatic consequences that ensued. The analysis also shows the tribes' decision to return to the initial restrictions on the blood feud. The author further explores in depth the status and rights of women under the Kanun, providing a valuable holistic analysis of issues which have usually received one-sided criticism.

271. **Valentini, Giuseppe. Toldo, Antonio.** Të Drejtat e Shqipnisë Ethnike. 'Plejad'. Tiranë, 2013. BK: S 412 C 40

Originally published in 1944, and republished in 2013, the book is a legal-philosophical study on the legal grounds substantiating the claims for an ethnic Albania and its independence, aiming to highlight the ethnic and historical continuity of the Albanian people over the centuries. The work is organized in two parts. The first part deals with the concept of the nation and its historical developments according to schools of legal thought. The second part deals with the issue of the Albanian nation, its origins from the Illyrians and Thracians until the declaration of independence. One of the chapters analyzes some of the institutes of Albanian *kanun* law, such as the importance of blood ties, *besa*, the tribe, *bayrak*, and the assembly of men.

272. **Nopça, Franc.** Fiset e Malësisë së Shqipërisë Veriore dhe e Drejta Zakonore e Tyre. 'Eneas'. Tiranë, 2013. BK: S 427 F 74

The publication reflects the customary regime of the highlands of northern Albania, which due to the mountainous and isolated terrain had developed unique sociological characteristics, which in turn have always drawn the attention of researchers. In particular, the fourth and fifth chapters of this work are dedicated to the institutes regulated in the *kanun*, its origins and implementation among the Albanian highlanders.

273. **Stavileci, Esat.** The Truth about Kosova. Arguments and Facts in Support of its Independence. 'Valon J. Fetahu'. Prishtina, 2013. English Edition. BK: Al 42 39 D

The paper deals with the political history of Kosova, the Serbian genocide in Kosova and its right of self-governance. It also provides the text of Kosova's Declaration of Independence of February 17th, 2008 and its constitution, together with the constitutional amendments referring to the end of the international supervision, as published in the Official Journal of Kosovo, no. 25 September 7th, 2012.

274. **Sinani, Shaban.** Shqiptarët dhe Hebrenjtë. Monografi. 'Naimi'. Tiranë, 2014. BK: S 434 B 8
275. **Sinani, Shaban.** Codices, Statutes, and Jews in the Albanian History and Space. 'Naimi'. Tiranë, 2021. English Edition. BK: Ar 210 D 14

This monograph analyzes the special relations between Albanians and Jews, and the protection of the latter in Albania. The paper is rich with archival references to normative acts, mainly circulars and decisions of Albanian municipalities and prefectures, approved during the government of King Zog and during the Second World War. These acts attest to the support for the Jewish population in Albania during this period, their equipment with emigration visas, provision of facilities to exercise commercial activities and to practice their religion.

276. **Sinani, Shaban.** Kodikët Kronografikë të Shqipërisë – Shkrime dhe Dorëshkrime prej Rilindjes Europiane deri në Rilindjen Kombëtare. 'Naimi'. Tiranë, 2014. BK: S 439 B 36

The publication, one of the author's many works on the codices, offers a wide and in-depth analysis which aims to show the influence of the codices in the formation and strengthening of national consciousness among Albanians, as well as in the creation of regulatory regimes in Albanian territories. The analysis probes semantic arguments which help to understand the classification of old documents in the category of codices, and makes comparisons and corrections of previous classifications. The author clarifies that the term *chronographic* refers to codices that are not used for the recording of the divine message—the *logos* (codices previously classified also as philological codices)—but to codices of religious and secular institutions, which have recorded the developments of the material, transient human world.[35] In this category the author includes codices of church institutions, writings which do not

35 Sinani, Kodikët, p. 10–14.

deal with the divine message but with facts of community life, the statutory codices (city statutes), the guild codices, cadastral and notarial codices, as well as secular philological codices. The chapters gradually take the reader through the evolution of the codices from the church liturgy to the church codices of the *regest* typology,[36] from manuscripts to printing, from the monk scribe to the secretary, chancellor or notary compiler, from the rules that regulated the status and functioning of religious institutions and their community of believers to the guild codices, from codices to codification and city charters, from church registers, to cadastral registers and then to the comprehensive imperial *sigils*. Common elements of codices, which at first glance are very different from each other, have been underlined by the author as evidence of a process during which national identity and consciousness has been forged. Albeit not a typical legal work, we recommend that the book be considered as a premise for the study of the history of codices regime. In particular, chapters 1, 3, 4, 6, 8, and 9, as well as the rich bibliography, provide information and analysis of great interest in the field of legal history.

277. **Kadilli, Daja Zhuljeta.** Elbasani në Vitet 1892–1908 sipas Regjistrave Osmanë. 'Morava'. Tiranë, 2014. BK: AL 43 27 C

"Elbasan during the years 1892–1908 according to the Ottoman Registries" publishes for the first time some Ottoman registers pertaining to the years 1892–1908. The registers provide data on the area of Elbasan. Of interest to the legal researchers are various legal acts on real estates of the Sanjak of Elbasan and the different types of taxes applicable in this sanjak. In the second chapter, the author delves extensively into the organization and functioning of the city's guilds, their significant impact on economic and social life, their decline and the gradual transition from artisans' workshops to the first capitalist forms of organization in factories. Besides the registers, which are part of the Central State Archives fund, the work has also relied on other archival sources, as for instance the archival fund of Lef Nosi, the Archives of the Institute of History and private archives of some of the manor families of the city of Elbasan.

---

36 The codices held by the church in the register's form, give information not only on the rules of church or other rules mandatory for the believers but also record legal facts relevant for the community itself. See Sinani, Kodikët, p. 8, as well as for more Chapter I.

Codices kept by church institutions in the form of registers, which, in addition to aspects related to church rules, or other rules applicable to the believers' community, also registered events and legal acts of this community. See Sinani, Shaban, ibid, p. 8, as well as chapter I.

278. **Qazimi, Azem.** Komunitetet Fetare në Shqipërisë Komuniste. (Dokumente) Instituti i Studimeve të Krimeve dhe Pasojave të Komunizimit. 'West Print'. Tiranë, 2014. AQSh. 348(496.5) Kom 86

In this publication, the author presents in chronological order the regulatory frameworks of religious communities after the installation of communism in Albania. Among these references we note the law on the approval of the Statute of the Albanian Muslim Community, the law on the approval of the statute of the Albanian Bektashi Community, and the decree on the approval of the statute of the Autocephalous Orthodox Church of Albania. These documents display the legal relations between the Albanian government and religious communities after the installation of communism, as well as the gradual limitation of freedom of religion until its complete prohibition in the Constitution of 1976.

279. **Tirta, Mark.** Etnokultura Shqiptare: Ligji Dokësor. 'Mirgeeralb'. Tiranë, 2016. BK: S 497 C 5

The book deals with various aspects of the Albanian ethno-culture, and dedicates one of the chapters to the customary law. The author refers to different variations of the Kanun of Lek Dukagjin that were implemented in the northern areas of Albania, as well as to the customary codes of other Albanian regions. Part of the references are works on customary law by Albanian and foreign authors, from the period of the Albanian Renaissance and Independence.

280. **Bardhoshi, Nebi.** Antropologji e Kanunit. 'West Print'. Tiranë, 2016. BK: S 492 35C

The author analyses the Albanian customary law from an anthropological and historical point of view. He maintains that the Albanian customary law is based on the close bonds within the tribe, which constitute the foundation of the *kanun*, its principles and legal norms. The work analyzes the origin, the legal authority of the *kanun*, the myths of the past and their influence on the structure and legitimacy of the norm. He notes the institutionalization of the hierarchy based on age, gender and knowledge, and their influence on the creation of the enforceable norm.

281. **Elsie, Robert.** The Tribes of Albania: History, Society and Culture. I.B. Tauris, London, 2015. English Edition. BK: Pp 908 Els
282. **Elsie, Robert.** Fiset Shqiptare. Historia, Shoqëria dhe Kultura. 'Artini'. Prishtinë, 2017. Albanian Edition of the Tribes of Albania (History, Society and Culture). n.c.

This work of the well-known Albanologist is of interest to legal scholars, due to the elaborate insights that it provides with respect to the concepts of tribe and *bayrak*, which according to the *kanun* possessed the capacity of acting on behalf of the comunity and its individuals. The author analyzes the difference between the concepts of tribe and *bayrak* as distinguishable from one another, yet interconnected. He notes that the Albanian tribes are based on blood ties and common ancestry, while *bayrak* is a notion of a political-organizational character, within a certain geographical territory. The author analyzes the reasons for the creation of tribes as autonomous political and social units, the characteristics of the Albanian tribes and their coexistence with other Balkan tribes, where language and faith were not grounds for division. Both the Albanian and the English edition can be found at the National Library.

283. **Zamputi, Injac. Huta, Përparime.** Dokumente për Historinë e Shqipërisë të Shekullit të XV. Vol. III (1411–1415). Red. and Prepared for Publication by Malaj, Edmond. Botim i Akademisë së Studimeve Albanologjike. Instituti i Historisë. Tiranë, 2018. BIHGJL; BK: S 540 C 13

The publication is based on documents extracted from the Vatican State Archives, the Venice Archives and the Dubrovnik State Archives. The documents reveal the relations between Albanian and Ragusan merchants, the connections between Ragusa and the Albanian coastal cities, various private relation legal acts on the domain of inheritance, contracts and obligations and matters of a non-legal nature. The acts are of interest not only to researchers of medieval history but also to jurists who study the governance of medieval Albanian cities based on statutes. The documents are included in the original languages of Latin and Italian and translated into Albanian. The publication is accompanied with a list of these documents in Albanian and French and a glossary.

284. **Saraçi, Alvin.** Tregtia Adriatike e Shkodrës me Republikën e Venecies në Shekujt XVII–XVIII. Akademia e Studimeve Albanologjike.Tiranë, 2018. BIHGJL

The work analyzes the history of commercial relations between the city of Shkodra and the Republic of Venice during the 17th–18th centuries, based on the correspondence of the consuls of Venice in Shkodra and Durrës with the authorities in Venice—the Five Wise Men for Trade. The author notes that since the end of the 14th century, Albania became part of the Venetian Sea State and that the Republic of Venice granted various commercial privileges to Albanian entrepreneurs. The book is structured in 5 chapters. The first presents a general overview of the Sanjak of Shkodra and trade with the Republic of Venice, both in the Venetian and modern periods; the role of Albanian schools and merchants from Shkodra in the relations with Venice; as well as trade relations with the Ottoman Empire over the 17th and 18th centuries. The second chapter reflects the system of customs and duties in the 17th century and the role of the Venetian consulate in Durrës in opening a trade route between the two countries. In the third chapter, the author delves into the "internationalization" of the Port of Shkodra in the years 1733–1756 and the system of customs and duties implemented in Albanian ports, such as the tax of the commercial broker, taxes on sailing and renting ships, anchorage taxes, or port taxes. In the fourth and fifth chapters, the author focuses on the trade between the Pashalik of Shkodra and the Republic of Venice under the leadership of the Bushatli family in the years 1757–1979. It also discusses the trade of wool, which accounted for a significant part of the commercial exchange between the two countries. The work refers to archival sources from the archives in Tirana and Venice.

285. **Plasari, Aurel.** Arbni. Historik, Gjeografik, Kishtar dhe Politik. Akademia e Shkencave e Shqipërisë. 'Kristalina-KH'. Tiranë, 2020. BK: Ar 206 C 27

This book by Aurel Plasari is a comprehensive historical study on Arbëria. We draw attention of legal scholars particularly to the third chapter entitled "The political formation of Arbëria", where, amongst others, the author analyses the agreement between Dimitri of Arbëria and the Republic of Ragusa, which is thought to have been signed around the 1210s. By means of this agreement, Dimitri undertook to guarantee the citizens of Ragusa privileges and fiscal facilities in the exercise of trade in the territory of the Arbëria. The agreement, which is part by the fund of the Republic of Ragusa in the Archive of the Dubrovnik Municipality Library in Croatia, provides data of interest to researchers of international public and commercial law.

286. **Krasniqi, Afrim. Stojarova, Vera.** Shteti dhe Shoqëria në Shqipërinë Komuniste 1945–1990. 'Emal'. Tiranë, 2020. BK: S 581 B 6

This publication contains works by various authors who have analyzed one of the most difficult periods in Albania's history—the 45-year communist regime. Although the primary goal of this work is not legal analysis, several components are of interest to researchers in the field of law. We can mention **Krasniqi, Afrim.** The Governing System and Aspects of Political Representation 1945–1990, p. 53–83; **Boçi, Sonila.** Freedoms "Imprisoned": Freedoms and Human Rights During the Years of the "Dictatorship of the Proletariat in Albania", p. 84–111; **Dervishi, Kastriot.** Crimes against the State in the Legislation of the Communist State, p. 124–148.

287. **Mema, Albana.** Institucionet Përfaqësuese në Shqipëri. 1920–1924. Akademia e Studimeve Albanologjike. Instituti i Historisë. Tiranë, 2021. BK: Al 52 E 36; BIHGJL

"The representative institutions in Albania (1920–1924)" reflect, in an historical context, the events of the Congress of Lushnja and the legal nature of the main act approved by this Congress—the Basis of the Kanun of the High Council (*Bazat e Kanunores së Këshillit të Naltë*), also known as the Statute of Lushnja, which defined the main constitutional principles and the form of governance. The author analyzes the role of the National Council elected by the Congress of Lushnja, the political elections of 1921 and the legislative activity of the first Albanian parliament that emerged from these elections, the elections for the Constitutional Assembly of 1923, the Constitutional Assembly of 1924 and the political activity of Albanian opposition from 1920 to 1923. The monograph provides the acts published in the Official Journal for the years 1922–1924, the Extended Statute of the Albanian State as well as the circulars of the Ministry of Internal Affairs for the years 1920–1922.

288. **Mema, Albana.** Institucionet Ekzekutive në Shqipëri 1920–1924. Akademia e Studimeve Albanologjike. Instituti i Historisë. Tiranë, 2021. BK: Al 54 B 38; BIHGJL

"The executive institutions in Albania (1920–1924)" analyzes the creation and the competences of the High Council of the Regency, in the period between 1920–1924, as well as of the administrations that governed during this period. The publication relies on documents from the archives of various Albanian and foreign institutions. The work includes references to the official publications of the years 1920–1924, the constitutional acts of this period, as well as other various circulars, and government programs.

289. **Saraçi, Alvin.** Dokumente mbi Cënimin e Pronës në Periudhën Komuniste 1944–1946. Instituti i Studimeve për Krimet dhe Pasojat e Komunizmit. Tiranë, 2021. BK: S 619 C 30

"Documents on the violation of property rights during 1944–1946 communism period" explores the legal amendments that were adopted for the purpose of restricting the right of private property and opening way to the drastic economic reform that would engulf the country after the establishment of communism in Albania. The author delves into a series of legal acts and bylaws that restricted property rights; measures on confiscation; extra ordinary tax laws; as well as other acts of equivalent effect.

290. **Meta, Beqir. Krasniqi, Afrim. Bello, Hasan.** Shteti dhe Komunitetet Fetare. (Dokumenta Historikë). Vol. I (1948–1950). 'Emal'. Tiranë, 2022. BIHGJL

The book "The state and the religious communities (Historical Documents)", volume 1, provides a series of documents, ordered chronologically, that testify to the persecution of religious communities and clergy in Albania after the installation of communism. It exposes the establishment of a special supervisory structure called the Committee for Clerical Affairs under the Council of Ministers, mainly composed of soldiers and state security officers, and publishes for the first time the archival documentation of this committee, which operated from 1948–1950. In addition to documents, which are mainly correspondences and other acts of a non-normative nature, the book also contains references to legal acts, such as the Ordinance of the Council of Ministers for the implementation of the Decree-law on Religious Communities, dated December 16th, 1949, placing them under the control of the communist state; the decision to approve the new charter of the Autocephalous Orthodox Church of Albania on February 10th, 1950; as well as other acts that strengthened restrictive measures until the complete abolition of religious freedom.

291. **Ǘnlü, Mucize.** Vilajeti i Kosovës (1877–1912). 'Dituria'. Tiranë, 2023. n.c.

"The Vilayet of Kosova (1877–1912)", although a work of historical character, is of interest to legal scholars as it provides information regarding the administrative organization of the province of Kosova under the Ottoman occupation, during the period 1877–1912. It highlights the events that influenced the creation of this province and the changes that its administrative structure underwent until the independence of Albania in 1912. Among other data, it also sheds light on the fiscal regime applicable in this *vilayet*.

Catalogues

Duka, Eleni. Najdeni, Nexhi. Katalogu Sistematik i Dokumentave 1832–1912. Shteti dhe e Drejta. Vol. I. Tiranë, 1982.[37] AQSh (For internal use).

The systematic catalog of documents from 1832–1912, organized in three volumes, is a valuable tool for finding documents and legal acts pertaining to the justice system of the Ottoman Empire after the Tanzimat Reform, promulgated by means

37 The systematic catalog of documents 1832–1912 is organized in three volumes. The second and third volumes are dedicated to politics and religious entities. For the purpose of this paper, we have referred to the first catalog dedicated to the state and law.

of a Decree in 1839.[38] The reform, which was also applied in Albanian territories, aimed at reorganizing public administration according to a centralized model and strengthening the Turkish influence on occupied territories, including Albania. Difficulties in implementing this reform in the mountainous areas of Albania obliged the Ottoman Empire to allow the continued application of Albanian customary law. Evidence of the coexistence of the Albanian customary law and the Ottoman state law in the highlands of Albania can be found in the archival funds of administrative divisions—*vilayets, sanjaks* and *kazas*, as well as the funds of the religious courts (Sharia) of these centers, which are kept in the State Central Archives (Arkivit Qendror i Shtetit). A significant part of these can be accessed through the website.[39] The information contained in the catalog consists of two subsections: "Organization and operation of the state apparatus in the years 1832–1912" *(Organizimi dhe funksionimi i aparatit shtetëror në vitet 1832–1912)* and "Law in the years 1832–1912" *(E drejta në vitet 1832–1912).*[40] The latter provides researchers with data on the administrative division of the Albanian territories under the Ottoman Empire, the legislative bodies, and the process of institutional building after these reforms. The subdivision of "Law" *(E drejta)* and its rubrics include the files of the *Sharia* courts and other courts of various instances, as well as data on the criminal and civil legislation of this period. The documents are chronologically organized per year, and within each year they are further divided in sub-branches.

Sharrexhi, Afërdita, Basha Nermin. Vepra të Autorëve dhe Studiuesve Italianë për Shqipërinë dhe Shqiptarët (Shek. XV–XX). Katalog. (Opere di Autori e Studiosi Italiani sull'Albania e gli Albanesi (Sec. XV–XX). Biblioteka Kombëtare. Tiranë, 1995. Bilingual Edition in Albanian and Italian. Open access.[41]

The National Library's two-volume catalog on the works of Italian authors about Albania and Albanians provides information on publications which span from the 15th to the 20th century, including legal research.

The Albanian ethnic element is also an indicator of the early development of Albanian feudalism under Byzantine rule, demonstrating the slow creation of the Albanian feudal class in a period of history for which archival sources are few. The author highlights the differentiation between Albanian feudal lords, the

38 Duka, Eleni. Najdeni, Nexhi. Katalogu Sistematik i Dokumentave 1832–1912. Shteti dhe e Drejta. Tiranë, 1982. Vol. I, p. 1–11.

39 https://katalogu.arkiva.gov.al/ [last access 15.11.2023].

40 Duka, Najdeni, Katalogu, p. 5–6.

41 https://bksh.al/uploads/_/originals/61b90437-9ca9-4ef1-aad1-14699f112f19.pdf [last access 15.11.2023].

strengthening of their political positions and their influence on the creation of independent state structures.

Part 3:
PhD Theses and Articles

3.1 PhD Dissertations from the Faculty of Law, of University of Tirana

Luarasi, Aleks. Shteti dhe e Drejta Shqiptare para dhe gjatë Epokës së Skëndërbeut. Tiranë, 1981.

The doctoral thesis titled "The state and the law before and during the epoch of Skanderbeg" analyzes the feudal formations that preceded the state of Skanderbeg, beginning with the 12th century principality of Arbër and extending to other Albanian principalities of the 14th century and the early 15th century. A separate chapter is dedicated to the organization of the state apparatus and the law in force during the rule of Skanderbeg, relations with other countries, as well as international agreements concluded during his rule. Cities and their legal and political organization are also part of the discussion. The doctorate was published as a book in 1998 and is cited in the first part of this publication.[1]

Ballanca, Zejnulla. Historia e Shtetit dhe e së Drejtës në Tokat Shqiptare gjatë Shekujve V-XII. Tiranë, 1982.

The PhD thesis titled "The history of the state and law in Albanian lands during the 5th–7th centuries" is structured in three chapters and analyzes the historical, political, economic and social developments in Albanian territories during the cited period. The author analyzes the legal system applied in Albanian lands before the Byzantine rule; as well as during the period of feudalism in the 8th–12th centuries based on the system of free communities, their development and demise, and the formation of the Albanian nationality. The author delves into the social organization of Albanian society between the 5th–12th centuries, the Roman–Byzantine administration system, the tribal self-government model and the Byzantine and Bulgarian feudal administrative organization in Albania during the 9th–12th centuries.

Mandro, Arta. Organizimi Shtetëror dhe e Drejta në Pashallëqet Kryesore Shqiptare. Tiranë, 1992.

This thesis explores "The state organization and the law of the main Albanian *pashaliks*", with a particular focus on the Pashaliks of Shkodra and of Ioannina. The author analyzes two opposing positions on the nature of the Albanian *pashaliks*: the view that these developed as a state within the state, and the contrary opinion, which considers the *pashaliks* as common possessions of the Ottoman Empire. The author

---

1 Luarasi, Aleks. The Albanian State and Law in the Era of Skënderbeu. 'Luarasi'. Tirana, 1998. BK: S 196 F 81.

supports the idea that despite the presence of the Ottoman state, the Albanian *pashaliks* were characterized by completely original elements such as inheritance of the position within the family, as in the case of the Pashalik of Shkodra; or the development of a peculiar legal regime, demonstrated, for instance, by the ecclesiastical law and special privileges of the Christian population, which differed from the general regime of Ottoman law.

Anastasi, Aurela. Institucionet dhe Politika në Shqipëri (1925–1939). Tiranë, 1995.

"The Institutions and Politics in Albania (1925–1939)" focuses on the consolidation of the independent Albanian state during the period in question, the division of powers between the state's governing structures, the evolution of Albanian institutions, and the governing activity and legal reforms undertaken during this period. The study also considers the relations between the church and the Albanian state during the periods of the republic and the ensuing monarchy.

Jançe, Kristinka. Aspektet e Zhvillimit të Qyteteve në Mesjetë dhe Statutet e Shkodrës si Monumente të Vërteta të Shqipërisë Mesjetare. (Në Këndvështrimin e Historisë së Shtetit dhe së Drejtës, Vështrim Krahasues, Shek. VII–XV). Tiranë, 2011.

"Aspects of the development of Middle Ages cities and the statutes of Shkodra as real monuments of Medieval Albania. (From the point of view of the History of the State and Law, comparative view, 17th–15th centuries)" explores the emergence and development of the medieval Albanian cities, their governing institutions and the influence of the Venetian state on this area of the Western Balkans. The author analyzes the legal nature of statutes as regulatory acts of cities. A comparative analysis is drawn between the statute of Shkodra, as a source for the law of the city, and the legal institutes of the Kanun of Lek Dukagjin that operated in the highlands of the same area.

Nano, Ilirjana. Sistemi i Drejtësisë në Pashallëkun e Janinës. Tiranë, 2017.

"The justice system in the Pashalik of Ioannina" explores in depth the legal elements of the Pashalik of Ioannina under the reign of Ali Pasha Tepelena, highlighting his efforts to create a stable state apparatus with the aim of separating from the Ottoman Empire. The analysis extends to the diversity of legal systems implemented in this *pashalik*, as well as the organization and functioning of the judiciary. Also discussed are the legal regime of land and the main sources of income of this *pashalik*, and the different types of taxes applicable on different categories of inhabitants in the village and other areas. Of interest are also the diplomatic relations established by Ali Pasha Tepelena with various European countries, as international legal instruments which he used extensively.

3.2 PhD Dissertations from the Library of the Faculty of History

Lufi, Simon. Kisha Katolike në Shqipëri: në Vitet 1912–1939. Tiranë, 1999.

The dissertation titled "The Catholic Church in Albania in the years 1912–1939" explores the role of the Catholic Church within the historical and political developments of 1912–1924, and during the Kingdom of Albania from 1925–1939. Particular attention is paid to the role of the Vatican and King Zog's efforts to institutionalize relations with the Catholic Church through attempts to sign a concordat with The Holy See. The paper presents the opposing stance of the Catholic Church towards the Civil Code of 1929, which reviewed the institutions of family law and enabled divorce. In order to appease this conflict, King Zog attempted to sign a concordat with the Holy See, which did not ultimately materialize. The author also deals with the decree law no. 1868 "On the formation of religious communities" dated July 16th, 1929 and the law of July 16th, 1929 which regulated the freedom of religious belief.

Baze, Ermal. Qyteti Shkodrës në Gjysmën e Parë të Shekullit XIV. Tiranë, 2010.

The focus of this paper is the discovery of the statutes of Shkodra, and what they contain. It analyzes the governing institutions of the city of Shkodra under the regime of statutes; the economic development of the city, focusing mainly on crafts and trade; as well as Venetian influence on the city. The author provides a comparative analysis of the statute of Shkodra with the Kanun of Lek Dukagjin, as well as with similar regulatory acts of neighboring areas, such as the Codex of Stefan Dushan and the statutes of Budva.

Ruspi, Ermonela. Shteti dhe Dinamika e Lirive dhe të Drejtave të Njeriut në Regjimin Komunist: 1945–1990. Tiranë, 2011.

The dissertation "The state and the dynamics of human rights and freedoms during the communist regime 1945–1990" focuses on the framework for human rights and freedoms under the Albanian Constitution of 1946, the constitutional changes of 1950, and further limitation of rights and freedoms under the Constitution of 1976, in accordance with the Marxist-Leninist ideology in ascendance at the time. The comparison of the constitutional framework, as well as other legal acts, highlights the suppression of private property, freedom of belief, and the subordination of all state bodies under the control of the Communist Party, later known as the Labor Party.

Cana, Jaho. Institucioni i Kuvendit sipas së Drejtës Zakonore Labe. Tiranë, 2012.

The research presented in this paper deals with the main elements of the Kanun of Labëria, with a particular focus on the assembly (*kuvendi*) as a self-governing institution. The analysis is illustrated with examples from the asembly of Mesapik of 1847, the assembly of Gjirokastra of 1880 and their genuine parliamentary functions.

Sufaj, Femi. Sistemi i Ndëshkimeve në Shqipëri gjatë Regjimit Komunist: (1945–1990). Tiranë, 2012.

The paper deals with the evolution of the system of government in Albania after the Second World War, based on Marxist ideology and the influence that this ideology had on penal legislation and on the institutions of the criminal justice system. The analysis chronologically follows the development of the applicable penal system in Albania after the declaration of independence in 1912 until 1944. It further discusses the establishment of the criminal justice system at the initial phase of the installment of the communist system, between 1945–1952, culminating in the adoption of the Criminal Code in accordance with the newly established system. The author notes that the acts approved during this time served to establish the criminal justice system, courts, prosecution and the system of execution of criminal decisions, the infamous special courts and the political trials. The analysis continues with the developments of the legal framework adopted in the years 1952–1966, and from 1966 until the adoption of the new Constitution in 1976, a period characterized by intensification of the class struggle and the elimination of groups of political opponents. The author notes that after 1976, the criminal policy was dominated by the ruling ideology and policy of the Labor Party. This was also reflected in the adoption of the Criminal Code of 1977, which significantly increased the number of both criminal offenses and the provisions providing for death punishments as instruments of control of the party-state.

Hoxha, Artan R. Marrëdhëniet midis Regjimit Komunist dhe Kishës Ortodokse Autoqefale e Shqipërisë në Vitet 1945–1967. Tiranë, 2014.

"The relationships between the communist regime and the Albanian Autocephalous Orthodox Church during 1945–1967" highlights different aspects on the relationship between the church and the state during a period of dramatic restrictions on freedom of belief and the exercise of activities by ecclesiastical institutions. The dissertation examines the effects of the agrarian reform, undertaken after the installation of the communist system, on the immovable properties of the Orthodox Church. Also reviewed are the novelties of the law of 1949 on religious communities, as well as the new statute of the Albanian Autocephalous Orthodox Church (KOASH) approved in 1950 by Prime Minister Enver Hoxha and the Presidium of the People's Assembly. Under the dictates of the state, the statute determined that prayers would be formulated by the leadership of KOASH and approved by state bodies.

Miço, Heliona. Një Vështrim i Përgjithshëm mbi të Drejtën për Arsim në Shqipëri: Ecuria e kësaj të Drejte në Përputhje me Standardet Ndërkombëtare dhe Legjislacionin Evropian. Tiranë, 2019.

The dissertation discusses the historical evolution of the right to education in the years 1912–1939, the radical changes that understanding and application of this right underwent during the period of communism in the years 1944–1991, as well as its re-assessment after the collapse of the socialist system in the 1990s. The analysis draws a comparison between the development of these rights in Albania after the 1990s and evolving European standards.

Boseta, Bashkim. Veprimtaria Parlamentare në Shqipëri në Vitet e Monarkisë Shqiptare, 1928–1939. Tiranë, n.d.

"The parliamentary activity in Albania during the years of monarchy, 1928–1939" explores the historical circumstance that led to the proclamation of the monarchy in Albania, the activity of the Constitutional Assembly, the approval of the fundamental Statute and the new Codes during this period. The dissertation delves into the role of the parliament in agrarian reform, its role in relation to religious communities, and the legal framework regarding the media and women's rights.

Ivanova, Rozeta. Historia e Legjislacionit në Shtetin Shqiptar (1912–1924). Tiranë, 2021.

This dissertation explores the developments of Albanian legislation from the proclamation of Independence until 1924, from a historical perspective. The author analyzes the Interim Law of the Civil Administration (*Kanuni i Përtashëm i Administratës Civile*), the Law of Jury (*Kanuni i Zhurisë)*, other legal acts enacted by the first Albanian government, the role of the International Control Commission, and governance under Prince Wied and the Organic Statute of Albania. The study further focuses on the Statute of Lushnje and the institutions of the Albanian State, the electoral law, the first Albanian pluralist parliament, its legislative activity and the activity of the various governments that ruled in the mentioned period.

3.3 Journals and various periodicals: *Drejtësia Popullore*

The journal *Drejtësia Popullore* (People's Justice) was first published in 1948, as a joint publication of the Ministry of Justice, the Supreme Court and the office of Attorney General. Initially it was published every two months, and as of 1975 every three months.[2] Its publication continued until 1993, shortly after the fall of communism. Until the fall of the communism the articles published are characterized by the mandatory ideological tone, censure and self-censure. But despite the politicization and glorification of the communist regime, the articles provide legal analyses on aspects that should neither be forgotten nor ignored. Some, for instance, provide an overview of the legal acts that served as a basis for the establishment of the communist government, the deformed justice system and the economic legislation after the Second World War. Others analyze the development of the

---

2 Fjalor Enciklopedik Shqiptar. Akademia e Shkencave të Shqipërisë. Tiranë, 2008, p. 520. BK: Fe 40 D 15.

legislation and jurisprudence of a specific branch of the law. In 1962, the journal began publishing articles dedicated to Albanian customary law, which are relatively more neutral in terms of propaganda. Some editions provide a summary of their articles in French as well. The journal can be accessed at the Library of the Faculty of Law, University of Tirana.

Omari, Luan. Roli i Shtetit tonë në Ndërtimin e Shoqërisë së re Socialiste. No.1, January–February, 1962, p. 1–13.

The article reflects the activity of the Constitutional Assembly resulting from the elections of December 2nd, 1945 and the adoption of the Statute of the People's Republic of Albania based on the dictatorship of the working class.

Papuli, Nonda. Organizimi i Shtetit të Parë Shqiptar dhe Aktet e tij Legjislative. No. 5, September–October, 1962, p. 23–34.

The article deals with some of the decisions of the National Assembly of Vlora (1912) and the legal acts it approved. It notes that, between November 28th, 1912 and December 7th, 1912, the Assembly held seven sessions and approved acts that paved the way for the declaration of independence and formation of the initial structure of the independent state of Albania. The analyses include government decisions and the organization of different state structures.

Puto, Arben. Njohja Ndërkombëtare e Shtetit Shqiptar. No. 6, November–December, 1962, p. 9–22.

The article discusses the legal consequences of Albania's independence in the international arena. In particular, the author draws attention to the decisions of the Conference of Ambassadors in London in 1912–1913 and Albania's relations with Turkey and other Balkan countries.

Tedeschini, Emid. E Drejta Dokësore Shqiptare e Shqipërisë së Veriut. No. 5, September– October, 1963, p. 63–70.

The author analyzes the Kanun of Lek Dukagjin, focusing on the personal rights and the provisions which regulated the status, rights and obligations of the household. In the same issue, p. 69, Tedeschini presents a brief summary of an unpublished manuscript of Lek Çoba, of around 208 pages, found at the archive of the Chair of Catholic Church of Albania in Shkodër. Tedeschini notes that this manuscript is also dedicated to the *kanun* and refers to an older recollection, dating around 1868, of an author about whom very little is known.

Meksi, Vangjel. Çështje të Historisë së Shtetit dhe së Drejtës gjatë Pushtimit Turk. No. 1, January–February, 1965, p. 53–65.

The article analyzes the Albanian feudal state and its demise, which opened the way for the establishment of the Turkish feudal system. It underlines the fact that in the highlands of Albania, from Kosova to Chameri, the *timar* system was never implemented, despite the efforts of High Gate. For this reason, the Turkish Empire officially recognized some provinces as autonomous, effectively permitting the application of Albanian customary law. Other interesting points are the discussion of the Jibal Commission, the reform of Tanzimat in the Albanian territories, and its coexistence with the Albanian Kanuns.

Meksi, Vangjel. Disa Institute të së Drejtës Dokësore dhe Rëndësia e tyre për Popullin Shqiptar. No. 3, May–June, 1965, p. 66–73.

The article deals with the recognition of Albanian customary law by the Ottoman Empire, as the governing law of the Albanian highlands, which regulated all relations of the private and public domain. The author reflects on several key issues of customary family law, such as the regime on marriages between Albanians of different faiths, the recognition of limited polygamy for the purpose of giving birth to male offsprings—an institute that was accepted among Albanians regardless of religion or region—as well as the ancient Albanian institute of brotherhood and its purpose.

Tedeschini, Emid. Figurat e Vrasjes në të Drejtën Dokësore–Kanunore. No. 5, September–October, 1965, p. 68–78.

The paper provides researchers with an analysis on the types of murder regulated in Albanian customary law. He identifies two categories of murders: the first includes murders that are *de facto* unpunishable, for instance the inter-tribal murders; as well as murders that are *de jure* unpunishable, where the author includes murders committed by the authorities, murders in the family, or murders for blood vendetta. In the second category, the author includes murders that are *de jure* punishable murders, which included murders against public order, pregnant women, or provoked murders.

Meksi, Vangjel. Privilegjet dhe Detyrimet e Krahinave Autonome Shqiptare gjatë Pushtimit Turk. No. 6, November–December, 1965, p. 66–78.

The article deals with privileges and obligations in the Albanian mountainous regions during the Turkish occupation as well as the preservation of these privileges until the declaration of independence. The author gives evidence of the local self-governance of these provinces according to Albanian customary law within the Turkish Empire, the free exercise of religion, and the exemption from the system of *timars* and *zeamets*. The author illustrates his interpretation with the privileges of the areas of Himara (south) and Mirdita (north).

Meksi, Vangjel. Kanuni i Skëndërbeut dhe Kanuni i Lek Dukagjinit–Monumente Historikë me Vlerë të së Drejtës Shqiptare. No. 4, July–August, 1967, p. 52–59.

The article delves into a comparative analysis between the Kanun of Skanderbeg and the Kanun of Lek Dukagjini, encompassing key moments regarding the inception and development of Albanian law from the time of Illyrians. It discusses extensively the Albanian institute of brotherhood—an entirely Albanian institute, which, according to the author, has been mentioned since 285 in Illyria, and was not borrowed from the Slavic countries.

Baboçi, Sinan. Zakone, Kanune e Ligje, të gjitha Sanksiononin Pabarazinë e Gruas ndaj Burrit. No. 5, September–October, 1969, p. 78–83.

The author analyzes the gender inequalities and relationship between spouses according to the customary law, whilst highlighting the new role that Albanian women gained in the socialist order, as equal in rights to men. The author points out that family law in Albanian customary law was based on the model of a monogamous and patriarchal family, in which the husband had unlimited power over the wife. He provides illustration with the the institution of betrothal (*fejesa*), which the author interprets as a contract for the sale and purchase of the girl against a reward; and outlines how the absence of an age determination for betrothal in the *kanun* gave the parent the right to betroth her from the cradle or even before birth. The text shows evidence of the fact that marriage within the tribe was not allowed, and that marriage was usually considered a means of forming alliances for the protection of the tribe.

Meksi, Vangjel. Në Gjurmët e së Drejtës së Lashtë Iliro-Shqiptare. No. 2, April–June, 1978, p. 97–112.

The author emphasizes the continuity of Illyrian law with Albanian customary law, illustrating this with several examples of institutions regulated in both. A comparison is drawn between the inheritance regime of the community property of the Kanun of Lek Dukagjin (KLD) and the family co-ownership of the Illyrian law, where in both cases the estate is not divided to the heirs but kept in the form of co-ownership between the living adults. Another example is the similarity in the rights and duties of the family head and other members of the family under the Illyrian customary law and the KLD.

Omari, Luan. Mbi Problemin e Autonomisë dhe të Qeverisë së Përkohshme në Vitet e Lidhjes Shqiptare të Prizrenit, No. 3, July–September, 1978, p. 32–39.

The article focuses on the efforts for the creation of an independent Albanian state and the role of the Albanian League of Prizren in preserving Albanian lands after the Treaty of St. Stephen and the Congress of Berlin, which severed Albanian provinces to the benefit of the neighboring countries. It analyzes the first founding acts of the League and the request for autonomy within the Ottoman Empire.

Elezi, Ismet. Dënimi sipas të Drejtës Penale përpara Vendosjes së Pushtetit Popullor. No. 3, July–September, 1978, p. 49–59.

The article analyzes some institutes of the Illyrian criminal law which were transmitted into the Albanian customary law, such as expulsion, blood feud and fines. The author also deals with the punishments provided in the criminal law of the Albanian feudal states of the 9th–15th centuries, as well as the criminal punishments in the applicable legislation from the declaration of independence in 1912 until the occupation of Albania by Italy in 1939.

Krisafi, Ksenofon. Shteti dhe e Drejta në Iliri. No. 1, January–March, 1979, p. 85–100.

The article analyzes the birth of the Illyrian slave-owning state, its historical development, and its consolidation in the first half of the 4th century BC. The paper also deals with Illyrian society organized on the basis of tribes and with its customary law.

Gjata, Rustem. Prendushi, Mikel. Dokumente Kryesore dhe Akte Normative të Lidhjes Shqiptare të Prizrenit (1878–1881). No. 2, April–June, 1979, p. 71–95.

The article focuses on the normative acts approved by the Albanian League of Prizren. It includes the program of the League for preservation of the Albanian territories in an autonomous organization under the sovereignty of the sultan, the organization of the defense of the Albanian lands and the liberation of the territories occupied by Serbia and Montenegro. The paper provides a complete overview of the historical context in which these acts were approved as well as their contents.

Luarasi, Aleks. Qytetet Shqiptare në Mesjetë dhe Organizimi i tyre Politik. No. 2, April–June, 1980, p. 111–119.

The paper discusses the emergence and developments of Albanian cities in the Middle Ages based on charters, their developments as centers of craftsmanship, trade and handicrafts, the increased trade with other cities on the Adriatic coast and beyond in the Mediterranean. It highlights that the development of cities was accompanied by differentiation of social classes, although from a legal point of view the inhabitants of the cities were all free. The author analyzes the organizational structure of Albanian society and the governing bodies of the city, pursuant to their statutes. The paper also pays attention to the regime of contractual obligations and other commercial contracts that developed during this period.

Ballanca, Zejnulla. Çështje të Historisë së Shtetit të së Drejtës në Shqipëri gjatë Periudhës së Sundimit Bizantin (Shekujt V–XII). No. 2, April–June, 1982, p. 7–81.

The article delves into the formation of the Albanian nationality, in both an historical and legal context, during the times of the Roman and the Byzantine conquest. The author points out that tribal law developed within the feudal law in the Albanian lands during the period of the 5th–12th centuries, despite various invasions. The patriarchal social model of free peasant communities influenced the implementation of the feudal model and the subsequent formation of the state of Arbër. The article notes that the penetration by Byzantine law did not prevent the development of Albanian customary law, which has influenced the formation of Albanian nationality.

Tarifa, Fatos. Koncepti i Autonomisë në Mendimin Politik Rilindas të Viteve 1900–1912. No. 1, January–March, 1984, p. 75–81.

The author analyzes the concept of nationality in Albania; the efforts of key figures of the Albanian Renaissance for the unification of the Albanian-speaking territories in one autonomous state under the Ottoman Empire; and later, the gradual creation of an independent national state.

Haxhi, Paskal. Legjislacioni për Lindjen dhe Zhvillimin e Rendit Kooperativist në Bujqësi (Vitet 1944–1955). No. 3, January–March, 1984, p. 19–34.

The author deals with the nationalization of private property and the collectivization of agriculture after the establishment of communism. It provides information on the legal acts of the agrarian reform and the compulsory formation of cooperatives under the communist regime.

Çela, Elira. Feja dhe e Drejta Zakonore. No. 1, January–March, 1988, p. 62–74.

The article focuses on the influence of Christianity and Islam on the Albanian customary laws (*kanuns*), and religious tolerance in the country throughout the ages, which is manifested in the mixed marriages.

Naska, Kaliopi. Pikëpamjet e Ismail Qemalit mbi Formën dhe Ndërtimin Administrativ të Shtetit Shqiptar. No. 3, July–September, 1988, p. 104–110.

The article deals with the administrative division established by the first government after the declaration of independence, and discussions on the nature of this division. It notes that the government of Ismail Qemali was against the division of the country into cantons, with the aim of eliminating separatist powers and placing Albania under centralized direction as the most suitable way to build homogenous economic and social progress of the country. It analyses the pertinent law regulating the country's administrative divisions and local bodies, known as "*Kanun i Përtashëm*", approved in November 1913.

Zaçe, Valentina. Disa Veçori të Marrëdhënieve Martesore sipas të Drejtës Zakonore. No. 4, October–December, 1988, p. 69–77.

The article draws attention to the legal regime of the institutions of engagement and marriage under Albanian customary law, the rights and obligations of spouses, and the prohibition of marriages within the extended family and bloodline. It then details the exception, through the institute of *Levirati*, which determined that the brother or cousin—as a rule, the youngest in age—had the obligation of marrying the widow of the brother or cousin. In the same way, the Institute of the *Sororati* recognized the right of the husband to marry the sister of his deceased wife. The author also deals with the evolution of the regime of kidnapping a woman for the purpose of marriage, which gradually became punishable under the KLD, the Kanun of Skënderbeu and that of Labëria, and constituted a cause for blood feud. This change paved the way for the development of the institution of arranged marriages, which took an important role in customary family law. Attention is also given to the allowance for limited polygamy, which permitted the husband to take more than one wife, but only if the wife had not given birth to male children.

Nova, Koço. Organizimi Shoqëror sipas Kanunit të Lekë Dukagjinit. No. 1, January-March, 1990, p. 64–77.

The text interprets several institutions of the *kanun* and the organization of the tribe, focusing on the *bayrak* as a territorial administrative unit with military functions, as well as on the law of *Jibal*. The author notes that the latter delegated to *bayraks* the task of ensuring mandatory military recruitment within their territories, and the adjudication of inter-tribal cases by a panel composed of representatives of the tribes as well as including representatives of the Ottoman administration. The jurisdiction of the *jibal* court was weak in the highlands, although the author highlights that it was not absent, even in the secluded *bayraks* of Shala or Shoshi. The practical adaptation of the Ottoman administration to the rules of the customary law of the KLD aimed at enabling the penetration of the Ottoman power in the north of the country and limiting the autonomy of these areas. The article points out that for this purpose, there were efforts to codify the Albanian customary law, albeit unsuccessful.

Hoxha, Izet. Parablerja në të Drejtën Zakonore Shqiptare (Sprovë e Karakteristikave Historike). No. 2, January–March, 1990, p. 74–88.

The author notes the two opposing opinions with regard to the institution of the right of pre-emption under the Albanian customary law. According to one of them, the Albanian customary right of pre-emption has its origins in the Roman law of *jus praelationes*, while the other opinion suggests that this right has its origins in the Slavic customary law known as *'parvo prece kupnje'*. The author makes a detailed legal analysis of pre-emption in Albanian customary law, concluding that the institute of the Albanian customary law is not a creation of one specific year or a borrowing from another law, but rather has been gradually formed over the centuries, with characteristics similar to the right of pre-emption regulated by other rights, whilst also having its own unique features.

Omari, Luan. E Drejta Zakonore dhe e Drejta Zyrtare në Shqipëri (Shekulli XIX–XX). No. 3, July–August, 1990, p. 63–68.

The author analyzes the co-existence of Albanian customary law with the positive law of the Byzantine, Serbian, Bulgarian and later Ottoman state order. This co-existence continued to persist even after Albania's independence in 1912, when Albanian customary law continued to be applied.

Mandro, Arta. Disa Veçori të Organizimit Politik e Administrativ të Pashallëkut të Shkodrës, No. 1, January–March, 1993, p. 101–113.

In this paper, the author analyzes the political and administrative apparatus of the Pashalik of Shkodra, comparing it with the administrative and political structure of the Ottoman Empire, and highlighting the distinct features of the Bushatli family governance.

Elezi, Ismet. Marrëdhëniet Familjare Martesore sipas së Drejtës Zakonore në Labëri. No. 2, October–December, 1993, p. 41–52.

The article analyzes the institutions of customary family law according to the Kanun of Labëria and focuses especially on betrothal (engagement), which was not only a promise of marriage, but a binding legal agreement between the heads of the families. Breaching the agreement could result in serious consequences, including murder. The author draws a comparison with the regime of engagement in other Albanian *kanuns*. Also of interest is the analysis of marriage and its institution regulated in the Kanun of Labëria compared with similar instruments regulated in the Kanun of Lek Dukagjin, such as legal marriage, marriage upon reward, and kidnapping; whereas marriage by test was known under the KLD, but not in the south. The paper also delves into the structure of the Albanian patriarchal family and the relations between its members according to the Kanun of Labëria.

Anastasi, Aurela. E Drejta e Zgjedhjeve në Shqipëri në Vitet 1925–1939, No. 2, October–December, 1993, p. 69–77.

The article focuses on innovations regarding the modalities of the right to vote under the law of 1923, which created the conditions for the constitutional amendments of 1925. In this context, the author offers a detailed analysis of the law "On the election of the Chamber of Deputies" as it was approved by the Constitutional Assembly on February 23rd, 1925, published in the Official Journal on March 14th, 1925. This law constitutes a serious attempt to follow the developed models of European legislations on the electoral system and the right to vote.

3.3.1 *Studime Juridike*

Studime Juridike is a bi-annual publication of the Faculty of Law, University of Tirana, which has been publishing as of September 2001. The journal is available at the library of the Faculty of Law, University of Tirana.

Elezi, Ismet. Vështrim Historiko-Juridik për Veprën e Sh. K. Gjeçovit. Kanuni i Lek Dukagjinit. No. 1, 2001, p. 9–20.

The importance of Gjeçovi's work for the collection of the KLD constitutes the core of the paper, which also points out the regulatory role of customary law in Albanian society since ancient times. Another feature that the author highlights is related to "particularism", i. e., the development of different provincial *kanuns* sharing an ancient and common legal basis, adapted according to the dialects and traditions of different areas of the country. The paper also evaluates the contribution of local and foreign studies on Gjeçovi's work.

Anastasi, Aurela. Dita e Drejtësisë dhe 'Kanuni i Zhuriës'. Vështrim mbi Aktin që i dha Drejtësisë Shqiptare një Ditë Përkujtimore. No. 1, 2001, p. 71–81.

The paper highlights that the Law of Jury (*Kanun of Zhuri*) dated May 10th, 1913 and the Interim Law of the Civil Administration in Albania (*Kanuni i Përtashëm i Administratës Civile të Shqipërisë*) of November 22nd, 1913, constitute two of the most important acts adopted immediately after the declaration of independence. The Law of Jury laid the foundations for the organization of the justice system and judicial procedures, breaking away from the old Ottoman tradition. The author analyzes the Jury (eldership) as an expression of the people's participation in the administration of justice. It also delves into trial procedures, the organization of justice, the courts of first instance and the Court of Dictation, as well as the provisions for the development of a fair trial.

Omari, Luan. Zhvillimet Kushtetuese në Kosovë. No. 2, 2001, p. 14–24.

The author analyzes the provisions of the Constitution of Kosova of September 7th, 1990 and the referendum of 1991, in which 98% of Albanian voted for the independence and sovereignty of Kosova in response to Serbia's colonial policy. The paper discusses Kosova's interim constitutional framework for self-government, approved in May 2001, based on UN Security Council Resolution 1244 of June 10th, 1999 and the mandate of the United Nations Mission in Kosovo (UNMIK).

Luarasi, Aleks. Tradita Juridike e Popullit Shqiptar. No. 2, 2001, p. 33–43.

The author explores the legal tradition of the Albanian people as connected to the Illyrian-Albanian and Byzantine-Roman legal traditions, where Albanian customary law has served as an uninterrupted conduit. The latter coexisted first with the positive law of these regimes and later with the feudal law of the Ottoman Empire. The analysis also includes assessments of the legislation from the period of the communist regime, which is regarded as a step back in the field of law.

Salihu, Ismet. Ismet Elezi, Zhvillimi Historik i Legjislacionit Penal në Shqipëri. No. 2, 2001, p. 79–89.

The article provides a review of professor Ismet Elez's monograph "Historical development of criminal legislation in Albania" (*Zhvillimi historik i legjislacionit penal në Shqipëri*), and its contribution to the history of Albanian criminal law.

Anastasi, Aurela. Raporti midis Shtetit dhe Fesë në Çështjet e Lirisë së Besimit. Rasti i Shqipërisë. No.1, 2004, p. 10–34.

The article analyzes the legal framework for the relationship between the Albanian state and the country's religious communities, from the creation of the independent Albanian state in 1912. It highlights that the principles of state secularism and freedom of religion were embedded in the constitutional frameworks as of 1922, until 1976. After the Second World War, although freedom of religion remained a constitutional guarantee, restrictions imposed by other laws increased and in 1967 the control of the communist government over religious institutions was established by decree. The author highlights that this control was reinforced by Article 37 and Article 55 of the Constitution, adopted in 1976, which defined the principle of atheism and prohibited the creation of religious organizations. The author delves into the normative acts approved after the political changes of 1990 and the constitutional guarantee of freedom of belief in the Constitutional Provisions of 1991 and the Constitution of 1998. Of interest is also the analysis within the historical context of the Albanian legislation on the right of education within the perspective of the freedom of belief.

Puto, Arben. Marrëveshjet e 1926–1927, një Fazë e Re e Depërtimit Italian në Shqipëri. No. 1, 2004, p. 35–42.

The article deals with commercial agreements signed between Italy and Albania, which aimed at granting Italy and Italian companies concessionary contracts in strategic sectors of the country, such as oil and infrastructure. He notes that the economic penetration was also bolstered by the SVEA loan agreement (*Società per lo Sviluppo dell'Albania*), which would serve to create the Albanian National Bank. Also of interest is the legal analysis of the treaty between Italy and Albania, dated November 27, 1926. From a legal standpoint, the author considers this agreement as a hidden protectorate, which enabled Italy to intervene unilaterally in Albania's political, legal and territorial sovereignty, in violation of the principle of reciprocity. It also brought the reaction of third-party countries that had economic and geo-strategic interests in Albania, such as the British government.

Omari, Luan. Evoluimi i Sistemit Zgjedhor në Shqipëri. No. 2, 2004, p. 11–18.

The article provides researchers with an overview of the developments and legal changes that have occurred in the Albania's electoral system, starting with the first electoral law approved on February 4th, 1992 by the pluralist parliament, to the changes brought by the Electoral Code of 2003.

Sema, Eneida. Vështrim Historik mbi Trajtimin e Veprave Penale të Trafikimit të Femrave dhe të Shfrytëzimit të Prostitucionit, si Biznese të Paligjshme të Rrjeteve Kriminale. No.1, 2005, p. 228–238.

The author reviews the legal and historical evolution of criminal offenses related to trafficking of women and the exploitation of prostitution. The analysis includes the regime of Albanian customary law on the protection of life and honor of women, the penal regime against prostitution in the Penal Code of 1928, the penal codes of the communist period, approved respectively in 1952 and 1977, the new legal framework adopted after the 90s, law no. 8279, dated 15.01.1998 and law no. 8733, dated 24.01.2001 as amended.

Bushati, Endira. E Drejta Civile në Shqipëri gjatë Viteve 1944–1950. No.1, 2008, p. 65–89.

The article discusses the developments in civil law during the years 1944–1950, after the establishment of the communist regime. Part of the discussion is a particular moment in Albania's jurisprudence after the Second World War when the communist regime[3] undertook the review of all legislation in force, with the aim of abrogationing old norms and introducing a new revolutionary legal framework. This created a legal vacuum and major obstacle for the justice system. The article points out that to overcome this problem, interim acts[4] mandated that until the completion of the new civil legislation, the jurisprudence of the Plenum of the Supreme Court would serve as a precedent for the courts of lower levels in the resolution of similar conflicts, in absence of a new special legal regulation. Of interest is the historical trajectory of the legal amendments during the period 1933–1950, which brought radical changes to the civil law and its sub-branches.

3 Law no. 61, dated 17.05.1945, "On the Abrogation of the Legal Provisions Promulgated during Foreign Occupation", adopted by the Anti-Fascist-National Liberation Council of Albania".

4 Law no. 2359, dated 15.11.1956 "On Legal Actions and Obligations".

Katro, Kestrin. Një Vështrim Historik për Falimentimin. No.1, 2008, p. 323–357.

The second part of the article reflects the history of bankruptcy law in Albania, from its regulation in the sixth book of the Commercial Code of 1932 until the regime of law no. 8901, dated May 23rd, 2002 "On bankruptcy". The overview also includes law no. 7631, dated 29.10.1992 "On the bankruptcy of state-owned enterprises", which aimed at liquidating all state-owned enterprises that had operated in the country during the model of the centralized economy controlled by the state, which were in financial difficulties.

Muçollari, Orjona. Analizë e Ligjit nr. 8652, datë 31.07.2000 "Për Organizimin dhe Funksionimin e Qeverisjes Vendore". No. 2, 2008, p. 185–220.

Although the focus of the paper is the legal analysis of the law on the organization and functioning of the local government, the author provides an historical overview of the developments of the Albanian legal framework regarding the local governance and the fiscal decentralization.

Peto, Zhaklina. Lindja dhe Zhvillimi Historik i Sigurimeve Shoqërore në Botë dhe në Shqipëri. No. 2, 2008, p. 310–343.

The article delves into the historical development of the social security system in Albania, starting with the law "On Retirement and Pension for the Army and Civil Service", dated May 2nd, 1923, the Pension Law, no. 129 dated October 28th, 1927 and their by-laws. The paper provides the social insurance regulatory framework for the period 1946–1966, as well as law no. 7703 dated May 11th, 1993 "On social security", approved after the fall of communism.

Zaka, Kristina. Qytetet Shqiptare në Shek. XII–XV si Dëshmi e Qartë e Zhvillimit dhe Kulturës Mesjetare Shqiptare. No. 2, 2009, p. 91–119.

The article analyzes the main characteristics of medieval Albanian cities, their legal personality and development. The author deals with the governing institutions and applicable law in Albanian cities, the role of judges and notaries, as well as the economic and commercial relations between cities, using the example of the city of Durrës as an illustration.

Zaka, Kristina. Qytetet Shqiptare si Komuna Autonome në Mesjetë dhe Disa Aspekte të Administrimit më Vete të tyre. Vështrim Krahasues. No. 2, 2011, p. 47–73.

In this article, the author analyzes from an historical and legal standpoint the characteristics of Albanian cities as autonomous civic municipalities, with legal personality stemming from their statutes. The analysis delves into the role of the statute, the main characteristics of the autonomy of these cities, the functions of the council, legislative, administrative and judicial bodies, as well as the role of the notary. The right of the cities to administer the income secured by real and personal obligations is considered as an expression of their autonomy.

Likmeta, Engjëll. Vështrim Analitik i Krimeve kundër Personit në Kanunin e Dibrës. No.1, 2014, p. 97–112.

The text reflects the legal regulation of the Kanun of Dibra for two types of murders—murder for revenge and murder for blood feud, with details explaining the differences between these two institutions. The author also considers ambush and the criminal responsibility for aiding and abetting a murder, where he expands on the category of the hit man (*dorasi*). The analyses also cover the norms regulating murder after reconciliation, involuntary murder, and other types of murders that occurred in a family setting.

Treska, Katrin. Likmeta, Engjëll. Një Vështrim Historiko-Juridik mbi Institutin e Familjes sipas së Drejtës Zakonore. Rasti i Kanunit të Labërisë. No.1, 2015, p. 61–74.

The article analyzes the regime of family relations under the Kanun of Labëria (KL), including the roles, rights and obligations of family members. The focal points are the rights of the master and mistress of the house. The analyses include the KLD regime for some institutions of family law, such as guardianship, adoption, engagement, marriage and its types.

Basholli, Arbër. Likmeta, Engjëll. Kundërvajtja, një Përqasje midis Normës Kanunore dhe Bashkëkohore. Rasti i Kanunit të Labërisë. No. 2, 2016, p. 21–36.

The authors deal with the regime and evolution of the misdemeanor in the Kanun of Labëria. The process and rules for the investigation, the conduct of the trial, and execution of the decision are part of the analysis provided.

3.3.2 *Jeta Juridike*

The journal *Jeta Juridike* is a bilingual publication in Albanian and English of the Albanian School of Magistrates (SM) since 1999. As a journal of the institution that prepares and trains magistrates, the articles accepted for publication aim at supporting judges and prosecutors with the best theoretical and practical standards for interpreting the law. The same selection criteria also apply for other publications of the SM. For this reason, topics focusing on the history of law are scarce. However, the following articles offer at least in part an overview on the history of Albanian law, for the timeframe specified in each title.

Boti, Federica. Pasuritë e Bashkësive Fetare në Shqipëri midis Kthimit ose Kompensimit të Pronave të Konfiskuara dhe Blerjes së Pronave të Reja. No. 3, 2015, p. 27–50.

The author, a researcher at the University of Bologna, offers an overview of the historical developments on the legal regime of the properties of the religious communities in Albania, since the declaration of independence until the present day. The analysis is structured in four parts: the regulatory legal framework after the declaration of independence, the agrarian reform and the expropriation of communities by the communist regime, the legal regime after the democratization processes of 1990, and the return of the property of religious communities expropriated by the communist regime. In addition to this analysis, the article offers a comparative perspective on the history of these processes in other countries of the former socialist camp.

Hajdari, Artan. Largimi dhe Përjashtimi i Ortakut. No. 1, 2019, p. 67–93.

The article focuses on theoretical and practical aspects of the sell-out and squeeze-out rights in companies; in one subsection it offers a brief historical overview of the changes in the legislation on commercial companies since 1992.

Anastasi, Aurela. Mërkuri, Erind. Zgjerimi i Aksesit të Individit në Gjykatën Kushtetuese në Kuadrin e Reformës në Drejtësi (2015–2016). No. 3, Tiranë, 2018, p. 5–21.

The article analyzes the evolution of the instruments available for individuals' access to the Constitutional Court after the constitutional reform of 2016. Part of this overview, although within a relatively narrow time frame, is dedicated to the historical development of an individual's access to constitutional judgment since 1991.

Nushi, Kaliona. Aksesi i Individit në Gjykatën Kushtetuese. No. 1, 2019, p. 31–53.

The individual's access to the Constitutional Court is explored in this article as well. The author discusses in one subsection the historical evolution of the individual's right to constitutional appeal, according to all the constitutional changes since 1990.

Çani (Methasani), Eralda. Natyra e Mjeteve Ligjore Administrative. Vështrim Krahasues mes Kodit të Ri të Procedurave Administrative dhe atij të Vitit 1999. No. 3, 2019, p. 23–43.

The primary focus of the paper is on the novelties of the new code of administrative procedures compared with the previous legislation. In one of the subheadings, a partial overview of the historical development of this branch of law is also provided, by highlighting the most important features of the codes that have been implemented throughout different periods.

Islamaj, Fatri. Vështrim Analitik mbi Shoqëritë me Përgjegjësi të Kufizuar sipas Kodit Tregtar të Vitit 1932 në Shqipëri. No.1, 2020, p. 27–51.

The article provides a quick historical overview of the regulation of commercial entities, from the declaration of independence through the following stages of evolution of this regime: monarchy; communism; and, after the fall of this system, the establishment of the market economy. The author deals in detail with the features of private limited liability companies in the first commercial code, approved in 1932, comparing them to the current legal regime.

3.3.3 *'Avokatia'*

The Journal "Avokatia" is a scientific publication of the Albanian Chamber of Advocacy which began publication in the spring of 2011. The aim of the journal is to create a forum where lawyers, jurists and various scholars publish and analyse different legal issues of practical importance. Among these publications are some of a historical nature. The journal is available and can be consulted at the Library of the Faculty of Law, University of Tirana.

Sinani, A. Petrit. Pak Histori për Institucionin e Mbrojtjes. No. 3, July 2012, p. 197–204.

The article analyzes from an historical point of view the development of the institution of legal defense, from the declaration of Independence of Albania in 1912 until the establishment of the democratic system in 1990; and reviews the main acts that have regulated legal defense. Among other points, the author dwells on the first law no. 85 dated June 15th, 1931 "On Advocacy", approved on December 30th, 1922, after the Congress of Lushnja, which established the dependence of lawyers on the Ministry of Justice. The legal profession continued to be exercised until 1967, where by decree no. 4277, dated June 20th, 1967, this profession was abolished. This interruption of practicing the legal profession lasted around 20 years, until the fall of the communism and was regulated again by the decree no. 7382, of May 8th, 1990.

Lika, Afërdita. Maho, Besnik. Evoluimi tek ne i Institutit të Bashkëpronësisë mes Bashkëshortëve. No. 4, October 2012, p. 71–94.

Through this article the researchers have the opportunity to learn about the evolution of the institution of co-ownership between spouses, from the legal regime provided under the Civil Code of 1929 to the main changes made in the Family Code in 2003. Initially, the authors review the regulation of co-ownership legal relations between spouses in the period 1929–1948. Of interest are the regulations of this institute in the first years of communism in Albania, in particular the amendments approved during the years 1948–1955, and the novelties brought by the laws no. 6340, dated June 29th, 1981 "On the Civil Code of the People's Socialist Republic of Albania" and no. 6599, dated June 29th, 1982 "On the Family Code of the People's Socialist Republic of Albania". In conclusion, the authors dwell on the advancement of this institute with the radical changes of the 1990s and those that occurred in the Family Code in 2003.

Jaho, Saemira. Lindja e Institutit të Dorëzanisë në Jurisprudencën Shqiptare. No. 5, January 2013, p. 145–155.

In Albanian law, the institution of bail has been implemented according to provisions made by the Arab Civil Code, under the institution known as "*Mexheleja*". This regulation was implemented in Albania until the adoption of the Civil Code of 1929, which regulated the institution of bail pursuant to the best models implemented in the European countries. In this article, the author focuses on the analysis of this institute according to the definitions made in the Civil Code of 1929, also reflecting the analysis of various Albanian authors.

Sinani, A. Petrit. Institucioni i Avokatisë në 100 Vjet Drejtësi Shqiptare. No. 6, April 2013, p. 9–19.

In May 1913, the "Provisory Government" undertook a fundamental reform regarding the organization of the justice system. In this context, the institution of "Kadi" inherited from the Osman law was replaced with the "Courts of First Instance" of the sub-prefectures and the reorganization of the legal profession. The efforts to regulate this profession in an appropriate manner date back to November 28th, 1917, when the General Directorate of Justice under the leadership of Avni Dabulla drew up the document entitled "*Zadhanje*". The author reflects in an historical context on the development of this profession, its limitations, and its interruption during the communist dictatorship until its revival in 1990. In addition, the author treats in chronological order the amendments made until the beginning of the 2000s.

Elezi, Ismet. Kultura Juridike Shqiptare në Lidhje me Gjuhën Shqipe, Letërsinë dhe Folklorin. No. 12, October 2014, p. 143–156.

The article presents a particular analysis of Albanian legal culture and its evolution, based on a deep heritage of unwritten, traditional folk legal culture that draws on the Albanian language and literary tradition, linked to the rich folklore of Albania. The article summarizes the norms of customary law and those created by the professional legal culture, where scholars have contributed to the enrichment of these norms.

Koçollari, Irakli. Një Status i Rrallë Ligjor i Qytetit të Drishtit i Vitit 1468. No. 13, January 2015, p. 149–155.

The statutes of medieval Arbërian cities testify to the development of medieval Albanian society, in a way similar to other European cities. In this paper, the author emphasizes the importance of studying the statutes of Drishti's cathedral as documents with rare historical-legal value and evidence of the heritage of the ancient Albanian legal tradition. The author highlights the uniqueness of this act, due to the fact that it combines canonical Arbërian cultural law with medieval positive law and Albanian customary law.

Xhufi, Pëllumb. Statutet dhe Kanuni në Mesjetën Shqiptare. No. 14, April 2015, p. 185–197.

The statutes of medieval Albanian cities, including that of Drishti's Cathedral, are clear evidence of the coexistence of feudal, civil and customary law. According to the author, this coexistence dated back to the beginning of 1272 in the acts signed by Karli I Anzhu of Sicily with the representation of the Albanian feudal nobility of Arbër and the representation of the citizens of Durrës. Among other points, the author analyzes several institutes of customary law regulated in the statute of the city of Shkodra, such as that of honor, oath and blood payment.

Molla, F. Vladimir. Rrethanat e Krijimit dhe Veprimit të Kodit Civil të Parë Shqiptar. No. 15, July 2015, p. 177–188.

The author highlights the circumstances in which the first Albanian Civil Code was approved. The Code was drafted affording to the models of codes implemented in Western European countries. Of interest is the analysis of the civil law applied in the territory of Albania, characterized by a multitude of civil rights applied in the country. The practice and coexistence of three different religious belief systems, in reference to three different legal systems, have influenced and enriched the legal regimes applied in the country.

Jahollari, Heralda. Zhvillimi i së Drejtës së Sigurimeve. No. 19, July 2016, p. 171–186.

The author analyses from an historical point of view the evolution of laws on insurance and the creation of a complete legal framework. The article reviews the regulation of insurance law in our country since the amendments made under the Civil Code of 1929 until the legal reform brought by the law no. 52/2014 "On the activity of insurance and reinsurance".

Bendo, Vasil. Kanuni i Labërisë në të Drejtën Zakonore Shqiptare. No. 123, July 2017, p. 183–196.

The author emphasizes the importance of studying the Kanun of Labëria and the regulatory role played by its norms and principles, referring to the work of various Albanian authors who have conducted research in this field. In particular he underlines the contribution of Professor Ismet Elezi who has identified the characteristics and originality of this Kanun.

Sinani, A. Petrit. Institucioni i Avokatisë Përballë Regjimit Komunist. No. 25, January 2018, p.173–184.

With the decree no. 4277, dated June 20th, 1967, the institution of advocacy was replaced by legal aid offices, under the competence and supervision on the Supreme Court. For about 23 years, this profession could not be practiced until 1990, when democracy was restored. The author discusses the evolution of this institution in an historical context, by analysing a series of legal acts that the communist regime adopted with the aim to limit and completely abrogate this profession. Of interest is the analysis of decree no. 1143, dated September 11th, 1950 "On Lawyers' Collectives" or the Circular of the Ministry of Justice dated August 21st, 1966, which, among other points, determined for lawyers what physical work they should perform.

Sherifi, Elmaz. Refleksione mbi 100 Vjetorin e Kongresit të Durrësit. No. 27, July 2018, p. 179–195.

The article analyzes in a historical context the main events that preceded the development of the Congress of Durrës, the institutions that emerged from it and the role of the Albanian elite in organizing the Congress on December 25th, 1918. The author dwells on the nature of the National Assembly of Durrës, which combined the norms of customary constitutional law and positive law in coexistence to strengthen the constitutional legitimacy of this body.

Kondi, Thimjo. Reflektime për Traditën, Aktualitetin dhe të Ardhmen. Në Vitin e '90 të Kodit Civil të Parë Shqiptar. No. 32. October 2019, p. 157–178.

The author reflects the circumstances and the historical events in which the Civil Code of 1929 was adopted, with attention to its modernizations based on the analysis of published historical-legal studies of the time. The author further dwells on the issues and interpretation of the Civil Code of 1994 and the need for its amendments.

Elmazi, Sherif. Kur Nisi Themeli i Institucioneve të Shtetit Demokratik në Shqipëri. No. 33, January 2020, p. 219–234.

This article analyzes the historical conditions for the organization and establishment of Albania's institutions during the Congress of Durrës on December 25th, 1918, and the creation of the Government of Turhan Pasha. In particular, the author dwells on the characteristics of Albanian institutions after the Lushnje Congress on January 21st, 1920.

Skrame, Olti. Njëzet e Dy Vjet Kushtetutë e Republikës së Shqipërisë. No. 35, July 2020, p. 199–228.

The focus of this article is analysis of the main amendments of the Albanian Constitution in a historical and chronological context. The author further brings to the reader the jurisprudence of the Constitutional Court and interpretations of its various provisions.

Skrame, Olti. Kontratat e Humbura nga Kodi Civil i Vitit 1929. No. 38, April 2021, p. 205–218.

Readers have the opportunity to obtain a better knowledge of several contracts initally regulated in the Civil Code of 1929. The author analyses the consequenses of the new Albanian Civil Code of 1994, approved after the fall of communism; also reviewed are the effects of this reform on some contracts that underwent fundamental changes, or were no longer regulated under the new regime.

Muratej, Andi. Transferimi i Sistemit të Paraburgimit në Varësi të Ministrisë së Drejtësisë. No. 43, July 2022, p. 183–204.

The author analyzes the evolution of the detention system in the Albanian legislation since the 1990s until the most recent amendments, which were implemented in accordance with European legislation. The article references some of the innovations of the law no. 7692, dated March 31st, 1993 "For an appendix to the Constitution law" no. 7491, dated April 29th, 1991, "On the main constitutional provisions" as well as on the transition of the prison system from the dependency of the Ministry of the Interior to the Ministry of Justice. Also of interest is the analysis regarding the rights of citizens in the Albanian detention system.

3.3.4 *Studime Historike*

The journal *Studime historike* has been among the publications of the Institute of History of the Albanian Academy of Sciences since 1964. Its articles focus on the history of Albania and touch upon different domains, including law. As of 2007, its editions are published online and are freely accessible to readers.[5] Until the 1990s, scientific articles were accompanied by a summary in French, after which summaries in English began to prevail. We reference in chronological order articles that discuss the history of the state and law in Albania. Scholars should be mindful of the standard mandatory ideological tones imposed on the writings published before 1990.

Puto, Arben. Disa Probleme Juridike të Pavarësisë Shqiptare. No. 1, 1965, p. 3–29.

The recognition of the Albanian state in the international arena following the international developments of 1913–1914 are at the core of this article's legal analysis. The neutrality of the Albanian state and the status of Albania during the First World War are part of the discussion.

Shkodra, Zija. Statuti ma i Vjetër i Esnafeve në Krahinat e Ballkanit nën Sundimin Turk. Kanunorja-Shexherea e Esnafit të Tabakëve të Elbasanit (14 maj 1657). No. 2, 1965. [Documents], p. 119–148.

The paper delves into one of the oldest statutes in the Balkans, which belongs to a guild in the town of Elbasan (*Esnafit të Tabakëve*). The statute, or *shexhereja* according to the Ottoman terminology, was written in Ottoman Turkish during the mid-17th century and contains valuable information about the Albanian guilds' organization during this period. The author analyzes the economic and social circumstances in which this document was drawn up and focuses on the analysis of its provisions. It documents the organization of the guild and its way of functioning under Turkish rule. The document, as the only copy of this type that survived the ages, constitutes an important resource for scholars.

Mitrushi, Llambrini. Kodiku i Manastirit të Shën Kozmait. No. 3, 1965, p. 175–182.

The article analyzes the Codex of the Monastery of St. Kozma, which contains ample data not only on the ecclesiastical aspects of the life of this monastery, but also on private legal relations and administrative matters under its jurisdiction. The author notes that the codex reflects the life of the Myzeqe area in the first half of the 19th century; and that it records marriage contracts from 1819 to 1843, divorces, betrothal contracts, wills and a number of other legal acts. He emphasizes the fact that the data recorded in the codex show that the sultans had recognized the right

5 http://asa.edu.al/site/ih/?page_id=826 [last access 05.09.2023].

of self-administration to the Monastery of Saint Kozma, according to the customs and canons of their non-Muslim faith (Orthodox Christian). The article analyzes the family law customs of the region of Myzeqe, and explores the text of some of the contracts registered in this codex. The article is accompanied by a summary in French.

Zojzi, Rrok. Aspekte të Kanunit të Skënderbeut të para në Kuadrin e Përgjithshëm të së Drejtës Kanunore. No. 4, 1967, p. 173–182.

The article analyzes the Kanun of Skanderbeg on the assumption that all Albanian *kanuns* have a shared legal foundation, despite being independent organic units. Throughout his paper, the author draws comparisons between the Kanun of Skanderbeg and other Albanian *kanuns*.

Pepo, Petraq. Materiale Dokumentare mbi Veprimtarinë e Zantaçinjëve të Korçës e të Voskopojës në Shek. XVIII–XIX. No.1, 1967, p. 165–182.

The paper brings to the reader's attention parts of the Codex of the Metropolis of Korça and Selafor of 1707. The focus of the paper is the tradition and requirements for conducting professional training with an experienced master (*usta*) in the Korça region. Researchers also find important information about the organization and functioning of guilds (*esnafeve*). At the end of the paper there is also a summary in Greek.

Nova, Koço. Pozita e Gruas sipas së Drejtës Zakonore të Labërisë. No. 2, 1969, p. 101–114.

The role of the Albanian woman in socialist society and the need for her emancipation are addressed in the article, highlighting the impact of the old customary law on her life. The article considers examples from the provisions of the Kanun of Papa Zhulit, which recognized the right of the husband—but not of the wife—to request the dissolution of the marriage, a rule that was also extended to engagements of minors. The absence of women's property rights under the customary law is illustrated by the fact that the wife did not have rights over her own properties, and if a deed of donation was made to her, the latter was merged with the property of the household. The author draws attention to the qualitative reform of the Kanun of Laberia by Idriz Suli, which provided women with the opportunity of generating income from their work; in agricultural production, in cutting wood, and in gardening. The paper is accompanied by a short summary in French.

Hysi, Gramoz. Krijimi i Aparatit të ri Shtetëror gjatë Luftës Nacionalçlirimtare. No. 1, 1970, p. 65–77.

In this paper, the author delves into the creation of the National Liberation Councils and the General Council, as organs of the new administrative apparatus of the Communist Party. The paper contains a short summary in French.

Hysi, Gramoz. Organizimi i Shtetit Shqiptar sipas Vendimeve të Kongresit të Lushnjës. No. 2, 1971, p. 3–22.

The article presents the main aspects of the Statute of Lushnja, which defined the state organization and the monarchy as a temporary form of governance in Albania. The author analyzes the reasons why this governing model was chosen and its main characteristics, focusing on the role of the Supreme Council (*Këshillit të Naltë*).

Nova, Koço. Hetimi dhe Gjykimi i Çështjeve sipas Kanunit të Labërisë. No. 2, 1971, p. 99–123.

The paper analyses the regime of investigation of criminal offenses and the conduct of trials under the Kanun of Labëria. It highlights the initiation of investigation by the elders, and the procedures for delivering a final decision. The paper is accompanied by a summary in French.

Nova, Koço. Aspekte nga Veprimtaria Gjyqësore Revolucionare gjatë Luftës Nacionalçlirimtare. No. 4, 1971, p. 95–124.

The paper delves into the organization and activity of the partisan courts, from their embryonic creation in the army units during the Second World War, until the liberation of Albania. The paper focuses on the issuance of specific acts and instructions from the army leadership, the proceedings of these trials, and illustrates with some of the decisions they delivered. The article is accompanied by a summary in French.

Doci, Pal P. Të Dhëna për 'Djelminë' e Shalës në Kapërcyell të Shekullit të XX. No. 4, 1972, p. 33–50.[6]

The paper focuses on the institution of the "youth of the tribe" (*Djelmia*), also known as the Commoners (*Vegjëlia*), as an important institution of the customary law of the North; especially in the plain of Dukagjin, where the Kanun specified that no decision of the elders or the chiefs could be implemented without the consent of the commoners. This latter category included all men capable of carrying and using weapons, who had the right to participate in the assembly and were not considered leaders according to the definitions of the Kanun. The author reflects the activity of the commoners of Shala (*Djelmia e Shalës*) and the criteria for membership. The paper is accompanied by a summary in French.

Ballvora, Shyqyri. Një Vështrim Historik mbi Legjislacionin Kushtetues të Paraçlirimit. No. 2, 1976, p. 71–77.

In this paper, clearly written within the ideological framework and under censorship, the developent of the governance of the Communist Party (CP) is analyzed from the perspective of the time. The analysis encompasses the CP's decisions in the Congress of Përmet (May 24–28th, 1944), which was regarded as the event that laid the foundations for the dictatorship of the proletariat.

Frashëri, Kristo. Mbi Kanunin e Skënderbeut. No. 2, 1977, p. 125–143.

---

6 This article can be find as [Separate] at the National Library with the code: Ar 17 11 C.

In this paper, the author deals with the main developments of the Kanun of Skanderbeg in a historical context, focusing mainly on its regime of public law and the social organization of the highlanders. The paper has a summary in French.

Shkodra, Zija. Kontribut për Historinë e Panaireve Shqiptare. No. 4, 1977, p. 149–184.

The article highlights the role of Albanian fairs in increasing the volume of commercial exchanges in both civic and rural economies. The author analyzes their development from the Byzantine Empire in the year 996, their subsequent reorganization during the Ottoman occupation, and their splendor in the mid-nineteenth century. The author provides details on the cities and the way in which fairs were organized, their main characteristics, as well as a quick glance at trade exchanges with other Balkan provinces and beyond, with Venice, Ragusa, Thessaloniki, Austria, or Germany.

Hysi, Gramoz. Sistemi i Ri i të Drejtave dhe i Detyrave të Shtetasve dhe Zhvillimi i tij Historik. No.1, 1979, p. 3–30.

The article discusses a series of documents from the period of the World War II national liberation, which later laid the foundation for the adoption of the Constitution of Albania on January 11th, 1946, and the declaration of the form of governance as a People's Republic. The author analyzes in an historical context the main elements of the Constitution, its amendments and the changes brought about by the new system of rights and obligations of Albanian citizens, based on the dictatorship of the proletariat.

Zamputi, Injac. Autonomitë e Qyteteve Shqiptare të Principatës së Balshajve. No. 3, 1980, p. 169–187.

The statutes of Albanian cities as constitutional acts; their regime on the institutional, administrative and judicial organization of the cities; as well as the relations between the cities are at the core of the article. From the analysis of the statutes, the author highlights the influence of the Venetian state. The article is accompanied by a summary in French.

Nova, Koço. Ndërtimi dhe Veprimtaria e Gjykatave të Shtetit në Vitet 1912–1939. No. 3, 1981, p. 99–125.

The paper deals with the historical development of the courts in Albania during 1912–1939. The analyses encompass the institutions of customary law of the (court of the elders) and the assemblies which influenced the traits of the new judicial system after the declaration of independence. Legal acts of the time, such as the Law of Jury (*Kanuni i Zhurisë*), and other laws passed after independence, illustrate the evolutionary stages of the justice system. The discussion extends to the organization and functioning of the regular courts and the religious courts during the time of King Zog. The paper has a summary in French.

Zoga, Kadri. Hilmia, Sabah. Organizimi i Sistemit Unik Financiar në Shërbim të Ndërtimit të Socializmit në Shqipëri (1944–1948). No. 1, 1983, p. 41–60.

The reform of the financial system according to the Albanian socialist ideology and the reforms undertaken for this purpose by the Communist Party after rising to power in 1944 are discussed through references to the main legal acts adopted in the first years of the installation of this system. Some of the cited acts include the decree-law of 1947 on state-controlled economic enterprises, the ordinance on the creation of insurance funds, the nationalization of private banks, the creation of the Albanian State Bank, and the approval of its organic law in 1945. A short summary in French is provided at the end.

Thëngjilli, Petrika. Aspekte të Shthurjes së Sistemit të Timarit në Tokat Shqiptare Shek. XVII–XIX. No. 3, 1986, p. 169–192.

The article provides an overview of the decline of the *timar* system in Albania and the transition to the feudal system. The interpretation provides the categorization of land ownership in Albanian territories, (i) in state lands (*erazi-mirie*), which included the sub-categories of *timar, zeamet* and *hasse*; (ii) in the category of private lands of special feudal lords (*erazi-mülk*); (iii) as well as in the lands of religious institutions Muslim (*eraz-i waqf*). It then provides accurate data on the number of *zeamet(s)* and *timar(s)* in Albania, at the end of the 16th century and the pursuant changes.

Ushtelenca, Ilir. Organizimi Politiko-Administrativ i Pashallëkut të Janinës. No.1, 1987, p. 137–156.

The author presents the main aspects of the state organization of the Pashalik of Ioannina and its function as a state independent from the Ottoman Empire. The paper is accompanied by a summary in French.

Karabeci, Kaliopi Naska. Organizimi i Drejtësisë dhe i Xhandarmërisë në Shtetin Kombëtar Shqiptar (1912–1914). No.1, 1990, p. 131–150.

The paper delves into the series of acts aimed at organization of the state apparatus after the declaration of independence. It focuses on the organization and functioning of the Ministry of Justice, of the judiciary, of the Ministry of Internal Affairs, of the gendarmerie and their role during this period.

Pulaha, Selami. Mbi Statusin Juridik Fiskal të Tokave Shtetërore – Mirie, në Viset Shqiptare gjatë Shekujve XV–XVI. No.1, 1990, p. 191–198.

The author analyzes in an historical context the features of state ownership of land and its fiscal status during the 15th–16th centuries, as well as the development of legal relationships over these lands. The work reflects the classification of the types of land owned by the state, where it mentions arable land, fields and meadows, distributed according to the model of *timar, ziamet* and *hass*. Using as illustration acts from 1583 and 1613, it presents the taxes and duties applied on the various contracts concluded for the use of the land, where religious appurtenance influenced the level of the levied tax.[7] The author also analyzes the legal status of the *raja* lands, which referred to the possessions of the land by the Spahis and members of the military class, as well as the taxes of the *raja* peasants.

Nova, Koço. Zbatimi i Normave Kanunore mbi Kishën dhe Fenë në Malësinë e Veriut. No. 4, 1990, p. 137–152.

This article presents the provisions of Albanian customary law that regulated the status and rights of the Catholic Church in the northern Albanian highlands, with a particular focus on the regime of the Kanun of Lek Dukagjin in this matter. The discussion encompasses the influence of the church in Albanian customary law, whereby illustration is provided with the Church's opposition to marriages by test.

Buda, Aleks. Problemi i Shteteve Mesjetare në Shqipëri. No. 4, 1990, p. 153–162.

"The issue of Albanian medieval states" is a presentation by the chairman of the Albanian Academy of Sciences at the Congress of the International Association of Southeast European Studies (AIESEE) in Belgrade in 1984, published originally in "*Studia Albanica*", no. 2 of 1986. It explores the medieval cities of Albania at the end of the 12th century and the beginning of the 13th century. According to the author, these formations not only testify to the consolidation of the Albanian ethnic element, but are also an indicator of the early development of Albanian feudalism under Byzantine rule. The article demonstrates the slow creation of the Albanian feudal class, in a period of history for which archival sources are few. The author highlights the differentiation between Albanian feudal lords, the strengthening of their political positions and their influence on the creation of independent state structures.

Bata, Nezir. Pronësia Tokësore dhe Shitblerja e saj në Zonat Fushore dhe Kodrinore të Sanxhakut të Elbasanit (Vitet 1880–1900). No. 3–4, 1991, p. 55–72.

The author analyzes the agrarian reforms in the Sanjak of Elbasan within the framework of the *tanzimat* reforms. He reviews evidence of the large fiefdoms of *beys* and the largest fiefdom owners of this *sanjak*. The paper provides a summary in English.

Baci, Nevila. (Editor) Kazaja e Delvinës. Nga Defteri Osman i Sanxhakut të Delvinës i Vitit 1583. Translated and Transcribed in Albanian by Buharaja, Vexhi. No.1–4, 1992, p. 121–151.

The cadastral register for the year 1583, drafted by the administration of the Ottoman Empire, provides data for the Sanjak of Delvina, which also included the provinces of Gjirokastra and Çamëria. The author highlights that this province included 52 villages, a monastery, a church and 5 plots of land. The register details

7 The author notes that according to the Kanun of the Sanjaks of Vlora in 1583 and Ohrid in 1613, the use of the land by the Christian peasant was conditional on the payment of two supplementary types of taxes, in addition to the generally applicable tax of tithes on agricultural products.

data on the *raja* villagers of the Sanjak of Delvina, the state land, the feudal estates, estates of the *zaims* of the *sipahis*, and other categories. Also of interest are several judicial acts of the judges of Delvina and Kurvelesh.

Bata, Nezir. Sistemi i Taksave dhe i Detyrimeve në Ekonominë Bujqësore të Sanxhakut të Elbasanit (Fundi i Shek. XIX–Fillimi i Shek. XX). No.1–4, 1995, p. 43–58.

"The system of taxes and dues of the agricultural economy of the Sanjak of Elbasan. End of the 19th century–beginning of the 20th century" is based on archival documents from the fond of Shefqet Vërlaci (year 1912, ds. 14 p. 18) and other documents from the Central State Archive. The referenced documents are financial registers, registers of revenues of the feudal lords *(çifligarëve)* of Elbasan, as well as documentary fonds of the Bank of Elbansan and Peqin. The author points out that the *tanzimat* reform affected the Albanian peasantry little or very little, as it continued to be subject to the system of taxes and duties according to the old regime reflected in this paper. The paper is accompanied by a summary in English.

Anastasi, Aurela. Iliria dhe Organizimi i saj nën Perandorinë Romake. No.1–2, 1999, p. 7–22.

The author analyzes the organization of the province of Illyricum during the Roman rule as a praetorian prefecture, focusing on the influence that Roman law and Romanism have had on the Illyrian areas. During the occupation by the Roman Empire, according to the author, Illyria maintained a certain level of autonomy in governance based on the *lex provinciae*. The article reflects the installation of the protectorate regime in Illiricum, the organization of the province during the rule of different Roman emperors and the impact of the reforms they undertook. The paper is accompanied by a short summary in English.

Kordha, Hysen. Parlamenti Shqiptar–Institucionalizim i Unitetit Politik Shtetëror dhe i Demokracisë Parlamentare Shqiptare. No.1–2, 2000, p. 133–138.

The article analyzes the first pluralist parliament in Albania in 1921 and the role of the two largest parliamentary groups, the People's Party and the Progressive Party.

Prifti, Kristaq. Pavarësia dhe Shteti Shqiptar. No. 1–2, 2003, p. 123–136.

The paper delves into the activity of the temporary government of Vlora during its 14-month tenure, along with the acts it adopted for the purpose of organizing the institutions of the independent state of Albania.

Anastasi, Aurela. Vështrim Bashkëkohor i së Drejtës Shqiptare të Viteve 1912–1914. (Referat-Kumtesë). No.1–2, 2003, p. 159–170.

The paper analyzes the main characteristics of the Albanian state and law after the declaration of independence (1912–1914). It highlights the features of parliamentarism in the Assembly of Vlora, the evolution of Albanian law during this period and the efforts to draft a new contemporary legislation. The discussion focusses on three main issues: (i) the most important characteristics of governance during the first months after the declaration of independence; (ii) the period known as the "Condominium" (October 1913 to January 22nd, 1914), because of Albania's the intertwined governance by the Albanian government and by the International Control Commission; (iii) the period of "Xenocracy", which refers to Albania's rule by foreign factors, namely the International Control Commission and the six-month monarchy of Prince Wied.

Hysi, Shyqyri. Legjislacioni Fetar në Shqipëri në Vitet 1929–1949. No. 1–2, 2006, p. 169–180.

The paper analyses the legislation on religious communities during the period 1929–1949, including the law "On religious communities" decreed by King Zog on August 8, 1929, which determined the state's secularism, the legal changes that occurred after the Second World War and the establishment of the communist regime. The author reflects on the declaration of human rights, approved by the National Anti-Fascist-Liberation Council (KANÇ) in Berat (1944); the Constitution of 1946, which guaranteed freedom of conscience and the exercise of religious activity; and the law of 1949, which brought fundamental changes and manifested increasing institutional repressions and attempts to dissipate religious freedoms.

Baze, Ermal. Institucionet Qeverisëse të Komunës së Shkodrës (Gjysma e Parë e Shek. XIV). No. 3–4, 2008, p. 19–38.

The paper explores the governing institutions of the city of Shkodra, regulated by its statutes during the first part of the 14th century. It focuses on the role and broad powers of judges and the College of Judges, the role of the Council of Shkodra in governing the city and the powers of the king. It also draws a comparison with other models of medieval municipal organization in the Italo-Dalmatian region.

Duka, Kolçe Valentina. Nga Presidenca në Monarki: Çështje të Legjitimitetit. No. 1–2, 2010, p. 199–212.

The presentation delves into the internal political developments and diplomatic relations preceding the proclamation of the monarchy in Albania in 1928, and the reasons why this form of organization was not chosen in 1925, when Zog had the necessary majority in parliament. The author notes the fact that Prince Wied had never abdicated, and that this could have affected diplomatic relations and weakened the legitimacy of the new monarch. Whilst international recognition of the Albanian state strengthened gradually in 1928, the Constitutional Assembly unanimously approved two constitutional amendments declaring Albania a monarchy and granting the royal crown to the President of Albania, Ahmet Zog.

Malaj, Edmond. Kanonikët Mesjetarë të Kapitullit të Katedrales së Drishtit sipas Statuteve të saj. No. 1–2, 2015, p. 7–26.

The author analyzes the statutes of the Chapter of the Drishti Cathedral and the organization of its entities. The paper explains that the canon regulars were clerics of the Catholic religion, including women, who lived within a community according to canonic law. Around the 10th century, these communities developed into cathedral chapters or monasteries, supported by the revenues of the chapters. From there, the canon members were divided into two categories: canon regulars (*canonici regulares*) and secular canons (*canonici seculares*). The article notes that the former lived according to the rules defined in the statutes of the Chapter of the Drishti Cathedral, while the secular canon belonged to the class of the nobility. The article provides details on the status of each category and analyzes the applicable statutes.

Nano, Ilirjana. Marrëveshja si Burim i së Drejtës në Pashallëkun e Janinës. 1915 (Referat-Kumtesë). No. 3–4, 2015, p. 63–180.

The article highlights that in the Pashalik of Ioannina, the applicable legal regime was a product of interaction between the legal systems of Ottoman law, Albanian customary law, legal acts issued by Ali Pasha, as well as the ecclesiastical norms of different religions. The article draws attention to the international agreements as well as to internal regulations, as part of the positive law in this *pashalik*. These stand as evidence of the Pasha's efforts to create a state entity autonomous from the High Gate. The quoted materials are part of the Archive of Ali Pasha Tepelena.

3.3.5 Studia Albanica

Studia Albanica is a journal of the Albanian Academy of Sciences since 1964. The purpose of this journal has been to present important works in Albanology, by Albanian authors, to an international audience of scholars. Hence the articles, which appear here in translation into various foreign languages, were usually published previously in other Albanian journals or books. The selected articles which follow are writings by historians and legal scholars on matters of history or the law and state. The titles reflect the language in which they were published. As of 2019 publications can be accessed online.[8] The complete collection (1964–2010) is available at the Institute of History, whilst parts of the collection are also in the National Library and the Library of the Faculty of History, University of Tirana. A reminder of the ideological tone of articles published before 1990 is applicable on these writings as well.

Puto, Arben. Sur les Relations Extérieures du Gouvernment Démocratique de 1924 en Albanie. No. 2, 1964, p. 28–45.

The article analyzes the relations of the government of Fan Noli of June 1924 and its isolation at the international level. The paper highlights the reforms and progressive efforts undertaken by the Noli government.

Puto, Arben. La Question du Statut International de l'Albanie Devant la Société des Nationes et la Conférence des Ambassadeurs. No. 2, 1965, p. 18–44.

---

8 https://albanica.al/studialbanica [Last access 12.09.2023]

The paper offers a window into the perspective of public international law on the legal debates regarding Albania's admission to the League of Nations in December 1920, the international recognition of the Albanian government and the consequences of this recognition.

Naçi, N. Stavri. Le Pachalik de Shkodër Considere dans son Développement Economique et Social au XVIII e Siecle. No.1, 1966, p. 123–144.

The author explores the economic development of the Pashalik of Shkodra in the 18th century. It depicts the feudal class organization, the development of cities due to commercial exchange, and the role of the Albanian feudal families.

Zija, Shkodra. Le Marché Albanais au XVIIIe Siecle. No.1, 1966, p. 159–172.

The article analyzes the empowerment of Albanian cities in the 18th century, as well as the important contributions of the artisan and entrepreneurial classes. It reflects the main features of trade within cities, trade exchanges between Albanian cities, as well as with other cities in the region and beyond. It also provides statistical data on the commercial activity of Albanian cities.

Pulaha, Selami. Materiaux Documentaires en Langue Osmano-Turque des Archives Albanaises concernant l'Albanie du XVIe au XIX Siecle. No.1, 1966, p. 187–198.

The article interprets documents from the period of Ottoman Albania. The documents are part of the fund of the National Library and the Central State Archive. They are categorized into four funds: (i) The fund of the collection of registers of court decisions of Berat and Elbasan (from the second half of the 16th century to beginning of the 20th century), those of Tirana, Korça, and Peqin (19th century to the beginning of the 20th century), as well as other court decision classified according to territorial division, of the cities of Shkodra, Vlora, Delvina, Ioannina, Ohrid, and Kruja; (ii) the fund of the feudal system, whose documents testify to the replacement of the *timar* system with that of the fiefdom; (iii) the fund for the organization of corporations (guilds) in Albanian territories and their statutes (iv); and the fund on Ottoman legislation applicable in Albanian territories.

Elezi, Ismet. Sur la Vendetta Albanie. No.1, 1966, p. 305–318.

The paper analyzes the reasons for the survival of the institute of blood vendetta, despite the radical economic and social changes in the country and the state efforts to eliminate it. The author draws a comparison with the efforts of Ali Pasha Tepelena to limit it through sanctions under the norms of positive law.

Toçi, Veniamin. Les Contradictions entre les Puissances Impérialistes sur les Pétroles Albanais (1920–1925). No.1, 1967, p. 157–168.

The article analyzes a series of concession and monopoly contracts on strategic sectors of Albania granted in favor of foreign companies, mainly from Italy and the UK, during the period 1920–1925.

Pupovci, Syrja. Le Formalisme et la Besa dans le Droit des Obligations du Coutumier de Lek Dukagjine. No. 2, 1968, p. 143–150.

In contrast with the plentitude of legal writings interpreting the institute of *besa* as a public law instrument that guaranteed the protection of the guest, or in criminal law; little is known about its application in the domain of private (civil) legal relationships. The author analyzes the norms of the Kanun of Lek Dukagjin regarding the use of *besa* in civil obligations, and the legal consequences of giving and breaching *besa*.

Omari, Luan. De Certaines Caractéristiques de l'Etat Albanais de 1912–1913. No. 2, 1970, p. 25–29.

The author argues that the declaration of independence and the institutional construction of the new state was the doing of the Albanian people, and opposes the viewpoints that attribute these to international decisions. The author analyzes the legal nature of the acts of the National Assembly of Vlora, as acts of a constitutional and state-forming nature.

Naçi, N. Stavri. Le Facteur Albanais dans le Commerce Balanique du XVIIIe Siècle. No. 2, 1970, p. 37–42.

The article focuses on commercial and artisanal exchanges in Albania during the 18th century, and their influence on the development of Albanian cities. It explores the markets' structures and trade exchanges in the Balkans, illustrated with the example of several Albanian guilds (*esnafe*), including their commercial volume and export-import activities.

Mejdiaj, Bajram. Le Droit de la Femmes a Demandé la Rupture du Mariage. No.1, 1971, p. 91–101

The author discusses the evolution of women's rights, with a particular focus on the right of divorce. The analysis encompasses the Albanian customary law, the Civil Code adopted in 1929 and the legislation adopted after the installation of the communist system.

Pulaha, Selami. Les Kastriote Devant la Conquete Ottomane des Années 1420–1430. No.1, 1971, p. 104–127.

The article highlights the changes that the *timar* brought into the Albanian feudal system, in the social as well as the economic spheres.

Pulaha, Selami. Traces de L'influence des Insurrections Albanaises sur les Actes de l'Administration Ottomane des Années 30 du XV e Siecle. No. 2, 1971, p. 25–34.

This article explores the records of the register of Sanjak of Arvanit between the years 1431–1432, and the changes that the Ottoman administration introduced in relation to the *timar*. It also notes that at this time the *timar* system had not yet penetrated the northern areas of Albania.

Islami, Selim. L'Etat Illyrien, sa Place et son Rôle dans le Monde Mediterraneen. No. 2, 1972, p. 77–104.

The article considers various opinions of Albanian and foreign authors on the origin and characteristics of the Illyrian state, as well as the Illyrians' relations with their neighbors.

Puto, Arben. Les Gouvernements Démocratiques de 1924 et la Solution des Différends sur la Délimitation des Frontières de l'Albanie. No. 1, 1974, p. 31–53.

The article analyses the diplomatic efforts of Fan Noli's government for determining the state borders of Albania.

Elezi, Ismet. La Lutte contre les Survivances du Droit Coutumier en Albanais. No. 2, 1975, p. 33–42.

The article highlights the reforms undertaken by the public administration during the communist regime in efforts to limit the application of customary law in Albania. Especially targeted were several early institutions of this law, such as marital and family relations, as well as the settlement of disputes between tribes.

Shkodra, Zija. Les Esnaf ou Corporations dans la vie Urbaine Balkanique des XVII–XVIIIe Siècles. No. 2, 1975, p. 47–74.

The author presents the evolution of corporate organizations of Albanian craftsmen and merchants throughout a century, focusing on their characteristics and the role they played in protecting and promoting the interests of their members. The paper contains interesting data, especially for researchers of the history of commercial law.

Year 1976, No. 1

In this year, the new Constitution was approved, which declared Albania a People's Socialist Republic and drastically deepened the class struggle, repression and state control, eliminating the fundamental rights of Albanian citizens such as the right of religion and that of property. It paved the way for the further isolation of Albania and the progressive tightening of measures against those perceived as political opponents, turning the country into a giant prison. The issue contains several articles, written in propagandistic language, mainly by very high figures of the communist nomenclature who lacked a legal background. The writings, in addition to the state-approved legal interpretations of the provisions, provide a window into the essence of the new dictatorship, now consolidated and sanctioned in the constitution—the dictatorship of the proletariat. These writings reflect the political and economic ideology on which the new constitution was based, the supremacy of the dictatorship of the proletariat, the class struggle, the elimination of private property, and the centralization of economy and power.

Pulaha, Selami. Formation del Region de self Government dans les Malaises du Sandjak de Shkodër aux XV–XVIIe Siècles. No. 2, 1976, p. 174–179.

The author analyzes in an historical context the development of the self-governing areas of Shkodra's Highlands during the Ottoman rule, and the consequences that this autonomy had in the development of Albanian customary law.

Toci, Veniamin. Les Débuts de la Collectivisation Socialiste des Petits Producteurs Urbains (1945–1950). No. 1, 1977, p. 35–43.

The article deals with collectivization as the model for organization of the Albanian economy under the Albanian socialist model, and the changes it brought especially in the craft sector and in production. The paper provides an overview of agricultural cooperatives and their evolution.

Banja, Hasan. Toçi, Veniamin. Le Développement de l'Industrie Socialiste en Albanie dans les Années 70. No. 2, 1977, p. 25–36.

The authors analyze the transformative process of the transition of the country's economy from a feudal organization model to an industrial country, and the role in this transition of the agrarian reform and organization of the economy according to the model of cooperatives and programmed planning.

Pepo, Petraq. Les Matériaux des Cartulaires et leur Importance pour l'Histoire du Pays. No. 2, 1977, p. 163–170.

The publication presents a series of documents and codices drawn up during the rule of the Ottoman Empire that illustrate the organization of economic, social and political life in the regions of Korça, Voskopoja, Vithkuq, Delvina and Gjirokastra. These documents reflect the physiognomy of the economy of medieval Albanian cities and life in the Orthodox community. The codes constitute a rich source of information on the implementation of the *timar* system in these territories.

Zija, Shkodra. Aspects du Marché Albanais Durant la Période de la Renaissance Nationale. No. 2, 1978, p. 93–107.

The author analyzes the characteristics and development of the internal market, fairs, bazaars, commercial and craft activities of Albanian cities during the period of national renaissance. The growing market exchanges, according to the author, played an important role in the formation of economic communities during this period, and later in catalyzing capitalist relations. The author analyzes the feudal structure of the land and the decline of *timars* in 1839, which influenced the spread of large land ownership structures and the development of the monetary economy.

Puto, Arben. Introduction à l'Histoire Diplomatique de l'Indépendance Albanaise. No.1, 1979, p. 13–28.

The author analyzes the issue of Albania's declaration of independence in an historical and diplomatic context.

Omari, Luan. Le Pouvoir d'État en tant que Questions Centrales dans la Lutte Antifasciste de Libération Nationale du People Albanais. No. 2, 1979, p. 55–58.

The author explores the radical changes that followed the end of the Second World War and the rise into power of the Communist Party. He draws a comparative analysis between Albania's trajectory and the issues of popular revolution in other countries of the communist bloc.

Toçi, Veniamin. Le Mode de Vie des Campagnes Albanaises de nos Jours. No. 2, 1979, p. 37–142.

The author analyzes the consequences of the agrarian reform of 1946, the socialist collectivization of agriculture and the newly emerging social relations, both in the city and in the countryside. The article reflects the socialist ideology on the centralized economy and the state-owned means of production.

Misja, Vladimir. De la Répartition Rationnelle de l'Industrie en Albanais, No. 2, 1979, p. 151–157.

The article analyzes a special aspect related to the rationing of industry in order to respond to the needs of the country. This principle guided the quantity and type of production according to the centralized planning of the economy. The article provides information and statistics on the issues addressed.

Zamputi, Injac. Le Potentiel Economique d'une Maison Feudale Albanaise au XVe Siècle. No.1, 1980, p. 209–222.

The author analyzes a notarial act dated April 28th, 1547, which certifies legal transactions performed on June 24th, 1515, in Drishti. The transactions, which are attached to the notarial act, are related to the expansion of the properties of an Albanian feudal family and its possession rights before the occupation of Drishti by the Ottomans.

Spahiu, Hëna. La Circulation Monétaire du Ve au XIII Siècles, Indice des Relations Ėconomiques sur le Territoire Albanais. No. 2, 1982, p. 109–114.

The paper sheds light on archeological discoveries which attests to well-developed economic relations, as well as monetary circulation in Albanian territories during the 5th century, as an important aspect of urban life. The interpretation is accompanied by the analysis of monetary circulation in the Albanian territories during the Byzantine rule and its evolution.

Hysi, Gramoz. Le Statut Amende de Lushnje. No. 2, 1984, p. 109–124.

The author highlights the significance of the Statute of Lushnja, approved on January 31, 1920, and provides a legal analysis of the temporary monarchist model of governance.

Buda, Aleks. Mittelalterliche Staatenbildungen in Albanien. (Shtetet Mesjetare në Shqipëri). No. 2, 1986, p. 3–14.

The author argues in his writing that the first Albanian state formations date back to the end of the 12th century and the beginning of the 13th century. He further reflects on the positions of various Albanian and foreign researchers on the timeframe of creation of genuine state structures in Albania during the Middle Ages, before the creation of the feudal state of Skanderbeg.

Malltezi, Luan. Le Monopole de l'Etat de Venise sur les Cereales en Albanie au XVe Siecle. No.1, 1987, p. 139–160.

The paper demonstrates the primacy of the Principatte of Topia and the Principate of Balshaj amongst the most important political organizations of the 15th century, and highlights their efforts to create a centralized Albanian feudal state. These efforts were opposed not only by the Ottoman Empire, which sought to extend its rule throughout the Western Balkans, but also by the Republic of Venice, which aimed to maintain its control over Albanian coastal cities. These interests are illustrated with the case of the monopoly held by the Republic of Venice on Albanian grains and the trade relations between the two countries. The issue can also be found at the BFHFUT.

Verli, Mariglen. A Propos d'un Accord Conclu en 1924. No. 1, 1988, p. 105–118.

The author analyzes the historical context of the agreement between Ahmet Zogu and Nikolla Pasiç signed in 1924, which according to his views violated the country's independence. He illustrates this by citing Article 1, where Albania commits to join in union with Yugoslavia, Article 4 which determined that the Albanian Ministry of War would disintegrate and Albania would cease constructing its own national army, and Article 11 that determined the withdrawal of the Albanian Orthodox Church from the Patriarchate of Constantinople and its union under the hierarchy of the Orthodox Church of Belgrade.

Pulaha, Selami. Die Wissensschaftlichen Forschungen uber die Osmanische Periode des Mittelateres in Albanien (15 Jahrhundert bis Anfang des 19 Jahrhunderts). No. 2, 1988, p. 57–76.

The author interprets Ottoman sources to explain the position of the Albanian feudal class and the Albanian peasantry, which culminated with the resistance of Skanderbeg. Through these documents, the author reflects on the consequences of the establishment of the *timar* system in the Albanian territories, as well as its use as means for mitigating the resistance of the inhabitants.

Sadikaj, Dilaver. Le Développement des Coopératives Agricoles, un pas Important de l'Ordre Cooperatif a la Campagne (Fin des Années 1950–1070). No.1, 1989, p. 71–87.

The article analyzes the development of cooperative ownership as one of the forms of socialist ownership based on the dictatorship of the proletariat. The analysis traces its historical evolution from small collective economies to agricultural cooperatives, which eventually followed the model of a planned economy.

Omari, Luan. Droit Populaire et Droit Officiel en Albanie: XIXe et XXe Siecle. No. 2, 1990,[9] p. 79–86.

The author analyzes the coexistence and interaction between the Albanian customary law and the positive law from the Middle Ages, during the Byzantine and the Ottoman rule. It further delves into the coexistence of the customary law with positive law approved after the independence of 1912, during the period of Fan Noli's government, and the latter's attempt to extend the mandate of the positive laws to the Northern highlands, which were regulated according to customary law. The author notes the coexistence of Albanian customary law and positive law throughout the reign of Ahmet Zog and during the first years after the Second World War. Exceptionally, the communist regime, despite abrogating all previously

9 The issue can also be found at the National Library: BK Shp 60 12 C.

adopted norms in January 1946, allowed for the application of customary law in the resolution of the civil law disputes, until the adoption of a new legislation.

Pulaha, Selami. Sur le Statut Juridique-Fiscal des Terres d'Etat Mirie dans les Regions Albanaises au Cours des XVe–XVIe Siecle. No. 2, 1990, p. 87–96.

The article presents the features of the legal status of land during the 15th and 16th centuries, after the establishment of the *timar* system in Albania and the legal position of the *raja* peasant. It also discusses the dues levied on the land, illustrating with the *kanunname* of the Sanjak of Vlora (1583) and of Ohrid (1613).

Malltezi, Luan. La Ville et la Campagne dans la Societe Albanaise des XIe–XVe Siècles. No. 2, 1990, p. 98–106.

The author provides details on the social and economic organization in Albanian villages and cities during the 11th–15th centuries, highlighting class division and their characteristics.

Nasi, Lefter. La Conference Nationale de Mukje et les Conditions Historiques et Politiques dans Lesquelles elle fut Tenue. No. 1–2, 1992,[10] p. 37–47.

The article analyzes from an historical perspective the conclusions of the Conference of Mukje, (August 2nd, 1943), which culminated in the creation of the National Salvation Committee and the agreement on the cooperation of political forces in joint resistance against the German occupation. Of interest are the differing stances of the parties in this conference regarding the status of Kosova, as well as the compromise reached between them for the resolution of this issue by means of a popular referendum, after the end of the Second World War.

Stavileci, Esat. The Dissolution of former-Jugoslavia and the Albanian Question. No. 1–2, 1994,[11] p. 59–64.

The paper focuses on the analysis of the status of Kosova after the developments of 1990 and the dissolution of former Yugoslavia. Although not a legal analysis, the article is of interest to legal scholars as it analyses the early trajectory of Kosova's independence.

Lalaj, Ana. The Issue of Kosova between the National and International Impulses in the Last Decades of the XX Century. Year 1995–1999,[12] p. 53–64.

The status of Kosova according to the constitution of Yugoslavia of 1974, and the historical events of 1981 regarding the status of Kosova along with the arbitrary violent actions of the Serbian authorities, are at the core of this paper. The author dwells on the demands for Kosova's independence within Yugoslavia as an expression of the principle of self-government. The paper examines the historical course of events after the rise to power of the Serbian president Milosevic in 1985,

10 The issue can also be found at the National Library: BK Shp 60 14 C.

11 The issue can also be found at the National Library: BK: Shp 64 25 E.

12 The issue can also be found at the National Library: BK: Shp 64 27 E.

the limitation of the rights of Albanians—including those previously recognized in the Constitution of 1974—and the role of the international community in the resolution of the conflict between the parties.

Milo, Paskal. L'Incident du Canal de Corfou (1945–1946). Year 2001, p. 63–78.

The author analyzes in an historical and diplomatic context the incident of the explosion of the English ship that passed over mines located in the southern sea of Albania in 1946, a conflict that resulted in a case brought before the International Court of Justice.

Nasi, Lefter. Causes et Consequences des Protestations de 1981 en Kosovë. Year 2002,[13] p. 61–80

The paper provides important data to understand in an historical context the status of Kosova under the federal state of Yugoslavia from the end of the Second World War, as well as the political platform of the Albanians' peaceful protests of March-April 1981. Of interest is also the analysis of rights and duties of citizens of Kosova according to the Constitution of the Federal State of Yugoslavia of 1974.

Kristaq, Prifti. L'Independence et l'Etat Albanais. Year 2003,[14] p.1–16.

The author analyzes in chronological order the events that influenced the declaration of Albania's independence on November 28th, 1912 in Vlora, and the activities of the Provisional Government of Vlora. The paper focuses on the decisions of the Conference of Ambassadors in London on the Albanian issue, the memorandum presented at this conference by the Albanian delegation, as well as the decision of July 29th, 1913 for the creation of the International Control Commission.

Anastasi, Aurela. Up-To-Date Approach to the Albanian Law of the Period 1912–1914. Year 2003, p.17–29.

The paper focuses on analysis of legal acts adopted by the Albanian government in the period between 1912–1914. These acts reflect the legal features of the emerging Albanian state, which, as the author underlines, were those of a state with a monarchical character. Also of interest is the analysis of Albania's Independence in relation to the historical events taking place on the European stage at that time.

Andromaqi, Gjergji. Kodikët e Shqipërisë (Les Codex D'Albanie), une Publication de la Direction Générale des Archives d'Etat. Year 2004,[15] p.147–150.

The writing refers to the publication of the codices of Albania from the Central State Archive, prepared by a group of scientific researchers under the supervision of Prof. Dr. Sinan Shabani, and analyzes the importance of this publication. The author notes that the codices constitute a source of primary importance for the Albanian cultural heritage and emphasizes the importance of their study.

13 The issue can also be found at the National Library: BK Shp 67 68 E.

14 The issue can also be found at the National Library: BK Shq 66 45 C.

15 The issue can also be found at the National Library: BK: Shp 66 64 C.

Prifti, Kristaq. La Proclamation de l'Indépendance de l'Albanie et la Question d'un Etat Albanais Unifie. Year 2007, p.1–12.

The article delves into the declaration of Albania's independence and the main features of the emerging Albanian state. It further analyzes the evolution of the issue of Kosova's independence and the developments of 1998–1999.

Bicoku, Kasem. L'Étendue a l'Est des Possessions des Kastrioti. Year 2007, p.13–35.

Based on Ottoman cadastral registers of the 15th century, especially the cadastral registers of the Sanjak of Ohrid dated March 1467, the article considers the registered lands owned by Gjon Kastriot and his sons within this Sanjak and elsewhere.

Meta, Beqir. Albania in the Projects for a Balkan Federation in the Mid XX Century. No.1, Year 2008, p. 41–65.

The author offers an historical analysis of the events at the end of the Second World War, especially around May 1944, and the idea of creating a federal state as a means to prevent the spread of communist ideology in the Balkan countries.

Sinani, Shaban. Les Statues de Drisht et le Droit Urbain au Temps de l'Arbanon. No.1–2, 2009, p.13–35.

The article focuses on the Statute of the Cathedral of Drishti and emphasizes the fact that the tradition of governing cities and churches through statutes had already been established and that the Albanian territories were influenced by the era of European humanism.

Verli, Marenglen. La Question Kosovare, l'Intervention de l'OTAN et la Stabilité dans la Region. No.1–2, 2009, p. 105–117.

The paper explores the issue of Kosova, from the decisions of the Conference of Ambassadors of London in 1913, when the Great Powers decided to truncate the territories of Albania, until the declaration of its independence in 2008.

Frashëri, Kristo. L'Assemblée Nationale de Vlora et ses Principes. No. 2, 2012,[16] p. 5–9.

The declaration of Albania's independence from the Ottoman Empire and the creation of a pro-European government marked an important moment in the country's political and legal life, which the author discusses in this paper.

Schmidt-Neke, Michael. Warum Albanien kein Staat Werden Kann-Argumente gegen die Staatliche Unabhangigkeit. No. 2, 2012, p.159–175.

In this publication the author analyzes the establishment of the Albanian state as the last national state created in the Balkans. Among other points, he highlights the fact that the request of the Albanian people for Albania's independence was articulated late and was not unanimous, as there were objections to the secession from the High Gate by a part of the Albanian population. The author analyzes the

16 The issue can also be found at the National Library. BK: Shp 77 74 F.

first major political program of the Albanian national movement, the positions of the currents that demanded complete independence, and those who were for autonomy under the Ottoman Empire. The author draws a comparative analysis 100 years later to the debate on the status of Kosova and the international opinion on this issue.

Dushku, Ledia. Le Protocole de Corfou et Les Albanais (Mai–Juin 1914). No. 1–2, 2013,[17] p.103–123.

The paper focuses on the diplomatic relations between Albania and Greece in May–June 1914. The topic is of interest to legal scholars with respect to the terms of the agreement signed by both countries for the determination of the southern border between them. The author analyzes the Albanian-Greek negotiations, the recognition of Albania's independence by Greece, the establishment of diplomatic relations between the two countries and the role of the International Control Commission.

Baze, Ermal. The Social Status of Albanian Women in the XIV–XV Century. No. 2, 2019,[18] p. 17–42.

The article offers a comparative analysis on the social status of Albanian women in the 14th –15th centuries, in main Albanian cities and the rural areas. The author explores the status, rights, and judicial and criminal protection of women in the autonomous Albanian cities of Shkodra, Durrës, Ulqini and Tivari, based on documentary sources of the time. In comparison to the provisions of customary law applied during the same time in rural and mountainous areas, the author concludes that women in cities had more rights and guarantees under the legal framework of the city statutes. The article also provides information about the Albanian nobility during the end of the 14th century and the first half of the 15th century, their privileges, as well as their right to emigrate after the Ottoman occupation of the Albanian territories.

Meksi, Aleksandër. Arbanense Bishopric, Gjon Kastrioti and the Quarrel about the Borders of the Bishopric of Lezha. No. 2, 2019, p. 3–43.[19]

The article, although primarily an historical analysis, is of interest to legal scholars of ecclesiastical law. It analyzes the contention between the Arbanense bishopric and the Lezha bishopric, over the legal status and administration of several Catholic churches claimed by both bishoprics. The author notes the elements of the dispute between the two bishoprics, which are apparent in the letter of Gjon Kastriot addressed to the Republic of Venice, on April 3rd, 1407.

---

17 The issue can also be found at the National Library: BK: Shp 68 66 E.

18 Articles are freely accessible at https://albanica.al/studialbanica [last access 10.30.2023].

19 Idem.

3.3.6 *Studime Albanalogjike*

The journal *'Studime Albanalogjike'* is a scientific publication of the Faculty of History and Philology of the University of Tirana, which has been publishing since 1996. It can be found at the library of the Faculty of History and Philology, University of Tirana, and at the National Library. The following articles focus on matters pertaining to the history of law.

Nathanaili, Petrit. Disa Çështje të Pozitës Ndërkombëtare të Shqipërisë (1944–1946). No. 2, 1996, p. 27–37.

The paper provides an historical analysis of Albania's international status, its diplomatic relations with the Great Powers, concerns over the issue of its borders and its geopolitical orientation during the years 1944–1946.

Mullai, Abaz. Pozita Social-Ekonomike e Juridike e Fshatarit në Ekonominë Kooperativiste të Tipit Sovjetik. No. 1, 1997, p. 7–19.

The author analyzes the types of "agricultural community" according to the Albanian socialist system. The author notes that the cooperation model began in Albania in 1946 as a form of cooperation between villagers which enabled them to share the costs of production. In the first years after the installation, the agricultural community coexisted with the agricultural cooperative soviet model until it was completely replaced by the latter. The article provides their main features and the differences from agricultural cooperatives.

Laçi, Sabri. Aspekte të Zbatimit të Ligjit për Tokën dhe të Bujqësisë Familjare. No. 1, 1997, p. 177–183.

The process of transition from the system of state property and centralized economy to the free-market economy and private ownership system after the return of political pluralism in 1990, is the central focus of this paper. The author delves into the implementation and consequences of the law "On Land" dated July 31st, 1991 and provides a historical overview of the change of the regime of ownership over the agricultural land.

Shahu, Ajet. Veçori të Fillimit të Luftës për Likuidimin e Pronës Private në Fshat në Vitet 1946–1948. No. 2, 1997, p. 7–24.

The paper deals with the steps taken to create the collectivist system of agriculture in Albania during 1946–1948, which is also known by the term "farm labor cooperation" (*kooperimi* fshtatar *i punës*). The author points out that this system was introduced with features that differed from the Stalinist model of collectivization, becoming completely unique in its kind.

Shahu, Ajet. Kushtet Historike të Lindjes së Kooperativave Bujqësore dhe Funksionimi Organizativ i tyre. No.1, 1999, p. 63–82.

In this article as well, the author revisits the topic of the history of the collectivization of agriculture, a process which began at the end of 1946 after the installation of the communist system in Albania, and which was aimed at eliminating private property. The article analyzes the social and political circumstances in which the agrarian reform of 1946 and the subsequent process of collectivization were implemented. The author delves into the Congress of the Albanian Communist Party, held on February 15th–17th, 1949, which considered the collectivization of agriculture as one of the pillars of the new socialist economy, legislating the gradual elimination of private property in agriculture and the creation of collective property.

Shahu, Ajet. Incidenti i Korfuzit dhe Bllokimi i Marrëdhënieve Shqiptaro-Britanike. No.1, 2009, p. 255–240.

In this article, the author delves into Albania's relations with the United Kingdom throughout the 20th century and highlights two moments which marked history. The first concerns the London Conference of 1913 and the definition of the borders of the new independent Albanian state. The second impactful issue discussed in the paper is the incident of the Corfu channel in 1946, and the decision of the International Court of Justice on this issue, dated April 9, 1949.

Duka, Ferit. Shteti Osman dhe Krishtërimi në Tokat Shqiptare (Shek. XVI–XVIII). No.1, 2011,[20] p. 1–5.

The author discusses the relations between the different religions in Albania during the rule of the Ottoman Empire, the practice of uniatism[21] and secret Christianity, as forms of resistance against the *jizya* tax system, which was considered the main factor of the spread of the Islam among Albanians. The analysis encompasses the impact of the international treaties signed between the Ottoman Empire and European states, such as the agreement of Karlowitz (1699), that of Passarowitz (1718), and Sistova (1791), which regulated the rights of the Catholic believers under the Ottoman rule and their applicability in the Albanian lands.

Duka, Valentina. Institucionet Fetare gjatë Mbretërimit të Ahmet Zogut: Një Vështrim i Legjislacionit të Kohës (1928–1939). No.1, 2011, p. 47–56.

The presentation analyzes the development of the legal regime on religious institutions and the attention that King Zog dedicated to them since the proclamation of the monarchy. The article explains the law of July 16th, 1929, which regulated the administration of religious communities under an increased control of the state, and the opposition to this control from the religious communities. It also mentions the approval of the statute of the Albanian Muslim Community on the Regulation of Albanian Bektashians. Of interest is the analysis of the law on the removal of the burqa for women and the standardisation of the head covering for men, introduced as a personal initiative of King Zog. The article provides accurate references of the Official Journal in which the mentioned legal acts have been published.

---

20 The articles in this issue of the journal are based on the references held at the scientific conference "State and Religion in Albania 1912–2000" ('Shteti dhe Feja në Shqipëri 1912–2000').

21 The union of an Eastern Rite church with the Roman Church in which the authority of the papacy is accepted without departing from the liturgies or government by local patriarchs (Encycl. Britannica).

Rama, Fatmira. Shteti dhe Njohja e Kishës Autoqefale Shqiptare (1922–1929). No.1, 2011, p. 65–79.

Based on archival documents, the author delves into the recognition of the Albanian Autocephalous Orthodox Church (KOASH). It discusses the founding documents of the Assembly of Berat of September 1922, the proclamation and statute of the Albanian Autocephalous Orthodox Church, which established five metropolises and determined that their heads would be of Albanian origin. The article also discusses the Second Albanian Pan-Orthodox Congress of 1959, in which the new Statute of KOASH was approved.

Gurakuqi, Romeo. Çështja e Shkollave Private në Shqyrtimin e Lidhjes së Kombeve dhe Gjykatës Ndërkombëtare të Drejtësisë në Hagë, 1933–1936. No.1, 2011, p. 101–132.

The article deals with the relations between the Catholic Church and the Albanian state in the ten-year period of 1920–1930. It focuses on the restrictions on the religious schools imposed by the government of King Zog and the efforts of the Catholic Church to oppose this position. Of interest is the analysis of the recommendation of the Permanent Court of International Justice on this issue, taking into consideration the declaration made by the Albanian Government upon its membership in the League of Nations as an independent state guaranteeing the freedom of religion.

Sala, Gëzim. Shyqyri, Hysi. Reforma Agrare Komuniste dhe Pasojat e saj në Ekonominë Vakëfnore të Shqipërisë. No.1, 2011, p. 203–215.

After the installation of the communist regime, the latter adopted an agrarian reform (law no. 108 dated August 29th, 1945) which had a direct impact on the properties of religious communities. The article delves into the legal specification of these properties, the expropriation of religious entities and the culmination of this process with the decree of the Presidium of the People's Assembly no. 4262 dated April 1st, 1967, which determined the expropriation of all movable and immovable properties of religious communities and the transfer of these assets to the party committees and agricultural cooperatives.

Çuka, Fatjon. Kuadri Juridik i Shtypit: Krahasimi mes Mbretërisë së Zogut dhe Demokracisë Aktuale. No. 3, 2010,[22] p. 118–124.

The author analyzes the legal framework on the press, during a period spanning from the Congress of Lushnja (1920), during the rule of Ahmet Zog (1925–1939), and after the fall of the comunist regime in 1990. Attention is drawn to the "Press Law", approved on January 20th, 1931, and the pertinent bylaws, for which their respective reference at the State's Central Archive is provided. The author draws a

22 The issue can also be found at the National Library: BK: Alp 8 16 C.

comparison between this legal framework and the one adopted after the 1990s: the law no. 7756 "For the press" approved on October 11th, 1993, as amended.

In volume No. 4, Year 2013, the journal published the presentations of the scientific conference entitled "Albania in 100 Years of Independence" held in November 2012. From these publications, for the purpose of this bibliography, we mention: **Nexhipi, Adelina.** The Legal Basis of the Albanian State, 1990–2011, p. 21–34; **Jusufaj, Elvina.** The Evolution of State Formation in Kosovo, p. 163–176; **Yzeiraj, Elvina.** The Albanian Economy during the Period of Ahmet Zog, 1925–1939, p. 177–192; **Gishti, Engjëll.** Reflections on the Proclamation of the Albanian Monarchy, 1928, p. 189–202; **Halimi, Enis. Shabani, Fahredin.** Political Acts of National Renaissance and the Declaration of Independence (1908–1912), p. 203–215.

3.3.7 *Buletini Shkencor*

"Buletini Shkencor" is a publication of the Faculty of Economics and the Faculty of Law of the University of Shkodra "Luigj Gurakuqi", published during 2007–2015. Issues can be accessed at the Library of the University of Shkodra (*Biblioteka e Universitetit të Shkodrës*). These articles were published in Albanian, accompanied by an abstract in English.[23]

Bërhana, Ilir. E Drejta e Zgjedhjeve në Shqipëri në Periudhën 1912–1939. (The Election Right in Albania During the Period 1912–1939). No.1, 2007, p. 111–130.

The author discusses the history of the legal regime on elections and voting rights in Albania, from the declaration of Independence of Albania until the occupation of Albania by Italy. It underlines the general principles and the different electoral systems that were implemented under the different forms of regimes of the Albanian state during this period.

Bërhana, Ilir. Elezi, Alketa. Zhvillimi Teorik i Kodit Penal Shqiptar në Lidhje me Veprat Penale të Narkotikëve. (Theoretical Development of the Albanian Criminal Code Concearning the Criminal Acts related to Narcotics). No. 2, 2008, p. 253–261.

The authors explore the trajectory of the penal legislation on narcotics in Albania. The historical overview includes the regime of the Criminal Code of Zog, the Criminal Code of 1952 and the Criminal Code of 1977.

Bërhana, Ilir. Disa Aspekte të Përgjithshme të së Drejtës Zakonore Shqiptare. (Albanian Canon Law. General Issues). No. 3, 2009, p. 7–16.

This article delves into the research of different authors on the nature and origin of the Kanun of Lek Dukagjini (KLD). It emphasizes the works of Valentini, Castelleti

23 The English titles of the quoted articles reflect the title of the respective abstracts as published.

and Durham on the importance of the Albanian customary law and its distinctive elements.

Bërhana, Ilir. Instituti i Martesës sipas Kanunit të Lek Dukagjinit. (Institute of Marriage under Canon of Lek Dukagjini). No. 5, 2011, p. 249–256.

The KLD norms on the institution of marriage are at the core of the paper. The author analyzes the provisions and the types of marriages regulated by the KLD, its economic importance and the position of women under this regime.

Likmeta, Engjëll. Treska, Katrin. Një Ndalesë në Statutet. (Normat Penale në Statutet e Shkodrës). [A Short Insight in the Statutes. (Criminal Provisions in the Shkodra Statutes)]. No. 8, 2014, p. 117–129.

The article explores the penal regime of the statutes of Shkodra. In particular, the authors dwell on the provisions which aimed at guaranteeing the protection of life and health; the criminalization of murder and of various types of wounding; other intentional injuries, such as punching and beating; as well as criminal offenses against honour.

Kokaj, Gasper. E Drejta e Votës dhe Zgjedhjet në Statutet Shqiptare të Periudhës 1912–1944. (The Right to Vote and the Elections within the Albanian Statutes of the Period 1912–1944). No. 9, 2015, p. 39–50.

The author discusses the different electoral systems adopted in Albania since the declaration of Independence until the end of the Second World War. Particular attention is given to the regime of the constitutional laws of this period, known as *statutes*: (i) the organic statute of Albania of 1914; (ii) the statute of the Albanian state of 1922; (iii) the founding statute of the kingdom of 1925 and 1928. It notes the coexistence of the Western electoral models and the preservation of the influence of Ottoman law until 1944.

3.3.8 The Interdisciplinary Journal of Research and Development

"The Interdisciplinary Journal of Research and Development" is a publication of the University of Durrës 'Aleksandër Moisiu', as of 2014. Its articles are in English and can be freely accessed online, hence we cite herewith only the titles of the articles.[24] The selected titles pertain to the focus of this bibliography.

Kume, Andon. A Historical Overview and Analysis on the Albanian Right to Vote 1912–1991. Vol. 8, no.1, 2021, p. 1–9.

Kocaqi, Elena. The Democracy in the Albanian Canonical Law and in the Ancient Greece. Vol. 8, no.1, 2021, p. 58–67.

24 https://www.journal-uamd.org/index.php/IJRD [last access 05.06.2023].

Ahmetaj, Lavdosh. Karaj, Kamila. The Nature of the Legal Acts Produced by the Government Essentially Alienated the Nature, Spirit and Constitution of the Albanian State 1944–1948. Vol. 10, no. 1 (Special Issue), 2023, p. 150–158.

3.3.9 Albanian Studies

The journal "Albanian Studies" is a publication of the Academy of Albanological Studies. The journal publishes in English scientific articles by Albanian authors, which have been published in Albanian elsewhere. The articles can be accessed online, and hence we cite herewith only the titles of the articles that, although not primarily focused on the analysis of legal acts, can nonetheless be of interest to legal scholars.[25]

Malaj, Edmond. Some Aspects form Shkodra's Medieval Economy. No. 2, 2020, p. 55–85.

Saraçi, Alvin. The Role of the Venetian Consulate of Durazzo in the Protection of the Economic Interests of Venice at the Beginning of the XVIII Century. No. 2, 2020, p. 85–108.

Kadria, Sali. The Political and Financial Administration of Albania's Territory from Austro-Hungary during 1916–1918. No. 2, 2020, p.109–142.

Verli, Mareglen. The Kosova Question in the Albanian Parlamament 1920–1924. No. 1, 2021, p. 121–154.

Verli, Mareglen. The Fluctuations of the Big Powers and the Albanian Stand after the Congress of Lushnja. No. 2, 2021, p. 121–154.

Malaj, Edmond. Agreements and other Issues between Ragusa and Albanian Nobles. No. 2, 2022, p. 47–76.

Verli, Mareglen. The Question of Kosova and the Stablity of the Albanian State 1912–1999. No. 1, 2023, p. 77–91.

3.3.10 Other Periodicals in Different Periods

Cozzi, Ernesto. La Donna Albanese, con Speciale Riguardo al Diritto Consuetudinario. Wien, Druck und Verlag der Mechitharisten-Buchdruckerei. 1912, p. 309–335. Italian Edition. BK: 85 B 104

The work reflects the position of women under Albanian customary law, mainly in the mountainous areas of Shkodra. The author presents a series of customs that highlight the role and rights of women in the parental home and in the husband's household. He notes the duties of the housewife, her exclusion from the right of inheritance and restrictions on public life. Although divorce was not regulated

25 http://asa.edu.al/site/?page_id=7523 [last access 11.09.2023].

as a specific institute, the author highlights the similarities between the rules on separation from the wife and those of a woman leaving her home. Also of interest is the analysis of the criminal offenses that were applied to women, and related cases that could lead to blood feud. The paper contains an appendix on wedding customs in the north of Albania.

Valentini, Giuseppe. Prishja dhe Rilindja e Korporacjonit. Revista 'Leka'. 1934, p. 225–236. BIHGJL

"The decline and renaissance of the corporations" explores the role of guilds in Albania in the Middle Ages and their rise to splendor in the late 18th century. The author notes that among the causes that led to their collapse, besides the development of industry, was the decline in the internal mechanisms of control of the administration, the abusive benefits of the masters to the detriment of the apprentice and the denial of some basic rights for the latter.

Rizzo, Giambattista. La Unione dell'Albania con l'Italia. Personalità Giuridica e Qualificazione Internazionale dello Stato Albanese. Revista di Diritto Pubblico, Serie II-Anno, XXXI. Agosto–Settembre 1939, XVII, p. 497–522. Italian Edition. BK: 83 C 36; 84 B 29

The article analyzes the legal acts that enabled the union between Albania and Italy, as well as the consequences of this process in Albania's legal personality. The author discusses whether Albania could still be considered a subject of international law after this union, and the legal classification of the Albanian state with regards to domestic law.

La Torre, Michelle. L'Unione dell'Italia coll'Albania ed i Suoi Riflessi Politici e Giuridici. Revista Echi e Commenti, Anno XX-n. 13, 5 Maggio, 1939, p. 388–390. Italian Edition. BK: 85 A 17

The author analyzes the union between Albania and Italy, approved by the Italian law of April 16th, 1939-XVII, n. 580, and the legal implications of this act. Referring to the principle of reciprocity, the author focuses on three important aspects: (i) the organization of the state apparatus, (ii) the applicable legal framework, and (iii) economic, financial, and customs relations.

Valentini, Giuseppe. Rrethi i Kanunit. Revista 'Shkëndija'. No. 6, April 1943, p. 1–4. BIHGJL.

In this article, the author maintains that the Kanun of Lek Dukagjin in its entirety was implemented first in Dardania, where the tribe was an autochthonous mixture between Thracians and Illyrians, based on close family ties. According to the author, in the customary law of Dardania the family had its own legal personality, whereas the tribe was an extension of the family. The article notes that in other areas of Albania, including the areas of Kurvelesh, Himara and other regions of the South, where the movement of the population from one place to another brought about new special customs, the norms of customary law developed other features.

Valentini, Giuseppe. Patriarchato, Gerachia e Organizzazione Ecclesiastica nella Pensiola Balcanica al Principio di Medio Evo. Revista D'Albania. Accademia d'Italia. Centro di Studi per l'Albania. Anno V. fasc. I, Marzo, 1944, p. 10–23. Italian Edition. BIHGJL.

In this paper, which may be of particular interest to scholars of ecclesiastical law, Valentini provides detailed information on the organization and hierarchy of the Albanian Catholic Church at the beginning of the Middle Ages.

Villari, Salvatore. Codice di Lek Dukagjini. Instituto per gli Studi di Politica Internazionale. Revista Albania, Fase. 1. Marzo, Milano, 1942. (Estratto). Italian Edition. BK: 83 C 7

The paper, initially published in 1942, was reprinted in Albanian in Tirana in 2012, and is quoted in part I of this bibliography.

Villari, Salvatore. In Tema di Consuetudini Agrarie in Albania. Estratto dall'Archivio Vittorio Scialoja per le Consuetudini Giuridiche Agrarie e le Tradizioni Popolari Italiane. Vol VIII e IX. Tipografia E- Coppini, 194–1942, Firenze, (Separat), 8 f. Italian Edition. BK: 80 D 5

The article draws attention to some agrarian practices based on customary law. It refers to the conclusions of Professor Patetta, an historian and legal scholar of the time who analyzed the method of determining the boundaries of agricultural properties and other agrarian issues, in the customary law of the northern Albanian regions.

Pepo, Petraq. Dy Dokumente Mesjetare mbi Shqipërinë – Berati i Sulltan Bajazitit II dhe Vakëfnameja e Mirahor Iljaz Beut. Buletini për Shkencat Shoqërore III. Institutiti i Shkencave Albanologjike. Tiranë, 1956, p. 271–290. BIHGJL: II Shq B. 945

The article "Two documents on the medieval Albania – the *berat* of Sultan Bajazit II and *waqfia* of Mirahor Iljaz Bey" highlights the importance in legal history of the discovery of the two cited documents, which attest to the mechanisms of transferring of ownership in the 15th and 16th centuries, whilst also providing other detailed data. The paper is accompanied by a summary in French.

Cristofoli, Angelo Masotti. L'Evoluzione del Commercio Estero Albanese dopo il Distacco dalla Cina. Rivista "Studi e Ricerche". Anno XV, No. 4. Trieste 1984, p. 87–112. Italian Edition. BK: AL 15 D 40

In this paper, the author analyzes the trade relations of communist Albania, focusing on the cessation of trade relations with China; trade with other countries of the communist bloc; as well as trade relations with some Western countries, such as Italy and France. The paper contains statistical data that show Albania's levels of imports and exports.

Meksi, Aleksandër. Peshkopata e Arbërit. (Episcopatus Arbanensis). Revista 'Hylli i Dritës', No. 5–6, 1995, p. 30–43.

The author analyzes from an historical perspective the creation of the Bishopric of Arbër, and provides interesting details on issues of ecclesiastical law. This article reflects the relations between the Catholic and Orthodox churches in the Albanian territories and draws attention to the fact that during the Byzantine occupation, the Orthodox Church administration was extended to all the provinces of the administrative jurisdiction of the metropolises. The author estimates that the moment when Tivari and Ulqin were separated from the Durrës Orthodox mertropolis and connected with the Roman Catholic Church in 1022 is the moment that marks the beginning of the supremacy of the Catholic Church and of the Republic of Venice over the Orthodox Church. The article notes that by the middle of the 14th century the Catholic Church had managed to fully extend into Northern and Central Albania, increasingly limiting territories which, from the ecclesiastical point of view, depended from the orthodox Archbishopric of Ohrid.

Del Re, Emmanuela C. Albania in Transition: The Question of Identity and the Customary Law in State Building in the Balkans. Dilemmas on the Eve of the 21st Century. Edited by Bianchini, Stefano. Schöpflin, George. A Series of Balkan and East-European Studies. Longo Editore. Ravenna, 1998, p. 167–194. English Edition. BK: PP 949.7.Sta.

The article analyzes the issue of Albanian identity through the lenses of the customary law. The author reflects some concepts of the Kanun of Lek Dukagjin, the role of the tribe in the organization of the Albanian social order, the respect towards the *kanun* as reflected in the institute of the given *besa* (oath), the regulation of ownership, blood feuds, as well as the persistence over the centuries of Albanian customary law and its future prospects. It also discusses the transformative processes in the transition from communism after the 1990s.

Sinani, Shaban. Sixhilati i Sherijes së Beratit. Revistë Shkencore-Kulturore 'Perla'. No. 2, 2003, p. 82–92. BK: Shp 66 54 C

The article explores the Sicil of the Sheriya of Berat (the Register of the jurisdiction of Berat), which is one of the most complete registers compiled during the Ottoman rule and contains authentic documents, valuable notes, and research on the law applicable in the Albanian territories during this period. Its 211 volumes comprise various legal acts, including *fermans*, *buyurdi*, orders, *waqf* deeds, wills, and decisions, ordered chronologically from 1603 to 1913. These acts show how the central administration of the Ottoman Empire directed the local governments in the occupied lands. The author explains that according to the practice of the Ottoman administration, the documents of the central authorities were written in a single original copy. Then, the *kadis*' (judges') offices of the local government were tasked with confirming the receipt of the document, producing identical copies and returning the original document back to the central authority that had issued it. The documentation of the Sicil of Berat, which is an identical copy of the original, is accessible at the Central State Archive. The article points out that some of these documents have been translated into Albanian and therefore can be consulted not only in the Ottoman language, but also in Albanian. The author analyzes some of these acts, which attest to the coexistence between the ecclesiastical and the positive law, the protection of the rights of Christian (Orthodox) communities, the resolution of various civil law conflicts, as well as the approach of the central Ottoman administration with regard to the Albanian customary law and attempts to harmonize it with the Ottoman law.

Popescu, Stefan. Albanie dans la Politique Ėtrangére de la France, 1919–1940. Valahian Journal of Historical Studies. Târgoviste: Cetatea de Scaun. No.1, 2004, p. 24–61. (Separat). BK: AL 28 B 7

The article discusses the relations between Albania and France, with a focus on the role of the French military mission in the city of Korça during the period known as the "Republic of Korça", as well as the French administration of the southern border of Albania with Greece. Among the main acts approved during this administration, the author mentions the regulation on public accounting dated December 27th, 1916; normative acts that regulated income tax; the stamp on contracts; as well as various judicial acts. The article evidences the creation of the Provincial Court for the Territory of Korça (*Le Tribunal Prévôtal du Territoire de Kortcha*), on June 17, 1918, which was competent to adjudicate violations of regulations related to the public order, but did not impare the jurisdiction of religious courts, especially in relation to personal rights.

Boccia V. P., Antonio. L'Antico Sistema Normativo Albanese: tra Diritto Romano e Proto-Europeismo. Edizione Progetto Grafico. Lauria, 2014. Italian Edition, f. 35. BK: PP 3 (496.5) Boc

The author analyzes from an historical-legal point of view the evolution of the Albanian state and its legal system from ancient times to the present day, emphasizing the close relationship that exists between Italy and Albania. According to the author, the traditional Albanian legal system is based primarily on customary law. He highlights the analogies and connection of Albanian customary law with the Roman law, illustrating this with a comparison between the council of elders of Albanian customary law and the senators in Roman law, the role of "*pater familias*", the limited rights of women, the similarities between the medieval Albanian and Italian cities, as well as the influence of Italian law on the positive Albanian law adopted during the reign of King Zog.

3.3.11 Articles of Faculty of Law Lecturers

The followings scientific articles are authored by lecturers of the Faculty of Law, University of Tirana and lecturers of the University of Durrës 'Aleksandër Moisiu', published in different legal journals.

Likmeta, Engjëll. Scanderbeg's Canon and Crimes against Person in the Journal on European History of Law. No. 1, 2014, p. 177–181.

The article explores the legal system according to Albanian customary law, with a particular focus on the penal norms of the Kanun of Skanderbeg. The English abstract of the article can be accessed on the journal's website.[26]

Likmeta, Engjëll. Treska, Katrin. Crimes against Person Viewed under the Light of the Canon of Labëria. Europian Scientific Journal. No. 14, May, 2014, p. 239–248.

The authors delve into the regime on criminal offenses of the Kanun of Labëria, and interpret the different types of murders. The English abstract of the article can be accessed on the journal's website.[27]

Kromiçi, Armela. Tregtari dhe Shoqëritë Tregtare në Kodin Tregtar të 1932. Revista Shqiptare Social Ekonomike. No. 2, 2014, p. 167–176.

The author analyzes the main legal characteristics of the entrepreneur and commercial companies regulated by the Commercial Code of the time of the monarchy (1932). The code was drawn up by a group of Italian experts under the guidance of professor Vivante.[28]

Malltezi, Argita. L'Influence Française et les Rapports Commerciaux entre l'Albanie et la France dans une Perspective Historique. Revue Internationale de Droit Comparé. Société de Législation Comparée. No. 3, 2014, p. 818 –842.

The article explores the commercial exchanges between France and Albania and the influence of French legislation in Albania. The analyses span from the period of the Ottoman rule in Albania to Albania's legal reform after its independence, the exchanges during the communist regime and the legal reforms in the commercial domain after the fall of communism.

Treska, Katrin. Engjëll Likmeta. The Funds for the Execution of Obligations (Contract) According to the Albanian Customary Law. Journal on European History of Law. No. 2, 2015, p. 90–97.

The authors deal with the main instruments for carrying out obligations under Albanian customary law, presenting an analysis of the customary norms of the various *kanuns* implemented in Albania. The English abstract of the article can be accessed on the journal's website.[29]

Likmeta, Engjëll. Some Reflections on the Delicts of the First Criminal Code of the Republic of Albania. Journal on European History of Law. No. 1. 2016, p. 178–185.

The article analyzes the penal code of 1928, which was the first code adopted after Albania's declaration of independence. The paper notes that the code permanently

---

26 https://www.ceeol.com/search/article-detail?id=159769 [last access 14.07.2023].

27 https://eujournal.org/index.php/esj/article/view/3406[last access 21.07.2023].

28 https://www.bksh.al/details/418443[last access 11.04.2023].

29 https://www.ceeol.com/search/article-detail?id=307606[last access 21.07.2023].

abolished the remnants of Ottoman legislation that were still applicable in Albania, whilst highlighting its novelties, the Western influence, as well as the preservation of the Albanian legal tradition. The article in English can be accessed on the journal's website.[30]

Likmeta, Engjëll. Dimni, Enton. Historical-Legal View of the Freedom of Religion in Republic of Albania. Journal on European History of Law. No. 2, 2016, p. 139–149.

The article provides an overview of the legal mechanisms that have guaranteed the freedom of belief in Albania, during different periods in history. The English abstract of the article can be accessed on the journal's website.[31]

Likmeta, Engjëll. Albanian Assembly (Parliament) between Tradition and Development. A Historical-Legal Approach. Journal on European History of Law. No. 2, 2017, p. 58–71.

The author offers an analysis of the history of the development of parliamentarism in Albania. The paper includes analysis of assemblies and elders' meetings organized on the basis of customary law, the League of Prizren, the Assembly of Vlora and the parliamentary assemblies of the Albania since its independence. The article in English can be accessed on the journal's website.[32]

Kola, Tafaj Flutura. Çinari, Silvana. Historik i Zhvillimit të Arbitrazhit në Shqipëri në 100 Vite Shtet. Revista Shqiptare Social Ekonomike. No. 1, 2019, p. 23–32.

The authors discuss the history of arbitration law in Albania since its independence in 1912. The analysis includes the trajectory of the pertinent legislation immediately after the declaration of independence, its development during the regime of King Zog until 1939, the changes during the communist dictatorship, as well as the developments of arbitration law in Albania after the fall of communism in 1990, until 2012.

Islamaj, Fatri. Likmeta, Engjëll. Historical Aspects of the Contract of Sale According to Albanian Customary Law. Journal on European History of Law. No. 2, 2019, p. 168–174.

The authors provide a comparative and historical overview of the contract of sale under Albanian customary law, focusing on its characteristics according to different *kanuns*. The English abstract of the article can be accessed on the journal's website.[33]

Kruja, Keltis. Likmeta, Engjëll. Historical and Legal Aspects of Heritage Law in Albania. Journal on European History of Law. No. 2, 2020, p.147–156.

---

30 http://www.historyoflaw.eu/english/JHL_01_2016.pdf [last access 21.07.2021].

31 https://www.ceeol.com/search/article-detail?id=463201[last access 11.04.2023].

32 http://www.historyoflaw.eu/english/JHL_02_2017.pdf [last access 11.04.2023].

33 https://www.ceeol.com/search/article-detail?id=812685 [last access 11.04.2023].

The paper presents the evolution of the institution of inheritance from its regulation by customary law to the provisions of the current regulatory framework. The English abstract of the article can be accessed on the journal's website.[34]

Likmeta, Engjëll. Treska, Katrin. Crimes Against Jugdes in Albania. Juridical Defense of Justice Officials Provided by the Criminal Law. Journal on European History of Law. No. 2, 2021, p. 187–197.

The paper offers an historical overview of the provisions of penal legislation in Albania, which has guaranteed the protection of justice system officials and, in particular, judges. The analysis covers the regime of customary law, the legal protection that was provided to the officials of the judicial system during the monarchy, the development of this regime during the period of communism, and the legal framework currently in force. The English abstract of the article can be accessed on the journal's website.[35]

Pepa, Eugen. "Institutiones Iuris" of Albanian Consuetudinary Law. Academic Journal of Interdisciplinary Studies. No. 2, July 2015, p. 337–348. Italian Edition.[36]

Musa, Elton. Shkëmbi, Aldo. Legal Position-International Recogntion of Kosovo and the Right to "Self-Determination". European Journal of Social Sciences. Vol. 2, Issue 3, May–August 2015, p. 43–50.[37]

3.4 Editions of Works from Scientific Conferences

The publications of this section are collected in special editions dedicated to specific events or scientific conferences.

Pepo, Petraq. Kodiku i Madh i Korçës si Burim Historik. Kumtesë në Konferencën e Parë të Studimeve Albanologjike (15–21 Nëntor 1962). Tiranë, 1965, p. 1–7. BK: Al 7 D 40

In this presentation, the author reviews the Codex of Korça, which depicts the town's life from the 17th–20th century; a period during which Korça was a Diocese, initially under the Patriarchate of Ohrid until 1767, and latter transferred to the jurisdiction of the Patriarchate of Istanbul. The article deals with the organization of the Christian Orthodox community of Korça, the feudal lords and the economic life of the Christian community.

Konferenca e Bujanit. Materiale nga Sesioni Shkencor Kushtuar 55 Vjetorit të Konferencës së Bujanit. Akademia e Shkencave e Republikës së Shqipërisë. Instituti i Historisë. Tiranë, 1999. BK: S 197 G 21

---

34 https://www.ceeol.com/search/article-detail?id=919813 [last access 11.04.2023].

35 https://www.ceeol.com/search/article-detail?id=1004356 [last access 12.09.2023].

36 https://www.richtmann.org/journal/index.php/ajis/article/view/7176/6878[last access 04.11.2023].

37 https://revistia.com/files/articles/ejser_v2_i3_15/Elton.pdf [last access 04.11.2023].

In this publication of the Academy of Sciences, several papers by different authors analyze the decisions of the Conference of Bujan, held from December 31st, 1943, until January 2nd, 1944. Of interest to legal scholars is the Resolution issued by the Conference of Bujan, which sought the union of Kosova and the Dukagjin Plain with Albania, as well as papers that delve into the more contemporary matters of: (i) resolution no. 3 dated August 6th, 1998 of the People's Assembly of the Republic of Albania on the issue of Kosova (*Kuvendit popullor të Republikës së Shqipërisë për çështjen e Kosovës*), or (ii) the temporary agreement for peace and the self-governance of Kosova issued by the Conference of Rambuje in 1999, as well as other acts on this matter.

Verli, Mariglen. Pavarësia e Shqipërisë dhe Sfidat e Shtetit Shqiptar gjatë Shek. XX (Përmbledhje Studimesh). Konferencë Shkencore me Rastin e 95 Vjetorit të Shpalljes së Pavarësisë së Shqipërisë. Instituti i Historisë dhe Fakulteti i Historisë dhe Filologjisë. 'Klean'. Tiranë, 2008. BK: S 284 25 F

This collection of historical studies provides some presentations that touch upon different aspects of Albanian independence, the challenges of the Albanian state and its history of law. We note **Prifti, Kristaq.** The Declaration of Independence of Albania and the Question of a United National State, p. 19–30; **Krisafi, Ksenofon.** The Issue of Albania's Borders at the Conference of Ambassadors in London (1912–1914), p. 119–144; **Naska, Kaliopi.** The Role of the National Council in the Defense of Independence and Territorial Integrity, p. 171–187.

Plasari, Aurel. Bashota, Sali. Përlindja e Shqipëniës. Prishtinë, 2012. BFDUT

On the occasion of the 100th anniversary of the Independence of Albania, the National Library of Albania and the National and University Library of Kosova republished a selection from the issues of the newspaper *"Përlindja e Shqipëniës"*, the first newspaper of the Albanian government after its independence. The reprint is based on documentation stored in the archives of the National Library of Albania. This publication contains some of the first legal acts adopted by the bodies of the independent Albanian state since 1912.

Qëndra e Studimeve Albanologjike. Instituti i Historisë, 100 Vjet Pavarësi. Aktet e Konferencës Shkencore Ndërkombëtare. Tiranë, 26–27 Nëntor 2012. Botimet Albanologjike. Tiranë, 2014. Albanian and English Edition. BFHFUT

The proceedings of the international conference "100 years of independence" contain several presentations that focus on the history of legal developments of the period 1912–2012. Among them we mention: **Krisafi, Ksenofon.** The Affirmation of the Albanian State with the Status of a Legal Subject of International Law, p. 393–424; **Kurti, Teki.** Institutions of Local Government in the Years 1913–1939, p. 539–548; **Ljarja, Nertila.** Independence of Albania and the Creation of a Secular State (1912–1939), p. 77–91; **Musaj, Fatmira.** Administrative Reforms in Albania and their Effects (1925–1928), p. 99–108.

Malltezi, Argita. Kromiçi, Armela. The Tradition of Public-Private Partnership and Concessions in Albania. International Conference Organized by University of Tirana, Faculty of Law, Tirana Court of Appeal, Max Planck Institute for Comparative Law and Private International, Hamburg, University of Kadir Istanbul. Tiranë, 2013, p. 26–38. BFDUT

The presentation includes an extensive list of concession contracts on Albania's natural resources, granted by the High Gate and the Albanian governments until the year 1939, as well as analysis of the legal regime on PPPs and concessions during the periods 1912–1939, and 1990–2013.

Shteti dhe e Drejta Shqiptare në 100 Vjet Pavarësi. Universiteti Europian i Tiranës. Revista Shkencore e Fakultetit Juridik, Univeriteti Europian i Tiranës. No. 8, 2014. BFDUT

This edition of the Scientific Journal of the European University of Tirana Faculty of Law, titled "The Albanian State and Law in 100 Years of Independence", provides articles from various authors, on different legal and historical issues. For the purpose for the topic of this bibliography we mention: **Krisafi, Ksenofon.** Affirmation of the Albanian State as a Subject of International Law (Afirmimi i Shtetit Shqiptar si Subjekt i të Drejtës Ndërkombëtare), p. 5–27; **Duka, Ferit.** Governance, Institutions and the Law in Albania During World War I: the Austro-Hungarian Zone of Occupation (1916–1918) (Qeverisja Institucionet dhe Ligji në Shqipëri gjatë Luftës Së Parë Botërore: Zona Austro-Hungareze e Pushtimit (1916–1918)), p. 28–41; **Ahmetaj, Lavdosh.** The Procedure of the Transition of Albania from Republic to Monarchy and the Central Institutions (Procedura e Kalimit të Shqipërisë nga Republikë në Monarki dhe Institucionet Qendrore), p. 52–61; **Kola, Tafaj Flutura.** History of Sources of Albanian Civil Procedural Law in 100 Years of Statehood (Historiku i Burimeve të së Drejtës Procedurale Civile Shqiptare në 100 Vite Shtet), p. 62–75; **Arbi, Mimoza. Ikonomi, Luljeta.** Legislative Reform of Criminal Law during the Reign of Ahmet Zogu and its Impact on the Consolidation of Criminal Law (Reforma Legjislative në Kuadrin e të Drejtës Penale gjatë Mbretërimit të Ahmet Zogut dhe Ndikimi i saj në Konsolidimin e të Drejtës Penale), p. 76–92; **Çani, Methasani Eralda.** Reforming the Legislation on Public Administration. Challenges and Perspectives (Reformimi i Legjislacionit për Administratën Publike. Sfida dhe Prespektiva), p. 104–120; **Nano, Ilirjana.** The Constitutional Position of the Head of State in Albania (1912–2012), his Relationship with the Judicial Bodies (Pozita Kushtetuese e Kreut të Shtetit në Shqipëri (1912–2012), Raporti i tij me Organet e Drejtësisë), p. 133–145.

Anastasi, Aurela. Konstitucionalizmi si një Përpjekje në Historinë e Konsolidimit të Shtetit Shqiptar të Pavarur. Presentation in the Conference 'Albanian Parcourse to Independence'. 2022, p. 1–5. Access Online.[38]

The author analyzes the development of the Constitutional law and the Albanian legal tradition during the period 1912–1939. It emphasizes the principle of constitutionalism, materialized in a series of norms in the fundamental statutes of the Albanian state, drafted in the period 1920–1939, which aimed at limiting the arbitrary exercise of power. Part of the analysis is the role of the State Council created in 1928, which represents the first constitutional body for the protection of constitutionality.

38 https://www.researchgate.net/publication/365686655_Konstitucionalizmi_si_nje_perpjekje_ne_historine_e_konsolidimit_te_shtetit_shqiptar_te_pavarur[last access 30.10.2023].

Part 4: Materials from the Archive of the Institute of History. (Albanologjia)

The Institute of History, in the Ethnography section, keeps manuscripts and original documents locatable by their reference code. Some of the files with no year or author's name listed are identified only based on the archive entry code. For this reason, unlike other sections of the bibliography, the coordinates of the manuscripts here are given before the title. The archive also contains translated parts of works that have been published abroad, for which data on the original publication is provided. Some of these manuscripts have been used in subsequent publications by different authors, and are reflected elsewhere in this bibliography. However, they are also included in this part for those researchers who want to consult the original versions.

4.1 Section on Ethnography

E. I. 3 **Ibrahimi, Sokol.** About our Legal Folklore

In this paper, the author highlights the fact that at the core of all Albanian customary rules is the "family community", in which the oldest members play an important role. The chairman elected amongst them was the head of the family and had a major role in making decisions. However, for important decisions affecting the family, he was obliged to consult the other members of the community in advance. The head could dispose of the family's wealth as he wished, unlike the Roman model of organization. Consequences of each member's actions weighed on all members of the community, especially in the case of a blood feud. The author notes that since the time of primitive Albanian tribes the blood vendetta was considered a sacred debt, to be repaid by the relatives of the murderer. He points out that over time, blood feud norms were softened and Albanian customs were enriched with the institution of reconciliation. The old traditions regulating all aspects of the daily social life became unwritten codes, known as *Kanun*. The customary law of the north, from Mirëdita to the Great Highlands of Gjakova, was called the Kanun of Lekë Dukagjini. According to the author, the Albanian customary judicial law contained within its rules the traditions of the Illyrian tribes organized in family communities. He notes that these rules were influenced by the Romanist tradition, especially in terms of civil legal relations, from which the Albanian legal customs were enriched and widely influenced. The author sees the influence from the Slavic tribes as a reciprocal relation, in which the Albanian and Slavic tribes exchanged customs and traditions with each other. The author also discusses the institute of *besa*, its well known role in protecting the guest and settling blood feuds, and the less publicised, but no less important, usage in commercial relations.

E. I. 4 **Palojaku, A.** Vendime të Marra prej Krerëve të Fisit të Shalës më 8 Shkurt 1919

The manuscript contains several decisions adopted by the canonical bodies of the tribe of Shala—the commoners (*djelmnia*) and the *chiefs of the tribe*. The author delves into *Commoners of Shala* (Djelmija e Shalës) as a special organization, created in Shala in 1900 for the purpose of implementing the Kanun, in cases when the *bayraktar* and the Chiefs did not enforce it. The author notes that the emergence of the organ of *djelmnia* occurred at a time when it was believed that the *bayraktar* and the chiefs had begun to concede to Ottoman interventionism. The author illustrates in detail several decisions of "*Djelmnia e Shalës*" up to 1919, which affected various aspects of the criminal, civil and public *kanun* norms. Some of the rulings detail the regime of blood feud, with the aim of restricting the killing to a limited proximity of the family males, and also to limit murders among the Shalians. Also of interest are the decisions on the regulation of co-ownership of the means of production (working animals) and their regime in the event of a criminal conviction on the property of one of the co-partners. Other decisions laid down the rules (i) for the separation of the property of a convicted murderer from the property of his cousins who were exempt from punishment, (ii) for the functioning and protection of the fortified tower *(kulla e ngujimit)*, (iii) for the guarantees and rules for the protection of life and honor of the guest, (iv) for the punishments for killing the spouse or other relatives for the purpose of taking their property, and (v) for punishments for murders near the church.

E. I. 6 **Palaj, A. Bernadin.** Mbi Kanunin e Maleve (n.d)

"On the mountains' *kanun*" is a work cited by many Albanian and foreign authors who have written on northern customary law. The author refers to ethnographic studies that reveal how the guarantee of basic rights, such as the right of life, honor, faith, property, gender, religion and marriage of man, have been regulated by norms since ancient times in the Geg Mountains of Albania. The author notes that the Kanun of Lek Dukagjin is in fact a later compendium of this ancient canonical corpus, which originates from the Illyrian-Thracian heritage of the Albanians. The paper analyzes in detail some of the main institutes of Albanian customary law, emphasizing the role of the assembly and the elders in the interpretation of canonical norms and the mandatory force of their decisions, the role of the Youth (or the commons—*Djelmnia*) in the enforcement of the *kanun's* regime, as well as the functions of another executive body known as *puthadorët e kanunit.*[1] Another argument that the author delves into is the of the family, the role that each member of the family had according to the *kanun*, including the rights and role of women.

E. I.8 L'Organizzazione della Bandiera (Organizimi i Bajrakut)

This manuscript, written in Italian, for which the author and the year of edition are unknown, analyzes the distinction between the *bayrak* and the tribe. It notes that while the tribe is the community of families based on the blood line of males, the *bayrak* is the tribe-state composed of the brotherhoods of the same origin linked to a certain territory. The paper points out leading insitutions of the *bayrak*: the *bayraktari*, the chiefs and the youth (*djelmnia*).

E. I. 9 **Zef A. Valentini.** Shënime Paraprake të Përgjithshme mbi Kanunin e Lek Dukagjinit

Although Father Valentini's works have been widely published recently, we also mention this manuscript in Italian, in which he elaborates on the etymology of the word "Kanun", and on the theories and positions of different authors on this issue. He points out that one group of authors supports the idea that the term *kanun* derives from the legal term *"kanon"* or *"nomokanon"* of Byzantine law, whilst other authors seek the origin of the term in Ottoman law. The author supports the position that *kanun* law has its roots in Illyria, and analyzes some common characteristics between the Illyrian customary law and the ancient Longobard law (*diritto longobardo*); pointing out that the legal basis in both customary regimes is the family. The author emphasizes that in the internal organization of the Albanian tribe there is no *"Imperium domi"*, and decisions are taken by the "Council of Elders". The latter has the authority to change the rules of the kanun, while decisions related to war and peace must be taken by an assembly, a comprehensive collegial body, created according to the principle of 'one man from each house'.

E. I. 11 **Valentini, A. Cozzi, Zef.** Kanuni dhe Fiset

In this manuscript titled "The *kanun* and the tribes", the author delves extensively into the legal concept of justice, focusing especially on the *kanun's* regime of penal law and punishments. He groups the norms of this regime into four categories, profiling them in accordance with the notion of justice they transmit: (i) the norms of legal justice, which determined the duties of the individual towards society and towards the chairman, (ii) the norms of distributive justice, which stipulated the duty of leaders to partially distribute tasks to assistants and members of society, (iii) norms of the penal justice, which determined the rights of individuals and the cases when sanctions were warranted, and (iv) the commutative justice, which determined the obligation of the individual "to give to another what belongs to

1 The term refers to persons tasked with the enforcement of the *kanun's* rules. Literal translation: hand kisser of the *kanun*.

him'. The latter concept included norms regulating ownership rights, cases of theft, robbery, and fraud.

E-I20 **Ipen, Theodor (Ippen).** E Drejta Zakonore e Malësorëve Shqiptar (Paper Published in the Journal of Ethnology, in Berlin, Year 1901, no. 33, p. 43–57)

The translation in Albanian analyzes some of the main aspects of the customary law of the North of Albania. The author notes that the inhabitants of the highlands regulate the relationships amongst themselves on the basis of customary law. The paper extensively refers to the notes of the Italian missionary, Father Gabriel Copasci, who lived in the highlands of Northern Albania; Johann Georg von Hahn's book *"Reise durch die Gebrete den Drin und Vardar"* and his notes on the customary law of the tribes of Mirdita, as well as the articles of the two Albanian priests, Lazër Mjeda and Nikollë Ashta. The articles of the Albanian parishioners, which are cited below, are found at the archive of the Institute of History and bear the same location number as Ippen's writing.

E-I20 **Mjeda, Lazër.** E Drejta ndër Fiset e Dukagjinit

The author analyzes the Kanun of Lek Dukagjin and its regime of blood feud. He further delves into the ability of the *kanun* to change, according to the procedures provided in its provisions, and emphasizes the canonical changes that were intended to ease the consequences of blood feud by restricting the rank of cousins who could be killed for redemption. The article discusses *besa* between tribes and the consequences of its violation. It notes that the killing of a member of the tribe in breach of *besa* was considered as though the murderer had acted against the chiefs of his own tribe, since they were the guarantors of the allegiance to the other tribe. Hence, the case was treated as if the perpetrator had committed murder against a member of his own tribe. The author describes in detail the regime in case of injuries, protection granted by *besa* and reconciliation.

E-I20 **Ashta, Nikollë.** E Drejta Zakonore e Fiseve të mbi Shkodrës në Malësitë që Gjenden në Veri të Shkodrës

The author discusses the social strata of Shkodra, categorized into town inhabitants, farmers of the low rural areas and the highlanders. The two first categories were under the jurisdiction of the Turkish administration, whereas the highlanders of Shkodra province lived in tribes and were regulated according to their law—the Kanun of Lek Dukagjin. The author also explores the *kanun's* regime on murder, injury, damage to foreign property, pawn, inheritance, sale and purchase, as well as the role of *precedent* in the adjudication of analogous cases by the assembly. The paper analyzes the governing bodies of the *kanun* and their competences, as well as the institutions that were created in the late period of the Ottoman occupation—the special court established by the Ottoman administration in 1856, known as the Chamber of Mountains (Jibal Chamber). The court was competent for the resolution of disputes between large tribes. It was headed by a president (*serkerde*) appointed by the government and extended its jurisdiction over the entire highlands, except for the Mirdita tribes. It adjudicated its cases according to Turkish law. Each tribe was assigned a *serkeda* and a *bylykbash*.[2]

4.2 From the Section of Book Manuscripts Preserved in the Archives of the Institute of History

A-III-175 **Buda, Aleks.** Shqipëria në Shekullin e V–XV.

The historical paper sheds light on the legal regime that regulated legal relations in the Albanian lands during the 5th to the 15th century, after the division of the Roman Empire into the eastern and western empires and the collapse of the slave-owning order. The author points out that during these centuries, the destruction of the common property regime in the Albanian territories continued in a systematic and slow manner, confining its application only to the mountainous areas where collective property was held by the community. In these communities, elders played an important role in the interactions with the state apparatus. The paper deals with the role of the tax regime on farmers in Illyria, which aimed to keep the peasantry community connected to the land.

In parallel, the author explores the fiscal regime of the free citizens and their heavy tax burden, especially what is known as "*Krizajir*" tax, which was paid in silver and gold. *Kurials* were functionaries charged with collecting taxes from citizens and who guaranteed the succesful collection of the income tax due commensurate with their wealth. The author points out that with the decline of the civic economy and the middle class aristocracy, the curials could no longer meet the obligations towards the treasury of the empire. The need for income led the Byzantine emperors to concede the collection of taxes to private entrepreneurs.

The author suggests that the process of the emergence and development of feudal relations in the Albanian lands was spread over two periods. The first period covers the middle of the 7th century to the 10th century, when the old slave owning regime was destroyed and free peasant communities prevailed, while the new feudal order was in its infancy and the power of the feudal aristocracy did not yet dominate the free peasantry. The second period belongs to the 11th to the 13th centuries and was characterized by the intensive development of feudal relations, the growth of feudal property and of the feudal power over the peasantry until their dominance was complete. According to the author, feudal relations coexisted in the cities with

2 The article also explains the role of the *bylykbash*, as a representative of the government in each highland tribe. He was a person accepted by the tribe members and charged by the Turkish administration to collect fines or damages on behalf of the Turkish administration in cases of violations of Albanian customary norms.

the remnants of slavery, and in the mountainous areas of the north, with the local patriarchal order.

The author also deals with the characteristics of the peasant community, which continued to maintain the model of collective property, although during certain periods of time the land was redistributed among the members of the community. Slowly, private ownership of land began to prevail over collective ownership. The paper illustrates the disintegration of collective property pursuant to the Agricultural Law (Nomos Georgikos) of the 8th century, which reflects Byzantine-Slavic customary law on the land regime. Since the peasant community was simultaneously a fiscal community, the Byzantine state was interested in preserving these communities.

The author also analyzes the role of the church and monasteries as land owners. He notes that one of the consequences of the increase of the fiscal burden was the creation of two main classes, the large landowners—the *dinate* (the powerful), which included churches and monasteries—and the class of the poor, who did not own land, known as *panetes*. These changes are illustrated in the legislative developments of the time, as for instance the Byzantine legislation known as "Vasiliqi", of the 9th–10th century, that provides for a range of typical feudal obligations such as feudal rents, non-economic coercion on peasants tied to land and their obligations towards the lord of the land. The economic dependence turned into a legal dependence which is illustrated by the typical figure of the dependent farmer (*pariku*), evidenced in documents on Albania dating back to the beginning of the XI century.

The text also provides data on the organization of the *themes,* as new administrative-military units. Of interest is also the role of Venice in the Albanian territories, its monopolies for trade activities in a number of Albanian provinces, and the exemption from customs duties for the Albanian feudal lords.

A-III-178 **Shkodra, Zija.** Struktura Ekonomike – Shoqërore e Shqipërisë në Shekullin e XIX – Shkodër, 1955.

The work explores in depths the features of ownership in the village and the organization of cities in Albania during the 19th century. It explains the dissolution of feudal relations and the development of agriculture, the destruction of guilds (*esnafe*) and the first steps towards the development of industry. The author points out that the growth of trade exchanges with other countries in the region and beyond created suitable conditions for the development of maritime trade, especially in the second half of the 19th century. This manuscript was later included in the author's book entitled "The process of disintegration of feudalism and the emergence of capitalist relations in Albania during the century XIX", published by the Ministry of Education and Culture. Tiranë, 1957. BK: S 66 63 R, cited in the second part of this bibliography.

A. III.179 **Frashëri, Kristo.** Shqipëria gjatë Lulëzimit të Marrëdhënieve Feudale të Shekullit XI-XIV, Tiranë, 1955.

In this paper, the author analyzes the development of feudal relations during the 11th–14th centuries, upon the restoration of Byzantine rule in Albania. It notes the important economic and social role of the village and peasantry, which had lost its homogeneity. He points out that the main part of this model was dominated by free peasants who were small landowners. The paper further deals with the development of cities, crafts and manufacturing, the intensification of commercial exchange and the organization of corporations (guilds) in the main Albanian cities.

The author also deals with the formation of the State of Arbëria and the need for the creation of an independent political power. The cited sources testify to the existence of this state since the end of the 12th century, when the Byzantine Empire still maintained its influence. The paper highlights the good commercial relations that the state of Arbëria had with Ragusa, as evidenced by the agreements on allowing trade and recognizing the rights of citizens, concluded between the two countries. The paper offers a part of the treaty translated into Albanian, which establishes the obligations assumed by the Arbër side towards Ragusa.

The author dwells in detail on the flourishing of the feudal economy in Albania during the 13th–15th centuries, explaining that feudal relations developed mainly in the lowlands of Albania, whilst in the mountainous areas, especially of the northern highlands, a semi-feudal model emerged; the *bayrak* model continued to prevail and the regime of the customary law remained intact. The author details the structure of Albanian society under the feudal model, clarifying the legal implications for each category.

Attention is also given to the development of cities, craft and commercial corporations (guilds) in the cities, the development of trade fairs and caravans, and the different systems applied in each city for collecting taxes in cash and in kind. Customs agreements between Albanian and Italian cities, which aimed to reduce the fiscal burden of the caravans, are also discussed and illustrated with the the agreement between Durrës and Bari in 1305 and the agreement between Shkodra and Ragusa in 1334.

Based on the writings of the Croatian researcher Sufflay, the author summarizes the structure of high functionaries who led the cities, called communes *(commune civitatis)*, which in Albania were organized in the form of aristocratic republics. These were governed on the basis of their statutes. The Durrës charter, registered in the offices of Venice in 1392, is mentioned as an illustration, as well as the fact that from the middle of the 15th century the rule of foreign states in Albania was greatly weakened and Durrës was the first city to gain political independence.

A-III-192 No. Register 473, **Barkan, Omer Lutfi.** Kanunametet e Shqipërisë, Shekulli XVI-XVII. Translated from Turkish by Janina, Myqerem. Edition by Istanbul University, no. 256, 1945.

The handwritten translation provides information about the Kanunname of the Sipahis and the *timars* applied in the Rumelia region. The author also discusses the Kanunname of Shkodra, Ohrid, Tërhalla and Elbasan and the tax regime they provided for.

A-III-262 **Naçi, Stavri.** Shteti Feudal i Shqipërisë së Veriut.

The paper focuses on Northern Albania in the 18th century, and in particular on the Sanjak of Shkodra and the Pashalik of Bushatli. The work is mentioned as a reference in most of the publications of other authors dealing with Albanian feudal state organizations. The paper points out that before the establishment of the *pashalik*, the head of the Sanjak of Shkodra was the *mytesarif*, a governor holding the title of pasha or vizier. He held full military and civil power, as well as an apparatus of power whose functions he distributed among members of the feudal class and the Muslim high clergy.

According to the author, in the highlands of Shkodra, the court was not exercised by the Ottoman *kadis*, because the Kanun of the Mountains, which was applicable there, granted the power of adjudication over disputes to the elders. The grand-elders who were in charge of the village or tribe had the duty to deal with the collection of taxes or duties that were assigned to the village by the state or different feudal lords. The author identifies the so-called feudal anarchy as a distinguishing feature of Northern Albania, feudal wars and popular uprisings. All these slowed down the pace of commercial, artisanal and agricultural development and shaped the course of centralization and the accumulation of power from the Bushatli.

Appendix

Compendiums of Laws, Decrees, By-laws and Jurisprudence

This part is dedicated to the publications of constitutional acts, laws, by-laws and jurisprudence, adopted in Albania since the declaration of Independence. The titles are official publications of state institutions, but also compendiums of legal acts and jurisprudence prepared by different publishing houses. The inclusion of these publications in this bibliography aims at assisting the research of legal scholars but also the work of practicing lawyers. At the same time, they reflect the history of law and of the Albanian state, from the declaration of independence to the present day. The list of publications below is not exhaustive, but a selection which, in the authors' opinion, is helpful for practicing lawyers and scientific researchers.

The official legal acts of the Albanian State were first published in the *Dit e Re* newspaper, and as of July 30, 1922 in the Official Journal. In 1925, the Council of State undertook the systematization and publication in several compendiums of the legal acts adopted during the years of the Republic and of the Kingdom of Albania. The editions of the Official Journal from 1922 to 1944 are published on the official website of the National Library.[1] The official journal's edition published from 1945 onwards are accessible at the Central State Archive.

1. Constitutional Acts

Le Statut Constitutionnel de la République Albanaise. Bureau de la Presse. Tiranë, 1925.[2] BK: 82 S 47

Constitution: Republique Populaire d'Albania. Tiranë, 1947. BK: 81R 64

Kushtetuta e Republikës Popullore të Shqipërisë. 'NSHB'. Tiranë, 1952. BK: S 6 R 42

Kushtetuta e Republikës Popullore të Shqipërisë. Tiranë, Shtypshkronja 'Mihal Duri', 1960. BK: S 44 U 98

Kushtetuta e Republikës Popullore të Shqipërisë. Shtypshkronja 'Mihal Duri'. Tiranë, 1962. BK: S 41 U 51

Paraprojekti i Kushtetutës së Republikës Federative Socialiste të Jugosllavisë. 'Rilindja'. Prishtinë, 1962. BK: Ar 86 F 31

Constitution of the Peoples's Republic of Albania. Tiranë, 1964. BK: 71 U 15

1 https://www.bksh.al/burime/fletore_zyrtare[last access 05.10.2023].

2 Other constitutional acts as of 1912, are found in the official journals: https://www.bksh.al/burime/fletore_zyrtare [last access 05.10.2023].

Statuti i Lidhjes Socialiste të Popullit të Kosovës (Statut Socijalistiçkog Saveza Radnog Naroda Kosova). Prishtinë, 1971. Albanian and Serbo - Croatian Edition. BK: Ar 79 G 63

Amandamentet I-X për Ligjën Kushtetuese të Krahinës Socialiste Autonome të Kosovës, me Ligjën për Zbatimin e Amandamenteve I-X për Ligjën Kushtetuese (Amandmani I-X na Ustavni Zakon Socijalisticke Autonomne Pokrajine Kosova, sa Zakonom za Sprovodene Amandamana I-X na Ustavni Zakon). Sekretariati i Kuvendit Krahinor. Prishtinë, 1972. Albanian and Serbo-Croatian Edition. BK: Ar 76 G 84

Kushtetuta e Republikës Popullore Socialiste të Shqipërisë. '8 Nëntori'. Tiranë, 1977. Edition in Arab Language. BK: AL 7 F 69

Kushtetuta e Republikës Popullore Socialiste të Shqipërisë. '8 Nëntori'. Tiranë, 1977. BK: S 129 E 35

Diskutime për Amendamentet Kushtetuese në Kushtetutën e RS të Serbisë dhe të KSA të Kosovës (Diskusije o Ustavnim Amandmanima na Astav SR Srbije i SAP Kosova). Prishtinë, 1988. Albanian and Serbo - Croatian Edition. BK: S 171 G 30

Kushtetuta e Republikës Popullore Socialiste të Shqipërisë. 2 Edition.Tiranë, 1989. BK: S172 T 70

RPSSH. Kushtetuta, 1976: Constitution de la Republique Populaire Socialiste d'Albanie. 2 Edition. '8 Nëntori'. Tiranë, 1989. BK: S 179 S 54

Verfassung der Sozialistischen Volksrepublik Albanien. Auflage, '8 Nëntori', 1989. BK: S 177 T 82

Kushtetuta e Republikës së Kosovës. Kolegjiumi i "Zërit të Kosovës". Biel, 1990. BK: S 111 E 40

Projekti i Kushtetutës së Republikës të Shqipërisë. Tiranë, 1994. BK: S 86 E 6

Kushtetuta e Republikës së Shqipërisë. Miratuar nga Kuvendi Popullor. 21 Tetor 1998, Tiranë. BK: S 140 V 92

Kushtetuta dhe Materiale Shpjeguese. QAKAPP (Qendra për Koordinimin e Asistencës dhe Pjesëmarrje së Publikut). Tiranë, 1998. BK: S 215 G 12

Loiodice, Aldo. Shehu, Natasha. La Costituzione Albanese. 'Cacucci'. Bari, 1999. BK: PP 3(496.5) Lo

Kushtetuta e Republikës së Shqipërisë (Constitution of the Republic of Albania). Qendra e Publikimeve Zyrtare. Tiranë, 2003. BK: S 209 F 4

Ismajli, Rexhep. Islami, Hivzi. Stavileci, Esat. Ramajli, Ilaz. Akte të Kuvendit të Republikës së Kosovës: 2 korrik 1990 - 2 maj 1992. Akademia e Shkencave dhe e Arteve e Kosovës. Prishtinë, 2005. S 442 B 1

Alsula, Ardita. Kushtetuta e Republikës së Shqipërisë: me Interpretime të Gjykatës Kushtetuese. 'Alb Juris'. Tiranë, 2008. BK: S 293 G 37

Kushtetuta e Republikës së Shqipërisë. Tiranë, 2009. BK: S 305 G 20

Kushtetuta e Republikës së Shqipërisë. (Amended with the Law no. 9675, date 13.1.2007; Law no. 9904, date 21.4.2008). Qendra e Publikimeve Zyrtare. Tiranë, 2009. BK: S 326 D 21

Alsula, Ardita. Kushtetuta e Republikës së Shqipërisë: Miratuar dhe Shpallur në 1998 dhe Ndryshuar në Vitet 2007 dhe 2008. 'Alb Juris'. Tiranë, 2010. BK: S 338 G 1

Kushtetuta e Republikës së Shqipërisë. (Amended with the Law no. 9675, date 13.1.2007; Law no. 9904, date 21.4.2008). Qendra e Publikimeve Zyrtare. Tiranë, 2011. BK: S 383 C 9

Kushtetuta e Republikës së Shqipërisë. (Enriched with Intepretation of the Costitutional Court). 'Alb Juris'. Tiranë, 2012. BK: S 400 G 20

Kushtetuta e Republikës së Shqipërisë. 'OSCE' Editon. Tiranë, 2013. BK: S 428 G 43

Kushtetuta e Republikës së Shqipërisë. Qendra e Botimeve Zyrtare. Tiranë, 2016. BK: S 488 G 21

Kushtetuta e Republikës së Shqipërisë 2016. Varianti i Konsoliduar i Kushtetutës të Republikës së Shqipërisë, i Integruar me Projekt Amendamentet Kushtetuese. Version Approved by the Parlament of Albania on Date 22.07.2016. 'Pegi'. Tiranë, 2016. BKSH

Kushtetuta e Republikës së Shqipërisë. Qendra e Botimeve Zyrtare. Tiranë, 2020. BKSH

2. Codes

Thaçi Kolë (Ed.). Kanun i Doganës dhe Administrimi Doganor në Shqypënië i Zhvilluar sipas Ligjeve dhe Rregulloreve të Doganave Otomane të Përparëshme. Unique Text. Shpypshkronja e 'Zojës s'Papërlyeme'. Shkodër, 1920.[3] BUSH's Archive

Kodi Civil i vitit 1927. Botim i Ministrisë së Drejtësisë. Tiranë (n.d.). BK: S 59 A 96

Kodi Civil i vitit 1928. Botim i Ministrisë së Drejtësisë. Tiranë (n.d.). BK: S 10 R 97

Kodi Tregtar. Këshilli i Shtetit Tiranë. Shtypshkronja 'Tiranë'. Tiranë, 1929. AQSH: Vendi J.s4

Kodi Tregtar. Botuar nga Këshilli i Shtetit. Tiranë, 1929. BK: S 11 g 163

Kodi Penal Shqiptar. Ministria e Drejtësisë. Tiranë, 1929. BK: S 50 U 1

Kodi Penal Ushtarak. Shkolla e Nxansave të Plotsimit. Tiranë, 1931. BK: S 12 C 37

Procedura dhe Kodi Penal Ushtarak për Kohë Paqi. Shpallur në Fletoren Zyrtare no. 28 bis date 18.V. 1932. BK S 64 S 153

Tedeschini, Emid. Codice Civile del Regno d'Albania. Versione Italiana a Cura di Emid Tedeschini. Tipografia dell'Immacolata. Shkodër, 1939. BK: S 228 C 27

Tedeschini, Emid. Codice di Commercio e Leggi Commerciali del Regno D'Albania. Versione Italiana a Cura di Emid Tedeschini. Industrie Grafiche Italiane. Trieste, 1941. BK: P 531 B 4

Kodi i Familjes. Ministria e Drejtësisë. Tiranë, 1948. BK: S 59 G 83

Kodi Penal i Republikës së Shqipërisë. Tiranë, 1952. BK: 89 R 230; Ar 8 G 11

3 The publication contains an introduction from the editor and all the Ottoman laws and by - laws that were applicable in the customs domain as of 1863.

Kodi i Doganava. Aprovuar nga Kuvendi Popullor më 16.XI.1956. Ministria e Tregtisë. Tiranë, 1957. BK: S 15 R 41

Kodi i Procedurës Civile i Republikës së Shqipërisë. Ministria e Drejtësisë. Tiranë, 1958. BK: S 36 S 70

Kodi i Procedurës Penale i Republikës Popullore të Shqipërisë. Ministria e Drejtësisë. Tiranë, 1959. BK: S 24 S 37

Kodi Penal i R.P. të Shqipërisë. Ministria e Drejtësisë. Tiranë, 1959. BK: S 36 T 174

Kodi i Familjes i RPSH. Botuar nga Drejtoria e Botimeve të Universitetit Shtetëror të Tiranës. (n.d). BK: S 32 A 4

Kodi i Familjes i Republikës Popullore të Shqipërisë. 'Naim Frashëri'. Tiranë, 1965. BK: S 60 G 148

Kodi i Familjes i Republikës Popullore të Shqipërisë. Universiteti i Tiranës. Tiranë, 1969. BK: S 76 B 22

Kodi i Punës i Republikës Popullore të Shqipërisë. 'Naim Frashëri'. Tiranë, 1970. BK: S 67 V 128

Kodet e Republikës Popullore Socialiste të Shqipërisë. Përgatitur për Botim nga Byroja Juridike, Këshilli i Ministrave. Tiranë, 1982. AQSH: Vendi F/1.s 3

Kodi Civil i Vitit 1929. Mbretënia Shqiptare. Ministria e Drejtësisë. 'Toena'. Tiranë', 1998. Republish of Civil Code of 1929. BK: S196 E 68

Luarasi, Aleks. Kodi i Procedurës Penale: me Praktikë Gjyqësore. 'Luarasi'. Tiranë, 2002. BK: S 125 F 82

Kanoni Zhurisë. Botim i Qendrës së Publikimeve Zyrtare. Tiranë, 2009. BK: S 336 C 12

Kodi Civil 1929. 'Papirus'. Tiranë, 2010. BK: S 338 G 12

Kodi Zgjedhor i Republikës së Shqipërisë. Aproved with the Law no. 10019, date 29.12.2008 and Amended with the Law no. 74/2012. 'OSBE' Edition. Tiranë, 2012. BK: S 403 E 5

Kodi i Procedurave Administrative të Republikës së Shqipërisë. Qendra e Publikimeve Zyrtare. Tiranë, 2009. BK: S 326 D 25; Republished in 2010. BK: S 352 B 5

Kodi Civil i Vitit 1929 (i Kohës së Zogut). 'Alb Juris'. Tiranë, 2011. BK: S 363 B 1

Kodi i Procedurave Administrative. 'Alb Juris'. Tiranë, 2012. BK S 391 G 69

Kodi Civil dhe i Procedurës Civile. (Enriched with the Case Law and Updated with the Changes of 2012). 'Alb Juris'. Tiranë, 2012. BK: S 395 B 23

Buna, Gjok. (Collected and Selected) Kodi i Punës, i Përditësuar dhe me Praktikën Gjyqësore. 'Alb Juris'. Tiranë, 2013. BK S 424 G 1

Kodi i Procedurave Administrative të Republikës së Shqipërisë.(Updated). 'Alb Juris'. Tiranë, 2014. BK: S 445 F 64. Republished in 2015. 'Alb Juris'. Tiranë, 2015. BK: S 464 G 1

Kodi Civil dhe i Procedurës Civile. (Updated and Enriched with Case Law). 'Alb Juris', Tiranë, 2015. BFDUT

Kodi Penal dhe i Procedurës Penal. (Enriched with Case Law). 'Alb Juris', Tiranë, 2015. BFDUT

Kodi i Procedurave Administrative të Shqipërisë. Qendra e Botimeve Zyrtare. Tiranë, 2020. BKSH

Kodi Civil i Republikës së Shqipërisë. Qendra e Botimeve Zyrtare. Tiranë, 2022. BKSH

Kodi i Procedurës Civile. Qendra e Botimeve Zyrtare. Tiranë, 2022. BKSH

Kodi Penal i Repulikës së Shqipërisë. Qendra e Botimeve Zyrtare. Tiranë, 2022. BKSH

Kodi i Procedurës Penale i Republikës së Shqipërisë. Qendra e Botimeve Zyrtare. Tiranë, 2022. BKSH

3. Compendiums of Legal Acts and Jurisprudence

Kanoni i dëmeve Gjirokatër. Shtypëshkronj' e Qeverrisë. Tiranë, 1920. BK: 90 C 144; S 54 S 108

Shqipënija më 1937. Veprimi Shtetnor gjatë Njëzet e Pesë Vjetëve të Parë të Vetqeverrimit. Komisjonit të Kremtimeve të 25 Vjetorit të Vetqeverrimit 1912–1937. Vol. I. Shtypshkronja 'Kristo Luarasi'. Tiranë, 1937. BK: 88 C 56

Shqipënija më 1937. Veprimi Shtetnor gjatë Njëzet e Pesë Vjetëve të Parë të Vetqeverrimit. Komisjonit të Kremtimeve të 25 Vjetorit të Vetqeverrimit 1912–1937. Vol. II. Shtypshkronja 'Kristo Luarasi'. Tiranë, 1938. BK: 88 C 56

Raccolta di Provvedimenti di Carattere Legislative Riguardanti L'Albania. Ministero degli Affari Esteri. Tipografia Riservata del Ministero degli Affari Esteri. Roma, 1941. BK: 4 A 14

Kode, Ligje e Dekret Ligje Civile që Kanë Hy në Fuqi në Tokat e Çlirueme në bazë të D. Mëkambësuer no. 77 U 1.5.1942-XX. Tiranë, (No.1314 Gjyqit Shk. I-rë këtu).[4] BK: Ar 13 A 17

Aktiviteti dhe Roli i Kooperativave në Ekonominë Tonë Popullore. Botim i Komitetit të Përgjithshëm të Kooperativave Shqiptare. Stabilimenti 'Bashkimi'. Tiranë, 1948. BK 90 E 52; S 3 F 66; S 71 T 71

Çevi, Kristo. Meksi, Vangjel. Dhima, Dhimo. Kodifikimi i Përgjithshëm i Legjislacionit në Fuqi i Republikës Popullore të Shqipërisë (1945–1957). Vol. I, (A - I). Botim i Kryeministrisë. 'Mihal Duri'. Tiranë, 1958. BK: Al 3 B 21; 91 C 149; AQSH: Vendi 340. 13 K 78; BKSH

Çevi, Kristo. Meksi, Vangjel. Dhima, Dhimo. Kodifikimi i Përgjithshëm i Legjislacionit në Fuqi i Republikës Popullore të Shqipërisë (1945–1957). Vol. II, (K-P). Botim i Kryeministrisë. 'Mihal Duri'. Tiranë, 1958. BK: 91 C 154; AQSh: Vendi 340. 13 K 78; BKSH

Çevi, Kristo. Meksi, Vangjel. Dhima, Dhimo. Kodifikimi i Përgjithshëm i Legjislacionit në Fuqi i Republikës Popullore të Shqipërisë (1945–1957). Vol. III, (Q-Z). Botim i Kryeministrisë. 'Mihal Duri'. Tiranë, 1958. BK: 91 C 186; Al 3 B 23; AQSh: Vendi 340. 13 K 78; BKSH

4 Details are handwritten on the cover.

Çevi, Kristo. Meksi, Vangjel. Dhima, Dhimo. Kodifikimi i Përgjithshëm i Legjislacionit në Fuqi i Republikës Popullore të Shqipërisë (1945–1975). Aneksi 1958. Botim i Kryeministrisë. 'Mihal Duri'. Tiranë, 1959. BKSH;

Çevi, Kristo. Meksi, Vangjel. Dhima, Dhimo. Kodifikimi i Përgjithshëm i Legjislacionit në Fuqi i Republikës Popullore të Shqipërisë (1945–1975). Aneksi 1959–1960. Botim i Kryeministrisë. 'Mihal Duri'. Tiranë, 1959. BKSH

Dokumenta të Organeve të Larta të Pushtetit Revolucionar Nacional Clirimtar (1912–1944). Institutit të Historisë së Partisë pranë KQ të PPSh. Tiranë, 1962. BFHF

Përmbledhës i Përgjithshëm i Legjislacionit në Fuqi të Republikës Popullore Socialiste të Shqipërisë (1945–1971). Tiranë, 1971. AQSh: Vendi 340.13 P 60

Përmbledhës i Përgjithshëm i Legjislacionit në Fuqi të Republikës Popullore Socialiste të Shqipërisë (1945–1979). Vol. I. 'Mihal Duri'. Tiranë, 1971. AQSh: Vendi 340.13 (496.5) P 60

Përmbledhës i Përgjithshëm i Legjislacionit në Fuqi të Republikës Popullore Socialiste të Shqipërisë (1945–1979). Vol. II. 'Mihal Duri'. Tiranë, 1971. AQSh: Vendi 340.13 (496.5) P 60

Përmbledhëse e Akteve më të Rëndësishme të Pabotuara të Këshillit të Ministrave të Republikës Popullore të Shqipërisë (1945–1974). Tiranë, 1974. AQSh. Vendi: Js.3 Republished in 1976. AQSh. Vendi: Js.3. Republished in 1977. AQSh. Vendi: Js.3. Republished in 1978. AQSh. Vendi: Js.3

Përmbledhës i Përgjithshëm i Legjislacionit në Fuqi të Republikës Popullore Socialiste të Shqipërisë (1945–1985). Vol. I. Botim i Byrosë Juridike në Aparatin e Këshillit të Ministrave. Tiranë, 1986. BK: S 98 C 16

Përmbledhës i Përgjithshëm i Legjislacionit në Fuqi të Republikës Popullore Socialiste të Shqipërisë (1945–1985). Vol. II. Botim i Byrosë Juridike në Aparatin e Këshillit të Ministrave. Tiranë, 1986. BK: S 98C 21

Bufi, Zana. Hysenbegas, Vjollca. Shiroka, Rudina. Legjislacioni Shqiptar 1991–2000. Treguesi 1991–2000. Thematic Bibliographic Index. Vol. I. Tiranë, 2001. BKSH

Bufi, Zana. Hysenbegas, Vjollca. Shiroka, Rudina. Legjislacioni Shqiptar 1991–2000. Treguesi 1991–2000. Thematic Bibliographic Index. Vol. II. Tiranë, 2001. BKSH

Veleshnja, Mbaresa. Indeksi i Akteve Ligjore të Shqipërisë. Botuar në Fletoren Zyrtare Gjatë Viteve 1990–Korrik 2001. Tiranë, 2001. BKSH

Bufi, Zana. Bibliografia e Akteve Ligjore 1920–1939. Botim i Kuvendit të Shqipërisë. Tiranë, 2000. BKSH

Bufi, Zana. Bibliografia e Akteve ligjore 1939–1944. Botim i Kuvendit të Shqipërisë. Tiranë, 2000. BKSH

Alsula, Ardita. Vuçini, Elona. Përmbledhëse Legjislacioni në Fushën e Përmbarimit. Botim i Qendrës së Publikimeve Zyrtare. Tiranë, 2002. BKSH

Bufi, Zana. Lamani, Marita. Bibliografia e Akteve Ligjore 1945–1955. Botim i Kuvendit të Shqipërisë. Tiranë, 2010. BKSH

Përmbledhëse Legjislacioni për Pushtetin Gjyqësor dhe Sistemin e Drejtësisë. 'Alb Juris'. Tiranë, 2010. BKSH

Reforma në Sistemin e Drejtësisë. Analiza dhe Strategjia. Vol. I. Part I. Kuvendi i Shqipërisë. Tiranë, 2018. BKSH

Reforma në Sistemin e Drejtësisë. Analiza dhe Strategjia. Vol. I. Part II. Kuvendi i Shqipërisë. Tiranë, 2018. BKSH

Reforma në Sistemin e Drejtësisë. Analiza dhe Strategjia. Vol. II. Part I. Kuvendi i Shqipërisë. Tiranë, 2019. BKSH

Reforma në Sistemin e Drejtësisë. Analiza dhe Strategjia. Vol. II. Part II. Kuvendi i Shqipërisë. Tiranë, 2019. BKSH

Reforma në Sistemin e Drejtësisë. Analiza dhe Strategjia. Vol. III. Part I. Kuvendi i Shqipërisë. Tiranë, 2019. BKSH

Reforma në Sistemin e Drejtësisë. Analiza dhe Strategjia. Vol. III. Part II. Kuvendi i Shqipërisë. Tiranë, 2019. BKSH

Legjislacioni Shqiptar 1956–1990. Alphabetical Bibliographic Index. Kuvendi i Shqipërisë. Tiranë, 2021. BKSH

Përmbledhje Legjislacioni për Sistemin e Drejtësisë. Euralius, Ministria e Drejtësisë. Shtypshkronja 'Morava'. Tiranë, 2021. BKSH

4. Compendiums of Judgements of the Constituional Court and of the High Court of Albania

Besides being published in the Official Journal, the decisions of the Constitutional Court and the unifying decisions of the High Court have been published in special publications over the years. Some of them are also published online,[5] but the complete series is available at the Library of the Albanian Parliament (Biblioteka e Kuvendit të Shqipërisë).

Jurisprudenca Shqiptare, Vendimet e Diktimit (Civile dhe Ndërshkimore). Ministria e Drejtësisë. No. 1–10. "Mbrothësija" Kristo P. Luarasi. Tiranë, 1924–1938. BK: Ar 13 A 51

Vendime të Gjykatës Kushtetuese të Republikës së Shqipërisë, 1997–1999. Gjykata Kushtetuese e RSH. Qendra e Publikimeve Zyrtare. Tiranë, 2000.

Vendime të Gjykatës Kushtetuese të Republikës së Shqipërisë: Procesi Zgjedhor 2001. Gjykata Kushtetuese e RSH. Tiranë, 2001.

Vendime të Gjykatës Kushtetuese të Republikës së Shqipërisë: 1992–1996. Gjykata Kushtetuese e RSH. Qendra e Publikimeve Zyrtare. Tiranë, 2001.

5 https://qbz.gov.al/search;q=Permbledhje%20te%20vendimeve%20%20unifikuese%20te%20gjykates%20se%20larteKërkim më i plotë mund të bëhet në faqen zyrtare të Qendrës së Botimeve Zyrtare https://qbz.gov.al/ [last access 21.07.2023].

Vendime të Gjykatës Kushtetuese të Republikës së Shqipërisë: 2000–2001. Gjykata Kushtetuese. Tiranë, 2002.
Vendime të Gjykatës Kushtetuese të Republikës së Shqipërisë: 2002. Gjykata Kushtetuese e RSH. Tiranë, 2003.
Vendime të Gjykatës Kushtetuese të Republikës së Shqipërisë: 2003. Gjykata Kushtetuese e RSH. 'Dita 2000'. Tiranë, 2004.
Vendime të Gjykatës Kushtetuese të Republikës së Shqipërisë: 2004. Gjykata Kushtetuese e RSH. 'Dita 2000'. Tiranë, 2005.
Vendime të Gjykatës Kushtetuese të Republikës së Shqipërisë: 2005. Gjykata Kushtetuese e RSH. 'Dita 2000'. Tiranë, 2006.
Vendime të Gjykatës Kushtetuese të Republikës së Shqipërisë: 2006. Gjykata Kushtetuese e RSH. 'ILAR'. Tiranë, 2007.
Vendime të Gjykatës Kushtetuese të Republikës së Shqipërisë 2007. Gjykata Kushtetuese e RSH. 'Grand Prind'. Tiranë, 2008.
Vendime të Gjykatës Kushtetuese të Republikës së Shqipërisë 2007. Gjykata Kushtetuese e RSH. Qendra e Botimeve Zyrtare. Tiranë, 2008.
Vendime të Gjykatës Kushtetuese të Republikës së Shqipërisë 2008. Qendra e Botimeve Zyrtare. Tiranë, 2009.
Vendime të Gjykatës Kushtetuese të Republikës së Shqipërisë: Parimi i 'Ndarjes dhe Ballancimit të Pushteteve' 1998–2011. Qendra e Botimeve Zyrtare. Tiranë, 2012
Vendime të Gjykatës Kushtetuese të Republikës së Shqipërisë 2012. 'Kristalina-KH'. Tiranë, 2013.
Vendime të Gjykatës Kushtetuese të Republikës së Shqipërisë 2013. 'Kristalina-KH'. Tiranë, 2014.
Vendime të Gjykatës Kushtetuese të Republikës së Shqipërisë 2014. 'Kristalina-KH'. Tiranë, 2015.
Përmbledhje e Vendimeve Unifikuese të Gjykatës së Lartë të Botuara në Fletoret Zyrtare 2013–2018. Qendra e Botimeve Zyrtare. Tiranë, 2020.
Përmbledhje e Vendimeve Unifikuese të Gjykatës së Lartë të Botuara në Fletoret Zyrtare 2014–2022. Qendra e Botimeve Zyrtare. Tiranë, 2022.

Glossary of Terms

Asqeri – Askeri: The high strata of the military of the Ottoman Empire, exempted from taxes.[1]

Bajrak – Bayrak – lit. The Flag: An administrative unit created pursuant to the Albanian customary law at the end of the 17th century in the highlands of the Northen Albania, which encompassed brotherhoods of the same tribe (see *vëllazëri*).[2]

Bajraktari – Bayraktar: The head of the *bayrak*. His competences in times of war and peace were established in the *kanun*.

Be-*ja* – Oath: Institute of the Albanian customary law which established rules for taking an oath as a means of proving one's innocence. The Kanun of Lek Dukagjin (KLD) determined which party had the obligation to take the oath, and recognized several types of oaths to exonerate someone from charges.

Be me sedije (Lit. *s'e dija, nuk e dija*) – Oath for not knowing: According to the KLD, a person could absolve himself from wrongdoing by swearing that he did not know the perpetrator of a violation, or the circumstances relating to it. False oath was, however, punishable (KLD, §569 et seq.). [3]

Be për derë – The oath upon the household: The oath performed by the head of the family by swearing on his honor and the honor of his family members. (KLD, §558 – §564).

Be mbë gurë, mbë kryq e mb'Ungjill: The oath upon the rock, upon the cross and upon the Gospel: Forms of oaths according to the Kanun of Lek Dukagjini (KLD, LXXXIX, §533 et seq). A person who wanted to absolve himself from an accusation would take an oath either upon the rock, upon a cross, or the Gospel.[4] The rock was a specially devised rock triangle with three holes, which served as a scale for weighing the candle wax that the person who swore would give to the church.[5]

---

1 https://www.encyclo.co.uk./meanning-of-askeri[lastaccess 11.10.2023]

2 Valentini defines the *bayrak* as "the entire tribe, including the *Anas* (brotherhoods who were found on the lands where the tribe is established and who rely on the tribe's support), and also nephews from the daughters of the tribe, all of whom bear the same name and live in the same mountain (or forest) ....Whilst the tribe is constituted by the bloodline of the men and their wives and daughters, the *bayrak* is the tribe as a state..." Valentini, Giuseppe. Studime dhe Tekste Juridike. Prepared by Kulla, Ndriçim. Thomollari, Dritan. 'Plejad'. Tiranë, 2009, p. 213.

3 Gjeçovi K., Shtjefën. The Code of Lekë Dukagjini. Kanuni i Lekë Dukagjinit. Edited by Fox, Leonard, Gjonlekaj. New York, 1989. Albanian and English Edition, p. 122.

4 Idem, p. 120.

5 Gjeçovi, Kanuni, Prepared by Tedeschini, Emid, p. 145; Gjeçovi K., Shtjefën. The Code, p. 120.

Be për krye të djemve – Oath on the sons' head: The accused would take the oath in front of his sons and his accuser that he did not do what he was accused of doing. According to the KLD, it was a procedural means to absolve the accused of the charge. (§565 - §568).

Beja e rreme (e gënjeshtërt) – False oath

Bejlerë – Beylerbey: Ottoman title of land owners, a high functionary of a province, but lower in rank than the *pasha.*

Berat (e) Berat – Decree: Imperial instrument used for granting privileges, appointment of high functionaries and special benefits.[6]

Besa: An institution of Albanian customary law consituting a promise or allegiance. The meaning of *besa* has slight variations, according to the circumstance in which it is given. It consists of keeping a promise, giving the word of honor, and of honoring at all costs an obligation one has undertaken. It was relied on in circumstances of blood vendetta for providing grace periods to the murderer and his family,[7] but it is most famous for the protection it provides to guests. A guest was considered under the protection (*besa*) of the host, who hence was obliged to protect the guest up to a safe distance. If the guest was harmed or killed whilst under *besa* of the host, the latter was obliged to take revenge. The obligation in this case was more stringent even than the case of killing of a family member, in which the family of the victim could decide to settle and not start a blood feud; the killing of a guest could not be settled by the host, but had to be expiated by killing the murderer or a member of his family. *Besa* was also used in civil law matters.

Bestari – The truce negotiator, the trustee: Negotiators who would mediate a truce period between the family of the murdered person and the murderer, for the benefit of the latter and his family. If the truce was granted, the *bestari* was the protector of the murderer and his family during the period of truce.[8] This truce period was usually granted based on objective circumstances, such as the need to harvest the crops, if it was harvesting season, or to dispose of other worldy affairs.

Buyuruldu (Turkish) – **Urdhër** – Order: Written orders by high-ranking officials of the Ottoman Empire, which were sent for execution to the heads of the empire's provinces and judges.[9]

Burrëria – Manliness: Institute of the Albanian customary law identifiable with a man's honor.

Bylykbashi (Boluk-bashi) – Bylykbash: Functionary of the Ottoman Empire tasked with the collection of taxes and dues imposed by the empire. In the northern highlands of Albania his assignments included the collection of fines for breaches of the Albanian

---

6 Pepo, Petraq. Materiale Dokumentare, p. 171; Sinani, Shaban. Firatli, H. Erkan. Atmaca, Tayfun. Të Shkruash Historinë me Tolerancë. Fermantar. 'Arbëria'. Tiranë, 2005, p. 284.

7 Fjalor Enciklopedik Shqiptar, Akademia e Shkencave të Shqipërisë. Part 1, Tiranë, 2008. P. 220. BK: Fe 40 D 15.

8 Gjeçovi, The Code, p. 166.

9 Sinani, Të Shkruash, p. 284.

customary law provisions. He was a representative of the tribe near the Vali of Shkodra and a mediator between the highlanders and the Turkish government. His duty was hereditary within his family.[10]

Çekiçët – Hammers: Persons who, according to the Albania customary law, maintained the position of the assistant or counsel to the tribe's elders.

Çiflig (Chiflik) – Fiefdom: Large agricultural or livestock economy, not conditioned by any service, oriented towards market production. As a rule, the manor included a village and consisted of two main parts: private property *(mylk)* and state land *(mirie)*. The private property *(mylk)* consisted of a dwelling where the fief lord or fief administrator lived, a number of huts where the peasants lived, a stone tower for protection from rival fief lords, stables for animals, storehouses, furnaces and forges. The size of the fiefs differed in size from a plot of land that was plowed in the fields to hundreds of hectares.[11]

Çifligar – Fief's lords or feudal lords

Çifçiu – A landless rustic who works on the lands of the fief owner.[12]

Çiraku – Apprentice: The status of a novice training into a craft, under the system of guilds *(esnafe)*. After completion of the necessary training period and other conditions set by the guild, the apprentice could gain the status of the journeyman, and later that of the master.

Defter – Registry: Fiscal and cadaster register under the law of the Ottoman Empire.[13]

Diktimi (Gjykata e Diktimit) – Supreme Court: The High Court of Albania, and the highest judicial instance, during the period 1921–1939.

Dinatë – Dinate: A social stratus that emerged from the farmers' communities during the rule of the Byzantine Empire in Albanian territories. They were known as "the powerful" because of the land they accrued from poor farmers.[14]

Djelmnia, vegjëlia – The youths, the commoners: A body regulated by the Albanian customary law, composed of all men who were fit to use a weapon and were entitled to participate in the community assembly, and were not members of the elders or *bayraktar*. Their competences included actions that warranted the enforcement of the *kanun* by the elders and the *bayraktar*.[15]

Dorëzanë – Guarantor

Dorërasi – The hitman: According to the KLD, the person who carried out a murder on the account of someone else.

---

10 Gjeçovi, K. Shtjefën. Kanuni i Lekë Dukagjinit. Collected and Codified by Gjeçovi, Shtjefën K. Preface by Pupovci, Syrja. Enti i Teksteve dhe i Mjeteve Mësimore. Prishtinë, 1972, p. 76.

11 Thëngjilli, Petrika. Historia e Perandorisë Osmane. 'Libri Universitar'. Tiranë, 1997, p. 114.

12 Elezi, Ismet. Kanuni i Labërisë. 'Toena'. Tiranë, 2006, p. 273.

13 Caka, Eduart. (Sci. Ed.). Defteri i Regjistrimit të Sanxhakut të Shkodrës i Vitit 1485. Akademia e Studimeve Albanologjike. Tiranë, 2018, p. 132.

14 Idem, p. 484; Buda, Alex. Shkrime Historike. Akademia e Shkencave të Shqipërisë. Instituti i Historisë. 'Toena'. Tiranë, 2002, p. 27.

15 Fjalor Enciklopedik, P. 1, p. 497.

(e) Dhjeta – The tithes: A tax of ten percent of the produce.

Drishti-Drivast: A settlement of Illyrian origin, located in the territories of today's municipality of Postriba (Shkodër). In the 11th century it became an episcopal seat under the Archbishopric of Tivar. Until the 13th century Drishti was under Byzantine rule, whilst in 1396 it fell under the control of Venice. In the 14th century it gained the status of an autonomous city. In 1478 the city was attacked by the Ottomans who massacred the city's inhabitants. The city was never after rebuilt.[16]

Ekloga law: Law of the Byzantin Empire, dated 726.

Erazi Kanuni: The Ottoman Empire Law on Land.

Erazi Mamluk / mylq: Private real estate, including meadows, vineyards, and lawns; the ownership of which was certified by a deed (*tapi*) issued by the Ottoman Empire administration.

Erazi metruqe: Land category under the law of the Ottoman Empire, destined for collective use.

Erazi-mirie: State-owned land according to the Ottoman Empire law.

Erazi mevat: Abandoned or deserted land according to the Ottoman Empire law.

Esnaf – Guilds: The name by which the guilds, associations of craftsmen and merchants were known in the Middle Ages during the period of feudalization. They preserved the same characteristics as the *collegia*, a Roman law institution that spread in Illyria during the 1st–3rd centuries AD. Traces of *esnafe* are found in 13th century Durrës, and in 14th–15th century Shkodra, Prizren and Drisht. These organizations played an important role in political and military spheres. Albanian guilds lost their role in the 19th century.[17]

Fejesa – Betrothal: An institute of the Albanian customary law which generated specific rights and obligations for both parties.

Ferman – Firman: In this book the term refers to a decree of the sultan of the Ottoman Empire[18]. Ferman is a legal instrument used also by other eastern monarchies.

Fisi – Tribe: Albanian tribes were organized based on the paternal blood line. For instance, the Kanun of Skanderbeg established that "of the same tribe are all those who descend from a common father (ancestor), generation after generation, for as long as it can be remembered, and all of them are called brothers and sisters. The tribe is therefore made of the common paternal bloodline".[19]

Gjakmarrja – Blood vendetta, blood feud: An institute of Albanian customary law, according to which murder carried out for the purpose of redeeming the killing of a family member was not punishable by public authorities of the community, if carried out in accordance with the *kanun's* rules.

---

16 Idem, p. 533.

17 Shkodra, Zija. Esnafet Shqiptare (Shekujt XV–XX). Akademia e Shkencave të Shqipërisë. Instituti i Historisë. Tiranë, p. 8–13.

18 Sinani, Të Shkruash, p. 285.

19 Illia, Frano. Kanuni i Skanderbegut. 'La Rosa', Milot- Brescia, 1993, p. 20.

Gjobtarë – Bailiff: A body of the Albanian customary law, tasked with enforcing the decisions of the community assemblies.[20]

Gjykatave Popullore – People's courts: Lower courts, established pursuant to article 79 of the Albanian People's Republic adopted in 1946, and the laws no. 59 on the Temporary Judicial Organization and no. 60 dated May 17th, 1945 On the Election of People's Judges.

Gjyqi special (1944–1945) – Special Court: Special court created pursuant to a decision of the Anti-fascist National Liberation Council (KANÇ), of December 25th, 1944, with the competence to adjudicate Albanian and foreign persons, who were considered enemies of the people or war criminals by the communist government. The judicial panel was composed of nine members. The investigations were carried out by a special commission. Reportedly, between March 1st and April 13th 1945 this court conducted judicial proceedings against 60 persons for charges relating to collaboration with the invaders and sabotage, sentencing to death 17 of them; two were absolved of charges and the rest were given prison sentences.[21]

Hakuk mushaviri: The regulation on the legal representative and lawyers, adopted by the Ministry of Finance of the Ottoman Empire in 1886.

Haraç – (harac or kharj) – Taxes due: Tax levied on non-Muslim citizens, according to imperial Ottoman law. This tax was organized in two forms: *Haraç-I muvasaf*, which was determined based on the surface of the land in possession of the non-Muslim subject; and *Haraç-I mukaseme*, a form of tax calculated based on the income generated from the land.[22]

Hasse – Hase: Estates of property of the Ottoman Empire, with annual tax revenue of over 100,000 *akçe*, which the sultan gave to high functionaries of the Ottoman Empire upon conditions related to their status or service. The estate was free of dues, but was restricted from sale transactions.[23] The sultan's *hasse* included the most important revenues of a country that came from taxes levied from the sale of goods in the main markets, customs at the wharves, mines, livestock taxes and from village dues.[24]

Hasil –The amount of the tax

Hise – The Estate: The estate in possession or under lordship of the *timariot.*

Ixhmal: One of the methodologies used for drafting the cadastral registers of the Ottoman Empire. It registerd estates and their respective dues, starting with the biggest *timars*, to any possession of the small households.

Jazixhi- Sekretar – Secretaries

20 Gjeçovi, The Code, p. 207.

21 Fjalor Enciklopedik, P. 1, p. 872.

22 Rizvanolli, Masar. Vendosja e Sistemit të Timarit në Kosovë në Gjysmën e Dytë të Shekullit XV. Instituti i Historisë 'Ali Hadri'. Prishtinë, 2021, p. 521.

23 Pulaha, Selami. Pronësia Feudale në Tokat Shqiptare (Shek. XV-XVI). Akademia e Shkencave e RPSH. Instituti i Historisë. Tiranë, 1988, p. 183.

24 Thëngjilli, Historia, p. 47.

Jurati judices (lat.): Sworn judges of the Byzantine empire.

Kadi: Usually a judge or a senior official of the judicial system, responsible for the administration of justice and public services.[25]

Kallfa – Journeyman: The young craftsman who, according to the guild system, had completed the initial period of apprenticeship and gained work experience. The rise in the internal hierarchy of the guild was carried out according to predetermined rules of the guild. The journeyman was the master's main assistant, but subordinate to him.[26]

Kanon: A Byzantine law term indicating a law, regulating aspects of religious or secular life.[27]

Kanonikë – Canons, canon regular: Canon was an ecclesiastical or secular person who lived and worked in the administration of a monastery or cathedral.[28] Canon regular refers to the clergy of these institutions.

Kanun – Ligj – Law: Under the Albanian customary law, *kanun* is an unwritten law inherited through generations, and obligatory for all community members of the area under its jurisdiction.[29] According to Gjergj Fishta, the origin of the term *kanun* is believed to be from the Greek word *eaipi.*[30] A number of *kanuns* were applicable in different regions of Albanian territories, with some being variations of the same *kanun*. The word *kanun* was also used by the Ottoman law to denote a law.

Kanuni i Zhurisë – *Kanun* (Law) of Jury: *Kanuni i Zhurisë* (The law of jury) was amongst the first legislative acts following the proclamation of Albania's independence enacted on May 13th, 1913. It established the regulatory framework for the creation of a judicial system based on jury trial. Albeit widely used in customary law, it was a novelty for the conventional criminal judiciary under which justice was provided through collegial bodies, such as the elders or the assemblies. The law was first implemented in the city of Elbasan and was repelled after almost a year, with the adoption of the Organic Statute of Albania in April 10th, 1914.[31]

Kanunname – Compendium of laws: Compendia of secular laws of the Ottoman Empire, which applied alongside religious legislation. The term was also used for the special legal acts of the *sanjaks*, which determined the rights and obligations of Timarli feudal lords and peasants.[32]

---

25 See Egro, Dritan. Ligji Osman ndër Shqiptarët e Mesjetës së Vonë. Gjysma e Dytë e Shekullit të XV – Fillim Shekulli XVII. Qendra e Studimeve Albanologjike. Instituti i Historisë. Tiranë, 2012, p. 325.

26 Fjalor Enciklopedik Shqiptar, Akademia e Shkencave të Shqipërisë. Part. 2, Tiranë 2008, p. 1098. BK: Fe 40 D 17.

27 Pepo, Materiale, p. 174.

28 Pepo, Materiale, p. 174.

29 Illia, Kanuni, p. 215.

30 Gjeçovi, Kanuni, Preface by Fishta, p. 25.

31 Fjalor Enciklopedik, P. 2, p. 1076.

32 Luarasi, Aleks. Historia e Shtetit dhe e së Drejtës në Shqipëri. 'Maluka', Tiranë, 2018, p. 216; p. 231.

Kasneci – Herald: According to the Kanun of Lek Dukagjini, the herald was the messenger who announced and disseminated door to door the orders of the chief of the tribe. It was a hereditary right regulated by the *kanun*, together with the protection it guaranteed to the messenger.[33]

Kapitulacionet – Capitulations: Privileges provided by the Byzantine Empire (and later by the Ottoman Empire) to the Western European States and their citizens, offering jurisdiction, fiscal and custom dues exemptions (or preferential treatment) to the latter. These privileges extended to all provinces of the Empire, including Albania, and remained in force even after the proclamation of Albania's independence in 1912. They were also provided for by the Organic Statute of Albania of 1914, which was drafted by the International Control Commission.[34]

Kapucari – Informer: The person who reveals the author of a crime. Articles 1079 et seq of the Kanun of Lek Dukagjini (KLD) provided guarantees for the protection of the informer.

Kararname (Kararnamé): Ottoman term meaning Book of Decisions. The legal acts adopted by the Albanian League of Prizren (1878).

Katundi – Village

Kaza – A subprefecture: An administrative unit under the Ottoman Empire, in the rank of subprefecture, headed by a Kadi.[35]

Kodik – Codex (*lat*) - Code: A compilation of legal provisions, enactments.[36] In this publication *kodik* refers to the codexes compiled by churches and monasteries in Albanian territories. In their early form, these codexes contained religious scriptures, but over time their scope expanded to include rules applicable to the internal administration of the church and to the secular community, as well as registers on various legal matters of the community.

Regest – Register, ledger: In this publication the term refers to the codexes kept by the ecclesiastical institutions in the form of registers, which, in addition to church rules, or other ordinances applicable to the believers, also recorded events and private legal acts entered between the members of the community.

Kodikët katastikë – Catastic codex: Registers of ownership and property transactions, concessions, trade and currency regime.[37]

Komiteti Ekzekutiv i Këshillit Popullor të Qarku – Executive Committee of the District People's Council: The higher executive organ of a district during the communist regime in Albania.

Komisioni i Xhibalit – Jibal Commission: Also known as the Mountain Commission, it was created by the Ottoman Empire in the Northern Highlands of Albania for the purpose

33 Gjeçovi, The Code, p. 214.

34 Fjalor Enciklopedik, P. 2, p. 1116.

35 Pepo, Materiale, p.174.

36 Sinani, Shaban. Kodikët e Shqipërisë. Drejtoria e Përgjithshme e Arkivave. Tiranë, 2003, p. 280.

37 Sinani, Kodikët, p. 230.

of controlling the customary applicable law and the order of these areas. Its composition included Ottoman Empire officials and representatives of the Albanian tribes.

Komisionet e caktimit të kufinjve të Shqipërisë – The Commission for the delineation of the borders of Albania: Commissions created by the London Conference (1912–1913), which were tasked with delineating the northern and southern borders of the new Albanian state.[38] Their work preceded the partition of Albanian territories inhabited by Albanian speaking population in favor of the neighboring countries.

Komisioni Ndërkombëtar i Kontrollit (KNK) (1913–1914) – The International Control Commission: The International Control Commission was established in 1913 by the Conference of Ambassadors in London, for the purpose of controlling the new Albanian state and its institutional building.

Komiteti Antifashist Nacional Çlirimtar – Anti-Fascist National Liberation Committee: The highest body with executive competences and the shadow government established by the Albanian Communist Party before the end of the Second World War, on May 27th, 1944, and chaired by Enver Hoxha.

Konferenca e Ambasadorëve në Londër (1912–1913) – The Conference of Ambassadors in London: The Conference of Ambassadors in London, also known as the London Peace Conference, was summoned by the six great powers of the time: the British Empire, the Austrian-Hungarian Empire, Germany, France, Italy and Russia, represented by their ambassadors in London. It aimed to resolve the consequences and territorial claims in Balkan territories following the dissolution of the Turkish Empire. Its decisions are closely connected to the partitioning of Albania and the transfer of substantial territories inhabited by Albanians in favor of the neighboring countries.[39]

Konferenca e Bujanit (1943) – Conference of Bujan (1943): The founding conference of the National Liberation Council for Kosova and the Dukagjin Plain. It is considered an important milestone of Kosova's efforts for independence, as the resolution adopted by the parties addressed in clear terms Kosova's right for self-determination, including its right to join Albania, which would be decided by referendum at the end of the war.[40]

Konferenca e Rambujesë (1999) – The Rambouillet Conference: The conference convened by the leading NATO countries for the purpose of mediating between Kosova and the Serbia (formally the Federal Republic of Yugoslavia (FRY)). It concluded with a proposed accord, which was not accepted by Serbia.

Kontrata e dorëzanisë – Contract of suretyship

Kooperativa Bujqësore – Agricultural cooperatives: Following the 1946 agrarian reform undertaken by the government of the Communist Party of Albania, which re-distributed the land to the farmers, the government initiated the creation of the soviet model of

38 Fjalor Enciklopedik, P. 2, p. 1227.

39 Fjalor Enciklopedik, P. 2, p. 1242.

40 Stavileci, Esat. Reka, Blerim. Bajrami, Arsim. Kosova: Political, Constitutional and International Law Arguments. Kosova Law Review (Special Edition). Prishtinë, 1996, p. 64.

agricultural cooperatives, based on the reverse process—the collectivization of the land. The cooperatives became the centralized economic units of agricultural production.

Kolektiva bujqësorë – Agricultural collectives: Organized units which preceded the agricultural cooperatives. These were created for the purpose of sharing the efforts and costs of agricultural production by joining the labor, whilst the land, animals and the means of production remained private property of the owners.[41]

Krerët dhe malësorët – Chiefs and highlanders. *Also* Elders and highlanders: Representative public functionaries or entities, established by Albanian customary law, which provided them with clear decision-making competences.

Krisovulat – Chrysobullos: Imperial bulls, charters, legal instruments, establishing a legal regime, granting financial and administrative privileges.

Kujri-ja: Common property used by the members of a delineated community in accord with each other. Its regime was regulated by the Albanian *kanuns*. The members' rights over this property were non-transferable, whilst the right of usage could be object of transactions, within limited conditions.

Kulak – Kulak: was the term used by the communist system to define opponents of the economic reforms undertaken in the countryside. It referred to the rich peasantry, which was perceived as hostile towards these reforms. Over time the term gained political importance and even poor peasants who refused to hand over the little property they had were considered *kulaks*. The classification in this category was accompanied by social ostracization, restriction of civil and economic rights and possibly other punishments.

Kumbaria – Godparents: An institute of the Albanian customary law, which differentiated between godparenting of baptism, of marriage and "of hair" cutting.[42] The latter was a practice applied by Albanians regardless of their religion and often cases was used as a means of forging inter-religious bonds between families.

Kuvendi – Assembly: Also known as assembly of men, this was the highest decision-making body of a community (tribe, *bayrak*, province) according to the Albanian customary law. Its powers and function were established in each local *kanun*. Depending on the importance of the decision, as well as the community affected by the decision, the assembly could summon the men of a tribe, *bayrak*, or of a province.

Kuvendi i bajrakut – The assembly of *bayrak*

Kuvendi i dheut – The assembly of the soil: The assembly of all the men of a province.

Libri i Eparkut – the Book of Eparch: Legislation containing legal norms on the organization, operation and supervision of corporations of merchants and craftsmen; circa 10th century.[43]

---

41 Mullai, Abaz. Pozita Social-Ekonomike e Juridike e Fshatarit në Ekonominë Kooperativiste të Tipit Sovjetik, in Studime Albanalogjike, No. 1, 1997, p. 7–19.

42 Gjeçovi, Kanuni, Preface by Pupovci, p. 72.

43 Ballanca, Zejnullah in Historia e Shtetit të së Drejtës në Shqipëri. Omari, Luan. Luarasi, Aleks. (Sci. Ed.) Part I. 'Luarasi'. Tiranë, 1997, p. 74.

Ligji i Fotit – The law of Photius: The law which established the schism between the episcopal sees of Rome and Constantinople.[44]

Mbledhjet e pleqësisë – Meetings of the Elders: An institute of Albanian customary law, composed of the elders of each household or tribe, depending on the community affected by the decision making. More important matters were decided by the assembly of men, or the assembly of the soil.

Mbrapshtinat (kundravajtjet, shkeljet) – Offenses, infractions: Minor offenses regulated by some of the Albanian customary codes *(kanun)*. The Kanun of Lek Dukagjini regulated *mbrapshtinat* in its 10th book.

Mikpritja – Hospitality: The maxim of the Albanian customary law "the house of the Albanian is the house of God and of the guest" was accompanied by a clear legal framework on hospitality. It detailed the host's obligation to honor and protect the guest, but also the specific legal rights and responsibilities of both parties.

Miku – Guest

Mirahor – Functionary of the Ottoman government. Originally this term was used to identify the caretaker of the Ottoman sultan's stables. Later the term *mirahor* or *mirahur* evolved to denote a high administrative functionary.

Mohuesit – Deniers: A denier, according to the Kanun, is someone who refutes an accusation against him by using the pertinent legal means established by the *kanun*, such as the different types of oaths.[45]

Mucerred – Bachelor

Muhtasib – Market inspector

Mufassal– Accounting books

Mussal – Detailed: The methodology of entering detailed data in the cadastral registry, according to the Ottoman law.

Mytesarif (Sanxhakbeu alb.) – Mutasarif (Sanjak bey): Head of the prefecture under the Ottoman Empire.

Nahije– Nahiya: An administrative unit, smaller than a *kaza*.

Nomokanon: Ecclesiastical regulation, which unified the regime on specific issues pertaining to the life of the congregation.[46]

Oda e Miqve (Oda e Burrave) – Chambers of guests (chamber of men): Oda in literal translation means chamber. The Chamber of Men was an Albanian custom of holding a forum of the tribe's men and guests, hence also referred to as the chamber of guests. The chamber's conduct and discussion followed exigent unwritten customs and served to forge tribal and inter-tribal bonding, to informally discuss community issues and to

---

44 Gallagher, SJ Clarence. Patriarch Photius and Pope Nicholas I and the Council of 879 in https://muse.jhu.edu/article/610258/pdf [last access 11.10.2023].

45 Article 302 of Kanun of Lek Dukagjin.

46 Sinani, Kodikët, p. 288.

educate the young children, who were allowed to listen to the chamber's discussions, receiving a wisdom that was accrued through generations.

Odat e ekonomisë – Chambers of commerce

Paria – The elite of cities (chiefs of tribes).

Pasha – Pasha

Pashallëk – Pashalik: Administrative unit governed by the pasha

Pazar – Market

Pellazgëve – Pelasgians

Pengu – Pledge

Pleqtë – Elders

Porota – Articles 1044 et eq of the KLD defines *porota* as persons who testified under oath warranted, to exonerate a person that was accused of a violation of the KLD norms.

Porta e Lartë – High Gate

Principata e Arbrit – Principality of Arbër: The first feudal state formation of the Albanians in central Albania, as documented since the end of the 12th century.[47]

Pronia: Was an institute of the Byzantine Empire law, as of the 11th century, which has been implemented in Albanian territories as of the 12th century. *Pronias* were estates that the emperor distributed by imperial bulls to individual feudal lords, as a conditional possession. A *pronia* granted the feudal lord the possession, but not ownership of the land. Feudal lords thus had the right to collect various taxes from the peasant economy, but could not transfer possession of the *pronia*. The features of this institute were later used by the Ottoman Empire in the similar institution of *timar*.[48] Before the Ottoman conquest, *pronia* was also recognized by the Venetian legal system implemented in Shkodra, with distinctive features.[49]

Prostati – Prostate: High executive body, elected annually by the Council of Representatives of the Epirote Simahia.[50]

Qefalia (Kefalé) – High rank dignitary: Kefalia refers to the local body of state administration, also known as the province; *Qefalia* or *Kefalé* is thus a subordinate appointed to govern a particular province. As a rule, he was the commander of a castle or the governor of a city.[51] The term is known since Byzantine law, but even later in the Ottoman Empire.

Qefili – According to the *kanun* of Dibra (chapter 21), *qefili* is a guarantor, a person who acted as a guarantor for the seller in cases when the buyer did not pay for the goods

47 Plasari, Aurel. Arbni. Historik, Gjeografik, Kishtar dhe Politik. Akademia e Shkencave të Shqipërisë. 'Kristalina-KH'. Tiranë, 2020, p. 80.

48 Buda, Shkrime, p. 39; Luarasi, Historia, p. 71.

49 Zamputi, Injac. Regjistri i Kadastrës dhe i Koncesioneve për Rrethin e Shkodrës 1416–1417. Akademia e Shkencave e RPSSH. Instituti i Historisë. Tiranë, 1977, p. 5–6.

50 Luarasi, Historia, p. 50.

51 Luarasi, Historia, p. 93.

immediately, but promised to pay later, according to the conditions agreed to by the parties.

Raja – Raya: A land plot under the *timar* system, which was given for use to a *raya* peasant, towards the obligation to pay annual taxes to the ottoman administration and the *sipahi*.[52]

Reforma agrare – The agrarian reform: A legal reform on the redistribution or the imposition of new legal conditions on the regime of agricultural land. In Albania, the term very frequently refers to the reform undertaken in 1946 by the communist government, which expropriated, without compensation, the big landowners and transferred the land to the peasants.

Rektor – Rector: High rank dignitary of the Venetian administration.[53]

Regjistri i Koncesioneve – Register of Concessions

Renta feudale – Feudal rent

Revolucioni i Qershorit (1924): The revolution led by Fan Noli, in which other prominent figures of the time participated, with the aim of overthrowing Ahmet Zogu's government.

Rufet – Zanat, Profesion – Craftsmanship, profession: This term was also used by craft-commercial organizations of various trades, which had separate buildings for the gathering of their members and operated in the bazaars of various Albanian cities.[54]

Salname – Year book

Sanxhak – Sanjak: Administrative unit at the rank of prefecture. There were several court jurisdictions within a *sanjak*, called *kadilik*, where the word *kadi* comes from.[55]

Sanxhakbej – Sanjak-bey: See *Mutesarif*

Selasfori: Ancient name of an area in Albania, currenty called Devoll.

Seriye– Religious court: Religious court, which during the Ottoman Empire rendered justice based on the Shariah.

Shart – Decrees: Mandatory decrees for applying a decision, norm, rule or mandatory behavior. Mostly known for Shartet e Idriz Sulit, a compilation of decisions which modernized the customary law in Labëria with the evolving economic relations.

Sheriati – Sheria –Sharia Law: The corpus of religious legal norms of Islamic law was one of the constituent components of the law of the Ottoman Empire enforced by religious courts on the Muslim population. These provisions were applied by the religious courts to the Albanian Muslim population until April 1, 1929, when the Albanian Civil Code came into force. The Sharia applied in Albania mainly to resolve disputes in family and inheritance matters.[56]

---

52 Egro, Ligji, p. 317.

53 Zamputi, Injac. Huta, Përparime. Dokumente për Historinë e Shqipërisë të Shekullit XV. Vol. III (1411–1415). Akademia e Studimeve Albanologjike. Instituti i Historisë. Tiranë, 2018, p. 717.

54 Pepo, Materiale, p. 177.

55 Luarasi, Historia, p. 221.

56 Fjalor Enciklopedik Shqiptar. Akademia e Shkencave të Shqipërisë. Part 3, Tiranë, 2009, p. 2440. BK: Fe 42 D 17.

Sinjoria (Signoria): The main land owner, according to Venetian law which applied in Albanian cities that were under the Venetian rule.[57]

Sixhilate – Sicils – Register: Register of religious courts *(seriye)* during the Ottoman Empire

Sistemi i mileteve – The Millet system[58]: Autonomous self-governing religious community allowed to set their own laws and collect and distribut their own taxes.

Spahi – Sipahi – Military cavalryman: Military cavalryman of the Ottoman Empire that was rewarded with estates, in addition to the salary.

Strapleqtë – the grand elders: According to the Kanun of Skanderbeg, the grand–elders were the elders elected from the commoners, with four main functions: (i) to safeguard the equitable, fair and strict implementation of the *kanun*, (ii) to protect the interest of the commoners' strata, (iii) to chair the bailiffs, and (iv) to substitute elders, in case of absence of the latter, in assemblies. This was a hereditary status. The term is also used to indicate an experienced elder who arbitrated the dispute resolution in the community based on the *kanun's* norms.[59]

Subashët – Soubashi

Subash: Governor of an administrative unit, military commander in the Ottoman Empire.[60]

Shkuesija – Matchmaker: In addition to conventional role of arranging marriages, the matchmaker was also a role regulated by the Albanian customary law, which allowed for someone to act as a conciliator between families who were locked in blood vendetta with each other.[61] Marriage was one of the instruments that was used to seal the truce.

Talimati – Urdhëresë – Ordinance: Ordinance, a by-law issued for the implementation of a legal act that regulated organizational aspects of the army. The term *Talimat* is also used by the League of Prizren. The Talimat of the League was approved on the same day by the General Assembly of the League of Prizren (June 17, 1878) in implementation of the Book of Decisions (*Kararname*).[62]

Tapi – Vërtetim pronësie (mbi pasurinë e paluajtshme) – Land deeds.

Tanzimati – Tanzimat reforms; Reforms undertaken by the Ottoman Empire over the period of 1839–1856 and 1856–1876 in order to modernize it in pace with the rhythm of the European capitalism.[63]

Thema (Greek: θέματα, thémata) – Themes: Thema was the main administrative division of the Byzantine Empire created around the 7th century, to strengthen the defense system in face of the influx of Slavic peoples in the Balkans. The theme was a military administrative

57 Zamputi, Regjistri, p. 6.

58 https://www.britannica.com/topic/millet-religious-group [last access 11.10.2023].

59 Illia, Kanuni, p. 125; Gjeçovi, Kanuni, p. 205.

60 Duka, Ferit. Berati në Kohën Osmane (Shek. XVI–XVIII). Akademia e Shkencave e Republikës së Shqipërisë. 'Toena'. Tiranë, 2001, p. 302.

61 Gjeçovi, Kanuni, Preface by Pupovci, p. 91.

62 Luarasi, Historia, p. 308.

63 Fjalor Enciklopedik, P. 3, p. 2657.

division which replaced the old civil administrative system. In the system of Thema, the civil and military administration was concentrated in the hands of a single *strategos* (commander), who was appointed and dismissed directly by the emperor. The Thema achieved their apex during the 9th and 10th centuries.[64]

Timar (et) – Timar(s): Land estates of the feudal system during the rule of the Ottoman Empire, bestowed by the Sultan as a reward, mainly to the Sipahis, and which yielded an income of up to 20,000 *akçe*.[65]

Timariot– Timariots; The *timar* possessor.

Usta – Master

Usull – Zakon, kanun – Custom, kanun.

Vakëf – Waqf, vakoufs: A charity instrument under the Islamic law, widely used during the rule of the Ottoman Empire. This usually consisted of donations in cash or in kind to support vulnerable groups, improve the infrastructure (construction of bridges, hospitals, schools, water supply systems), or to support the religious institutions, but donation of real estates was not uncommon.

Vakëfname – Waqfia: The waqf deed.

Vetëgjyqësi – Taking the law in your own hands.

Venome: Unwritten code of customary law. The term is used in the south of Albania, as a synonym of the word *kanun*. The term is well known for Himara's Venome.[66]

Vëllazeria – Brotherhood: Brotherhood, according to Albanian customary law, were "... all those brothers and tribes that derive from blood or from filiation".[67] Brotherhood is considered smaller than the tribe.[68] Another institution was the blood brotherhood, according to which two men who drank blood from each other were considered brothers.

Vilajet – Vilayet – Province: Administrative unit, a province, according to the law of the Ottoman Empire after the Tanzimat reform. The Albanian territories were divided into the *vilayets* of Kosovo, Shkodra, Manastir and Ioannina.

Xhelepi: Tax on the livestock, applied in the Albanian territories for the benefit of the Ottoman Empire. This tax was also levied by the independent Albanian state and was implemented until 1944.[69]

Xhibali – Jibal: See the Jibal Commission.

Xhizja – Jizya: Per capita tax levied by the Ottoman Empire on its male non-Muslim subjects.

---

64 Luarasi, Historia, p. 69.

65 Pulaha, Selami. Defteri i Regjistrimit të Sanxhakut të Shkodrës i Vitit 1485. Akademia e Shkencave e RPSH. Instituti i Historisë. Shtypshkronja 'Mihal Duri'. Tiranë, 1974, p. 4.

66 Luarasi, Historia, p. 259.

67 Gjeçovi, Kanuni, codificated by Tedeschini, Emid. p. 48, (Chapter III, art. 12–14).

68 Elezi, Mehmet. Hebrenjtë dhe Republika e Kanunit. Second Edition. 'Gjergj Fishta'. Lezhë, 2019, p. 325.

69 Fjalor Enciklopedik, P. 3, p. 2657; p. 2950.

Ziametet – Ziamet: Estates created on state-owned lands of the Ottoman Empire, which were given as reward by the Sultan to the feudal aristocracy.

Zil-Kade: The Ottoman Esmpire taxation law, adopted on 1839, which established a unified system of taxation for the Ottoman Empire.[70]

70 Shkoza, Haxhi. Financat e Shqipnis (1839 – 1934). Shtypshkronja 'Nikaj'. Tiranë, 1935.